P9-CDE-173

Android™ Phones and Tablets

2nd Edition

Android™ Phones and Tablets

2nd Edition

by Guy Hart-Davis

Visual
A Wiley Brand

Teach Yourself VISUALLY™ Android™ Phones and Tablets 2nd Edition

Published by
John Wiley & Sons, Inc.
10475 Crosspoint Boulevard
Indianapolis, IN 46256

www.wiley.com

Published simultaneously in Canada

Wiley publishes in a variety of print and electronic formats and by print-on-demand. Some material included with standard print versions of this book may not be included in e-books or in print-on-demand. If this book refers to media such as a CD or DVD that is not included in the version you purchased, you may download this material at http://booksupport.wiley.com. For more information about Wiley products, visit www.wiley.com.

Library of Congress Control Number: 2015941036

ISBN: 978-1-119-11676-9

Manufactured in the United States of America

10 9 8 7 6 5 4 3 2 1

Trademark Acknowledgments

Contact Us

For general information on our other products and services please contact our Customer Care Department within the U.S. at 877-762-2974, outside the U.S. at 317-572-3993 or fax 317-572-4002.

For technical support please visit www.wiley.com/techsupport.

Sales | Contact Wiley at (877) 762-2974 or fax (317) 572-4002.

Credits

Acquisitions Editor
Aaron Black

Project Editor
Lynn Northrup

Technical Editor
Andrew Moore

Copy Editor
Lynn Northrup

Manager, Content Development & Assembly
Mary Beth Wakefield

Vice President, Professional Technology Strategy
Barry Pruett

About the Author

Guy Hart-Davis is the author of various computer books including *Teach Yourself VISUALLY iPhone*; *Teach Yourself VISUALLY iPad*; *Teach Yourself VISUALLY MacBook Pro, 2nd Edition*; *Teach Yourself VISUALLY MacBook Air*; *Teach Yourself VISUALLY iMac, 3rd Edition*; and *iWork Portable Genius*.

Author's Acknowledgments

My thanks go to the many people who turned my manuscript into the highly graphical book you are holding. In particular, I thank Aaron Black for asking me to write the book; Lynn Northrup for keeping me on track and skillfully editing the text; Andrew Moore for reviewing the book for technical accuracy and contributing helpful suggestions; and SPi Global for laying out the book.

How to Use This Book

Who This Book Is For

This book is for the reader who has never used this particular technology or software application. It is also for readers who want to expand their knowledge.

The Conventions in This Book

① Steps

This book uses a step-by-step format to guide you easily through each task. **Numbered steps** are actions you must do; **bulleted steps** clarify a point, step, or optional feature; and **indented steps** give you the result.

② Notes

Notes give additional information — special conditions that may occur during an operation, a situation that you want to avoid, or a cross reference to a related area of the book.

③ Icons and Buttons

Icons and buttons show you exactly what you need to click to perform a step.

④ Tips

Tips offer additional information, including warnings and shortcuts.

⑤ Bold

Bold type shows command names, options, and text or numbers you must type.

⑥ Italics

Italic type introduces and defines a new term.

Table of Contents

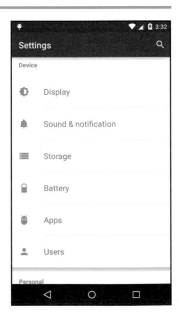

Chapter 3   Sharing Your Device with Others

Chapter 4   Working with Text, Voice, and Accessibility

Table of Contents

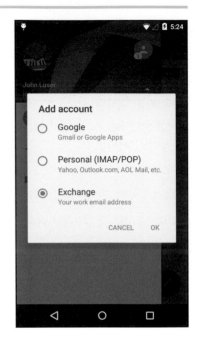

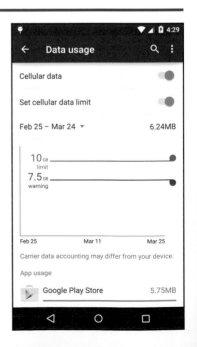

Chapter 7 Phoning, Messaging, and Social Networking

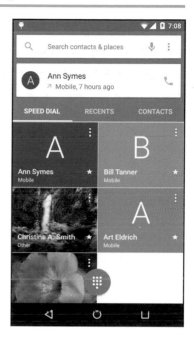

Chapter 8 Working with Apps

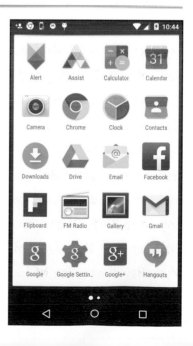

Table of Contents

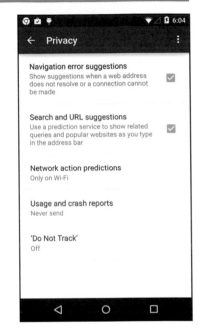

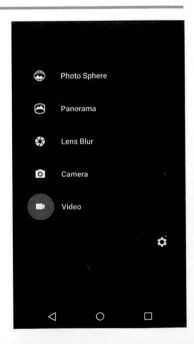

CHAPTER 1

Getting Started with Android

In this chapter, you set up your Android phone or tablet, meet its hardware controls, and learn to navigate it. You also learn to transfer files from your PC or Mac to your device.

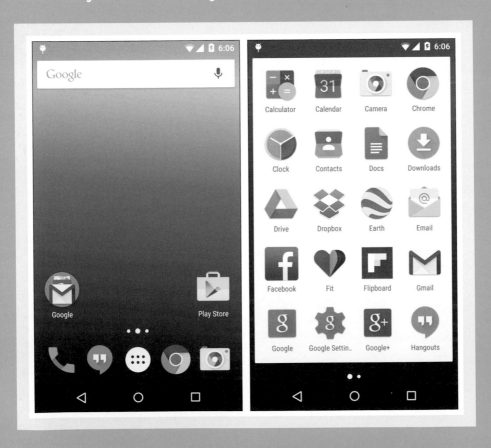

Discover the Types of Android Devices

Android is an operating system created by Google for use on mobile computing devices. Android runs on both smartphones and tablet computers and is widely used on both types of devices. Various hardware manufacturers install Android as the operating system for their devices, and as a result, you can buy many different Android devices with widely varying capabilities and prices. Android has a standard user interface that is referred to as *stock Android*. But some manufacturers add an overlay called a *skin* to Android, giving it a different look, changing its built-in functionality, and adding features.

Android Smartphones

Android smartphones are cellular phones that run on the Android operating system. Android provides a wide range of features, from sending e-mail and browsing the Internet to making phone calls and taking photos. Most Android phones include a rear camera with which you can take high-quality photos, using the screen as a viewfinder, and a front camera for taking self-portraits and for enjoying video chat sessions. Android phones also include one or more microphones you can use to record audio and voice memos.

Android smartphones come in many sizes, designs, and price levels. This book uses the Google Nexus 5 phone as a reference Android smartphone that runs unmodified Android version 5, which is known as Lollipop.

Android Tablets

Google designed Android to run tablet computers as well as smartphones. Tablets come in a wide range of sizes, ranging from pocket size to table-top size. Smaller tablets have screen sizes such as 7 inches or 8.9 inches. Full-size tablets have screen sizes such as 10 inches. Oversize tablets have screens sizes such as 13 inches. Monster tablets have screens as big as 22 inches. This book uses the Google Nexus 7 tablet as a reference Android tablet. In general, tablets are

larger than smartphones, although bigger smartphones now approach the size of smaller tablets. Smartphones have cellular phone capability, whereas tablets do not. Some tablets have cellular data connectivity but cannot make cellular phone calls.

Choosing an Android Device

Many hardware manufacturers make Android devices. Some manufacturers make both Android smartphones and Android tablets, whereas other manufacturers produce only smartphones or only tablets. When looking for an Android smartphone or tablet, you can choose from a wide range of devices, so spend time deciding exactly what you need and carefully researching suitable devices. Study the specifications for the devices and read both professional reviews and user reviews to learn their strengths and weaknesses. The Amazon website, www.amazon.com, is a good place to find user reviews of many devices.

Versions of the Android Operating System

As of this writing, Google has released nine main versions of the Android operating system. Each version has a code name from a sweet treat. For example, the code name for Android version 5 is Lollipop, and the code name for Android version 4.4 is KitKat. When Google releases a new version of Android, each hardware manufacturer must create a custom version for its phones and tablets. Each new version may take weeks or months to arrive — or a manufacturer may decide not to create a new version for its older phones and tablets. For this reason, when considering buying an Android device, you should check carefully the Android version it is running and updates that are available.

Android Skins

Android Lollipop is a full-featured operating system with an easy-to-use user interface. But hardware manufacturers can alter or extend the Android user interface by applying extra software called a *skin*. For example, Samsung adds a skin called TouchWiz to many of its Android devices, and HTC adds a skin called HTC Sense. A skin can modify many aspects of the standard "stock" or "pure" Android interface. For instance, the TouchWiz skin gives the Home screen and the Lock screen a different look, adds extra features and graphics to the Settings app, and replaces key apps such as the Camera app with custom versions.

Android Accessories

To get the most out of your Android device, you can add many different types of accessories. The following accessories tend to be widely useful:

- **Case and screen protector.** To keep your device in good condition, protect it with a case and apply a screen protector to the screen.

- **Extra charger.** If you need to be able to charge your device in multiple locations, keep a charger in each location.

- **TV connection.** You can make a wired connection using a SlimPort-to-HDMI cable or make a wireless connection using a device such as Google's Chromecast.

- **Wireless keyboard.** If you need to enter a lot of text on your device, buy a Bluetooth keyboard. You can choose from many stand-alone keyboards and keyboard cases.

Meet Your Device's Controls

Once you have your Android phone or tablet, take it out of the box, identify the components, and charge it if necessary. For a phone or cellular-capable tablet, insert a suitable SIM card if the device does not have one. When the battery has some charge, turn the device on and meet its controls. Although Android devices use many different controls and layouts, many devices have standard hardware buttons. Standard Android devices also have three soft buttons — Back, Home, and Overview — built into the bottom of the screen.

Meet Your Device's Controls

1 Press and hold the Power button on the phone or tablet for a couple of seconds.

As the phone or tablet starts, the Google logo appears on the screen.

A This is the micro-USB port. Google refers to this as the Charger/USB/SlimPort port.

B This is a microphone on the base of the device.

C This is the front-facing camera.

D This is the headphone socket.

E This is a microphone at the top of an Android phone.

F This is the rear-facing camera.

G This is the camera flash.

2 Turn the phone or tablet so that you can see the side that contains the volume button or volume buttons.

③ Press the upper part of the volume rocker to increase the ringer volume.

④ Press the lower part of the volume rocker to decrease the ringer volume.

Ⓗ This is the SIM tray. To open it, you push a SIM-removal tool or the end of a straightened paper clip into the hole.

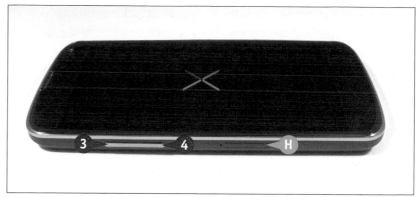

⑤ When the lock screen appears, touch the **lock** (🔒) and then drag upward until the screen unlocks.

The phone or tablet unlocks, and the Home screen appears.

Ⓘ You can touch **Home** (⬤) to display the Home screen.

Ⓙ You can touch **Back** (◀) to display the previous screen.

Ⓚ You can touch **Overview** (◼) to display a list of recent apps and screens.

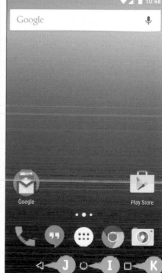

TIP

How do I insert a SIM card in my phone or tablet?

If the store or carrier has not inserted a SIM card, you will need to insert one yourself. Consult the device's documentation to learn which kind of SIM card it needs — for example, a micro-SIM or a nano-SIM — and get a SIM card of that type.

Consult the documentation about inserting the SIM card in the phone or tablet. Some devices, like the one shown here, have an external SIM slot that you open using a SIM ejection tool or the end of a straightened paper clip. Other devices require you to take the back off the device in order to access the SIM compartment and insert the SIM card.

Perform the Initial Setup for Your Device

To get your phone or tablet working, you must perform the initial setup routine. This is a one-time procedure in which you select essential settings and connect the device to a wireless network.

The first time you turn on your device, Android displays the Welcome screen. You can then choose the language, connect to a Wi-Fi network, set up your Google account, and choose other settings. If you already have an Android device, you can pick up settings from it by using the Tap & Go feature.

Perform the Initial Setup for Your Device

Begin Initial Setup and Connect to Wi-Fi

1 Turn on the phone or tablet by pressing and holding the Power button.

The Welcome screen appears.

2 Touch the language.

3 Touch **Next** (→).

The Select Wi-Fi screen appears.

4 Touch the appropriate network.

A If the Wi-Fi network does not appear in the list, touch **Add Another Network**. The network may be one that does not broadcast its name.

B If you do not want to connect to a network now, touch **Skip**.

5 Type the network password.

C You can touch **Show password** (☐ changes to ☑) to display the characters.

D You can touch **Advanced options** (☐ changes to ☑) to choose proxy settings or Internet Protocol settings.

6 Touch **Connect**.

Your device connects to the Wi-Fi network.

7 The Tap & Go screen appears.

You can now set up your device using Tap & Go, as explained in the next subsection, or manually, as explained in the subsection "Set Up Your Device Manually."

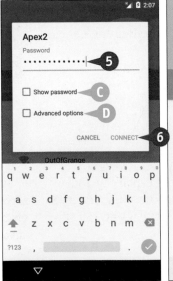

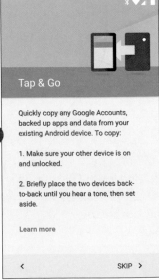

Set Up Your Device Using Tap & Go

The device you are setting up displays the Tap & Go screen.

① Turn on and unlock your other Android device.

② Bring the two devices back to back.

A tone plays when the NFC chips connect.

Note: You may need to move the devices around to line up the NFC chips.

Ⓔ The Check Your Other Device banner appears once the devices have established the NFC connection.

On the other device, the Copy Accounts and Data from This Device? dialog box opens.

③ Touch **OK**.

The device locks, and the screen for your chosen unlock method appears, such as the Confirm Your PIN screen.

④ Perform your unlock method. For example, type your PIN and touch **Continue**.

On the device you are setting up, the Getting Accounts and Data banner appears while Android transfers data.

The Google Services screen appears. Go to the subsection "Choose Google Services and Google Now Settings."

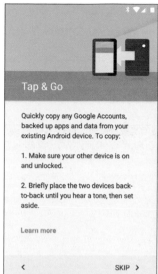
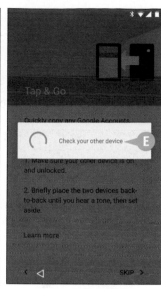
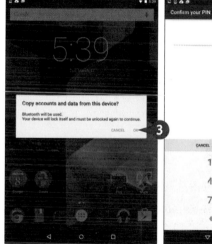

TIPS

Why does the Tap & Go screen not appear on my device?

The Tap & Go screen appears only if your device has Near Field Communications capability, NFC for short. NFC requires extra hardware, which involves additional cost, so many budget devices do not have it.

Should I use Google's location service?

Normally, Google's location service is helpful, because it enables apps to deliver information that is more relevant to your location. However, if the location service raises privacy concerns for you, you can turn it off by opening the Settings app and working on the Location screen.

continued ▶

During the setup routine, you can allow your device to use Google's location service, which helps apps determine your location and deliver targeted search results. You can also let apps and services scan for Wi-Fi networks — even when you have turned Wi-Fi off — to help improve location services, and allow your device to send diagnostic and usage data to Google anonymously.

You can also turn on Google Now, which delivers local information and updates but must use your location, calendars, and Google data to do so.

Perform the Initial Setup for Your Device (continued)

Set Up Your Device Manually

1 On the Tap & Go screen, touch **Skip**.

Note: On some devices, the About Your Privacy screen appears at this point. Touch **Privacy settings** to change your privacy settings. Touch **Accept and continue** to proceed.

The Add Your Account screen appears.

2 Touch **Enter your email** and type your e-mail address.

F You can touch **Or Create a New Account** to create a new account.

3 Touch **Next**.

The Password screen appears.

4 Type your password.

5 Touch **Next**.

The Terms of Service and Privacy Policy screen appears.

G You can touch **Terms of Service** to view the Terms of Service.

H You can touch **Privacy Policy** to view the Privacy Policy.

6 Touch **Accept**.

The Google Services screen appears, and you can proceed as explained in the next subsection.

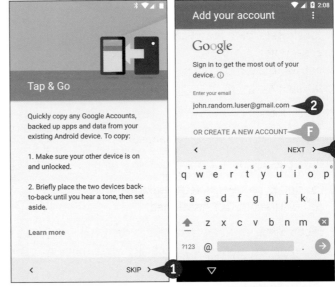

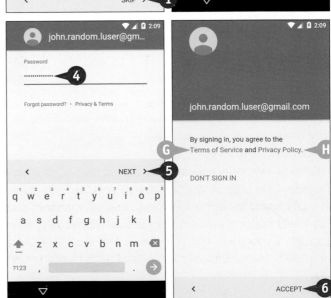

Choose Google Services and Google Now Settings

1 On the Google Services screen, touch **Use Google's location service** (☑ changes to ☐) if you want to turn off location services.

2 Touch **Help improve location services** (☑ changes to ☐) if you do not want to send anonymous data to Google.

3 On a phone, touch **More**.

4 Touch **Help improve your Android experience** (☑ changes to ☐) if you do not want to send diagnostic and usage data to Google.

5 Touch **Next**.

The Get Google Now screen appears.

6 On a phone, touch **More**.

7 Touch **Yes, I'm in** or **No, thanks** (○ changes to ◉), as needed.

8 Touch **Next**.

The Home screen appears, showing a Welcome message.

9 Touch **Got It**.

You can start using your device.

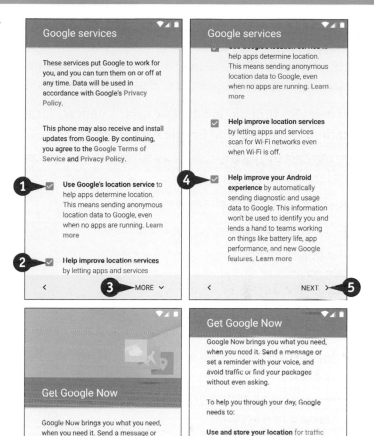

TIP

Should I back up my phone or tablet to my Google account?
Normally, it is a good idea to back up your Android phone or tablet to your Google account, because doing so enables you to recover your data and your device's configuration after hardware or software problems. But if you prefer not to entrust your data to Google, do not back up your phone or tablet to your Google account. Be aware that if you store a lot of content on your device, you may exceed the free storage allocation of your Google account and have to pay for extra space.

Connect to a Wireless Network

If you use your phone or tablet in multiple locations, you may need to connect to several wireless networks. You can quickly connect your device to wireless networks when you want to connect to the Internet. Many networks broadcast the network name, and often you need only provide the password to make a connection. If the network does not broadcast its name, you will need to type the name to connect. For some networks, you may need to specify an IP address or proxy server details.

Connect to a Wireless Network

Connect to a Wireless Network That Broadcasts Its Name

1. Touch **Home** (⊙).

   The Home screen appears.

2. Pull down from the top of the screen with two fingers.

   The Quick Settings panel opens.

3. Touch **Wi-Fi**.

   Note: Touch the **Wi-Fi** text label, not the symbol. Touching the symbol turns Wi-Fi on or off.

   The Wi-Fi screen appears.

4. Set the **Wi-Fi** switch to On (⬤ changes to ⬤).

5. Touch the appropriate network.

   A dialog box for connecting to the network opens.

   Note: If the network does not use security, Android connects to the network without displaying the connection dialog box.

6. Type the password.

   Ⓐ You can touch **Show password** (☐ changes to ☑) to display the password.

7. Touch **Connect**.

   Android connects to the network.

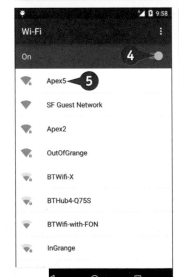

Connect to a Network That Does Not Broadcast Its Name

1 On the Wi-Fi screen, touch **Menu** (⦙).

The menu opens.

2 Touch **Add network**.

The Add Network dialog box opens.

3 Touch **Network name** and type the network name.

4 Touch **Security** and then touch the security type — for example, **WPA/WPA2 PSK**.

5 Touch **Password** and type the password.

6 Touch **Save**.

Connect to a Network and Specify Settings

1 On the Wi-Fi screen, touch the appropriate network.

2 Touch **Password** and type the password.

3 Touch **Advanced options** (☐ changes to ☑).

4 To set proxy server information, touch **Proxy**, touch **Manual**, and then choose the settings.

5 To set IP address information, touch **IP settings**, touch **Static**, and then choose the settings.

6 Touch **Connect**.

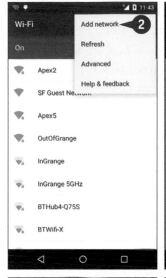

TIPS

How do I stop using a particular wireless network?

Tell your device to forget the network. Touch **Home** (⬤), touch **All Apps** (⬚), and then touch **Settings** (⚙). Touch **Wi-Fi** to display the Wi-Fi screen. Touch the network's name to open the dialog box for the network, and then touch **Forget**.

Can I set up a wireless network another way?

Yes, if the wireless network has *Wi-Fi Protected Setup*, or WPS, and you have physical access to the wireless router. If so, display the Wi-Fi screen, touch **Menu** (⦙), touch **Advanced**, and then touch **WPS Push Button.** You can then press the WPS button on the wireless network router to make Wi-Fi Protected Setup set up the network connection automatically.

Download and Install Companion Software

While you can use your Android phone or tablet as a stand-alone device, you may find it helpful to sync data such as contacts, photos, and songs between the phone or tablet and your PC or Mac. You can sync data between your Android device and your computer in two main ways. You can use companion software that syncs the data for you, such as the Samsung Kies app or the HTC Sync Manager app, or you can sync your data via your Google account or another online service.

Determine Whether Companion Software Is Available

Some manufacturers of Android phones and tablets provide companion software for syncing data to their devices. For example, Samsung provides the Smart Switch app for Windows and the Kies app for both Windows and OS X, whereas HTC provides the HTC Sync Manager app for Windows. The easiest way to find out if the manufacturer provides companion software for your device is to open your web browser and go to the manufacturer's website. If the manufacturer does not provide companion software, you may be able to find third-party sync software by searching on the web. Alternatively, you can copy files to your device manually.

Download the Companion Software

If you find suitable companion software or third-party sync software to use between your computer and your Android phone or tablet, download the software to your computer using your web browser. When downloading the installer file, your browser may offer you the choice between saving it and running it. Normally, saving the installer file is the better choice, because you can then run the installation again if necessary. If you locate the software by searching rather than by browsing the manufacturer's website, make sure you download it from the manufacturer's website rather than from a third-party site that may provide a version containing spyware or malware.

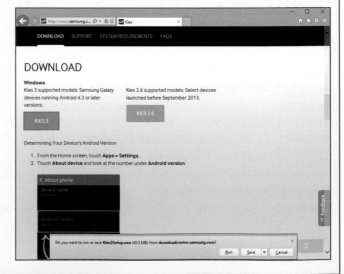

Install the Companion Software

After downloading the companion software, run its installer to install the software on your computer. On Windows, User Account Control prompts you to confirm that you want to allow the software to make changes to your computer; if you are not an administrator, you will need to provide an administrator password to proceed. On the Mac, you will need to authenticate as an administrator user in order to install the software for all users.

Follow through the installer, evaluating all options and choosing settings suitable to your needs. When installing third-party software, be careful to read all the on-screen prompts so that you can avoid installing any extra features, such as browser toolbars, that you do not want. After the installer finishes, restart your computer if prompted to do so.

Run the Companion Software and Sync Your Files

Run the companion software from the Start menu or from a desktop shortcut on Windows or from the Launchpad on OS X. The first time you run the software, you may need to choose which language to use and set some other options.

Connect your Android phone or tablet and verify that the app detects it. For example, in Samsung Kies, the phone or tablet appears in the Connected devices list in the upper-left corner of the window. You can then select items and transfer them between your computer and the device by dragging them from one to the other. Depending on the app, you may also be able to install new versions of Android on your phone or tablet and back it up to your computer.

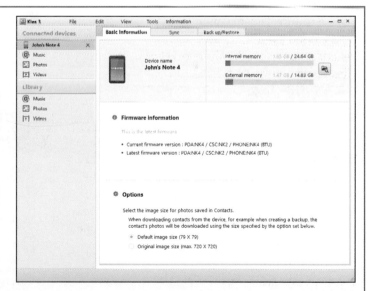

Transfer Files from Your PC to Your Device

You can load files on your phone or tablet by connecting the device to your PC via a USB cable and transferring files. If the manufacturer of your Android phone or tablet does not provide companion software for syncing files between your computer and the device, you can transfer files directly between the two. To do so, you can use File Explorer or Windows Explorer, the file-management programs that come built in to different versions of Windows. The storage space on your phone or tablet appears as a drive.

Transfer Files from Your PC to Your Device

1 Connect your phone or tablet to your PC via the USB cable.

Note: If the device's screen is protected with a PIN or password, unlock the device to allow your computer to access it.

Windows displays a banner prompting you to tap to choose what happens with the device.

2 Click or tap the banner.

The AutoPlay dialog box opens.

3 Click or tap **Open device to view files**.

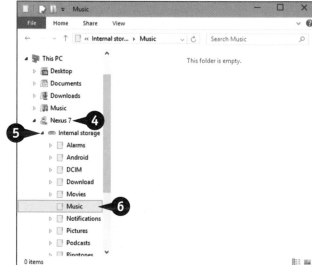

A File Explorer window or Windows Explorer window opens showing your device's contents.

4 Double-click your device's name.

5 Double-click **Internal storage**.

6 Click the appropriate folder. For example, if you want to copy music to your device, click **Music**.

The Windows Explorer window shows the contents of the folder you clicked on the device.

7 Open the folder or library that contains the files you want to copy. For example, right-click **Music** and click **Open in new window** on the context menu.

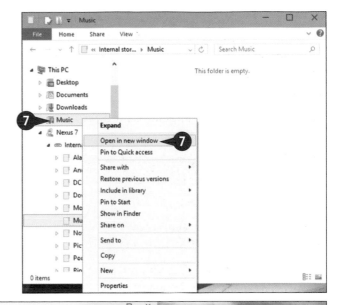

The folder or library you clicked opens.

8 Click the first item you want to copy.

9 Hold down **Shift** and click the last item you want to copy.

Windows selects the range of items.

10 Drag the items to the destination folder on your device.

Windows copies the files.

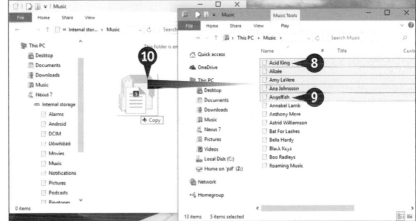

11 When Windows finishes copying the files, disconnect your phone or tablet from your computer.

TIP

How can I see how much free space my phone or tablet has?

Connect your phone or tablet to your PC and open a File Explorer window or Windows Explorer window. Click the device, click **Internal Storage**, and then look at the Internal Storage readout in the details pane. To see a pie chart showing how much space has been used and how much is left, right-click **Internal Storage** and then click **Properties** on the contextual menu.

Transfer Files from Your Mac to Your Device

If you have a Mac rather than a Windows PC, you need to add an app for transferring files to or from your Android device. Android phones and tablets do not appear in the OS X Finder, but you can use an app called Android File Transfer to transfer files. Android File Transfer is free, and it works well with standard Android devices. But if your device is designed to work with companion software, such as Samsung Kies, you should use that software instead of Android File Transfer.

Transfer Files from Your Mac to Your Device

Download and Install Android File Transfer

1. Click **Safari** (⊘) on the Dock.

   A Safari window opens.

2. Click in the Address box.

   The contents of the Address box become selected.

3. Type **www.android.com/filetransfer** and press **Return**.

   The Android File Transfer web page appears.

4. Click **Download Now**.

   The download begins.

5. When the download completes, click **Downloads**.

   The Downloads stack opens.

6. Click **androidfiletransfer.dmg**.

   A Finder window opens showing the contents of the Android File Transfer disk image.

7. Drag **Android File Transfer** (📱) to the Applications icon (🅰).

8. Drag the **Android File Transfer disk image** to the Trash (🗑).

   OS X ejects the disk image.

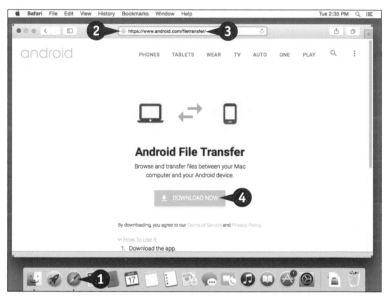

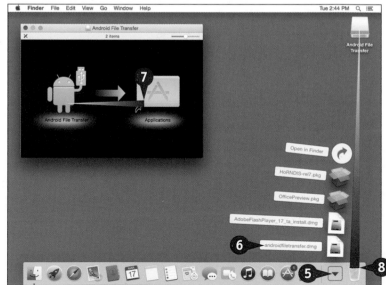

Launch Android File Transfer and Transfer Files

1 Connect your phone or tablet to your Mac via USB.

2 Click **Launchpad** ().

The Launchpad screen appears.

3 Click **Android File Transfer** (📱).

Android File Transfer opens and displays the contents of your device.

4 `Control`+click or right-click **Finder** (🙂).

The contextual menu opens.

5 Click **New Finder Window**.

A new Finder window opens.

6 Navigate to the folder that contains the files you want to copy to your device.

7 Select the files or folders.

8 Drag the items to the appropriate folder on your device. For example, drag song files to the Music folder.

Android File Transfer copies the files.

9 When you finish using Android File Transfer, disconnect your phone or tablet from your Mac.

TIPS

How can I see how much free space my device has?
After launching Android File Transfer, look at the status bar. The readout shows the amount of free space — for example, "5.55 GB available."

What other actions can I take with Android File Transfer?
You can delete a file or folder by `Control`+clicking or right-clicking it and then clicking **Delete** on the context menu. You can create a new subfolder by `Control`+clicking or right-clicking in the existing folder in which you want to create the subfolder, clicking **New Folder**, typing the name, and then pressing `Return`.

Explore the User Interface and Launch Apps

When you press the Power button to wake your phone or tablet from sleep, Android displays the lock screen. You then unlock the phone or tablet to reach the Home screen, which contains a Favorites tray of icons for running frequently used apps plus the All Apps icon for accessing the full list of apps installed on the device. You can add other icons to the Home screen as needed. When you launch an app, its screen appears. From the app, you can return to the Home screen by touching **Home** (⊙). You can then launch another app.

Explore the User Interface and Launch Apps

1 Press the Power button.

Note: If your device has a physical Home button rather than a soft button, you can normally press **Home** to wake the device instead of pressing the Power button.

The device's screen lights up and shows the lock screen.

2 Drag the **lock** icon (🔒) up to unlock your device.

Ⓐ You can swipe from the left to the right to go straight to the Phone app.

Ⓑ You can swipe from the right to the left to go straight to the Camera app.

The Home screen appears.

Note: If Android displays an app rather than the Home screen, touch **Home** (⊙) to display the Home screen.

3 Touch **All Apps** (▦).

The Apps screen appears.

4 Touch **Calculator** (▦).

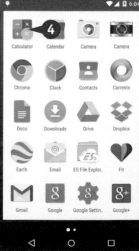

The Calculator app opens.

5 Touch the buttons to perform a calculation.

C Calculator displays a preview of the result.

D The result appears after you touch =.

Note: When your device is in portrait orientation, Calculator displays buttons for basic operations: addition, subtraction, multiplication, and division. Turn your device to landscape orientation to reveal more buttons.

6 Touch **Home** (◉).

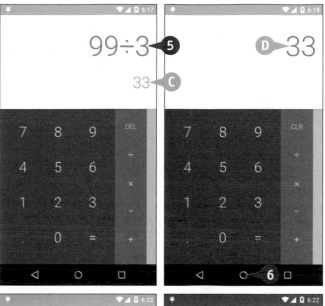

The Home screen appears.

7 Touch **All Apps** (⊞).

The Apps screen appears.

8 If the screen is full of apps, swipe your finger from right to left across the screen.

Note: If the Apps screen is not full, most likely there is no second screen of apps to display.

The next screen of apps appears.

9 Touch an app to launch it. For example, touch **Settings** (⚙) to open the Settings app, which you use to configure Android.

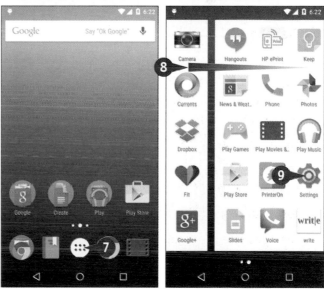

TIPS

Is there just one Home screen, or are there several?
Android provides multiple Home screens. You can navigate among them by swiping right or left when a Home screen is displayed. When you touch **Home** (◉), your device displays the Home screen you used last. Chapter 2 explains how to customize the Home screens.

Where do I get more apps to perform other tasks?
You can find a wide selection of apps — both free and ones you must pay for — in the Apps section of Google's Play Store. See Chapter 8 for instructions on finding and downloading the apps you need.

Understanding Skinned Versions of Android

Google's Android is currently the most widely used operating system for smartphones and tablets. At this writing, the latest version of Android is version 5, which is known as Lollipop. This book shows Lollipop in its regular form. But many manufacturers add overlays called *skins* to Android. The skins typically add extra functionality, modify the interface for existing apps and features, and make Android look different. If your Android phone or tablet uses a skin, you can still use this book, but you may need to consult your device's documentation to learn about differences and extra functionality.

Establish Whether Your Android Device Uses a Skin

You can easily establish whether your Android phone or tablet uses a skin. Touch **Home** (🔘) to display the Home screen, and then see if it looks like the left screen in the illustration or significantly different, as the right screen does. The left screen shows stock Lollipop; the right shows Lollipop with a skin. If your device's screens look like those in most of the screens in this book, your device uses stock Android Lollipop. But if your phone or tablet is from a manufacturer that uses a skin — such as Samsung, HTC, Motorola, or Sony — most likely it uses a skin rather than stock Android.

Major Android Skins

Many manufacturers apply custom skins to their devices. At this writing, Samsung's TouchWiz skin, HTC's Sense skin, and the skins from Motorola and Sony are the most widely used, but skins from Huawei, Xiaomi, OnePlus, and other manufacturers are also installed on many devices. Amazon's Kindle Fire devices also use a highly customized skin. Skins change Android's look in different ways and to different degrees.

Some manufacturers put skins on all their Android devices, whereas other manufacturers put skins on some devices but not all.

Advantages of Skins

Skins have several advantages over stock Android. First, skins can provide extra features and greater functionality than stock Android. For example, Samsung's TouchWiz skin includes support for the S Pen stylus in Android devices such as the Galaxy Note 4, enabling you to draw accurately on the screen and making note-taking easier. Second, a skin can provide greater integration with the specific hardware in a particular phone or tablet, so a manufacturer can make it easier for you to take full advantage of the hardware built in to the device. At the same time, the manufacturer can disable some of Android's stock functionality to encourage you to use the features it has added to the skin. Third, a skin can simply make Android look more attractive — or less so.

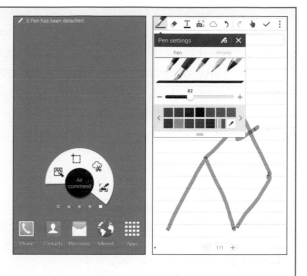

Disadvantages of Skins

If your phone or tablet uses a skin, you may not be able to update to the latest version of Android until a long time after its release. This is because after Google releases each new Android version, a manufacturer must create a new skinned version of Android customized to its phones and tablets. Often, manufacturers decide not to create a new custom version of Android for their older devices that are reaching the end of their product life cycles. This leaves the devices stuck on an older version of Android. If you are considering buying an older Android device, bear in mind that you may not be able to update it to newer versions of Android.

Skinned versions of Android may also run more slowly than regular versions. While high end devices can run skinned Android at full speed, you should test a device for speed before buying it.

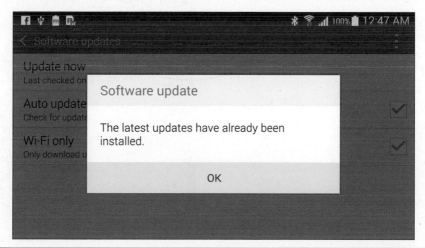

continued ▶

Skinned versions of Android typically customize first the areas in which phone and tablet users spend the most time, and second the features and apps from which users will derive most benefit. Four of the major areas in which skins often change the Android user interface are the Home screen, including the Favorites tray; the lock screen; the Notification shade; and the Settings app. Depending on the skin, you may also find that the manufacturer has provided an enhanced Camera app to make full use of the hardware features your device offers.

Home Screen

Most skins customize the Home screen, because it is a screen where each user will normally spend a lot of time taking actions. By providing different wallpapers, a manufacturer can give its Android devices a distinct look; and by building additional functionality into the interface, the manufacturer can make its phones and tablets faster and easier to use. Most skins customize the Favorites tray that appears at the bottom of the Home screen. For example, Samsung's TouchWiz skin rearranges the icons, putting the Apps icon on the right rather than in the middle.

Lock Screen

Most skins customize the lock screen, adding functionality to it in various ways. For example, in OnePlus' CyanogenMod skin, you can drag the lock icon to different icons arranged in a semicircle to unlock the device straight into specific apps, such as Phone, Hangouts, or Chrome. By contrast, in stock Android, you can swipe left from the lock screen to open the Camera app, which is useful for taking photos quickly. If your phone or tablet uses a skin, check the documentation to learn about any extra actions you can take from the lock screen, such as switching straight into apps or adding lock-screen widgets.

Notification Shade

The Notification shade, which you learn to use at the end of this chapter, brings together all your notifications — such as incoming calls and messages, app updates, and operating-system updates — into a single pane that you can easily access by dragging down the status bar at the top of the screen. Most skins customize the Notification shade to put frequently needed items right at your fingertips. For example, whereas in stock Android you can touch the bar at the top of the Notification shade to display the Quick Settings panel, the top of the Notification shade in TouchWiz displays a scrollable list of essential settings to give you instant access to a wider range of settings. TouchWiz also uses a more colorful look for the Notification shade than stock Android does.

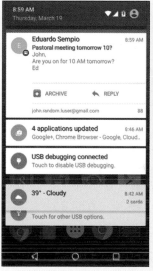
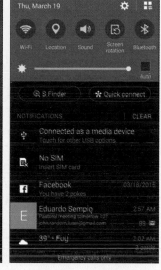

Settings App

Most skins also customize the Settings app, the app that you use to manipulate the settings on your Android device. Changes to the Settings app include adding settings for extra features; removing access to features that the skin disables; and changing the overall look of the Settings app itself for cosmetic reasons. For example, the TouchWiz skin changes the icon for not only the Settings app itself but also each of the settings categories. TouchWiz adds extra features, such as Blocking mode and the Power saving mode, to the main Settings screen. TouchWiz also provides access to Samsung's custom Application Manager app, which you use to control the apps that are running and to force-quit any app that stops responding to the user interface.

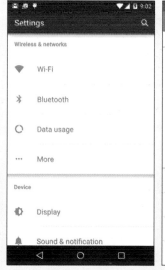

Navigate with Gestures

To navigate the Android user interface smoothly and swiftly, you can use seven main gestures. To trigger the default action for an item, you touch it and raise your finger. To access extra functionality, you touch and hold for a moment. To select text or zoom in to content, you double-tap.

To scroll from one screen to another, you swipe right, left, up, or down. To move a shorter distance, you drag a finger. To zoom in or out, you pinch apart or pinch inward with two fingers.

Navigate with Gestures

1 Touch **Home** (⬤), pressing your finger briefly to the screen and then lifting it.

The Home screen appears.

2 Touch **All Apps** (⬚).

The Apps screen appears.

3 Touch **Maps** (▨).

Note: If Maps (▨) is not on the Apps screen that appears first, scroll left or right until you find Maps (▨).

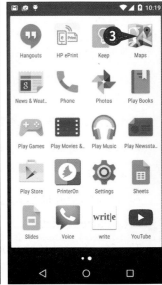

The Maps app opens and displays the area around your current location.

4 Swipe left by moving your finger rapidly from the right side of the screen to the left side.

The map scrolls, following the direction you swiped.

5 Double-tap with one finger an item or area of interest on the screen.

Note: The double-tap gesture is also called "double-touch."

The map zooms in on the area you double-tapped.

Note: In the Maps app, double-tap to zoom in by increments; double-tap with two fingers to zoom out.

6 Place your thumb and finger close together on the screen and then move them apart. This is the "pinch apart" or "pinch open" gesture.

The map zooms in on the point where you pinched apart.

Note: To zoom out, place your thumb and finger apart on the screen and then pinch them inward. This is the "pinch in" or "pinch close" gesture.

7 Touch and hold a road on the screen for a moment.

A A dropped pin (📍) appears.

B A banner appears.

8 Touch the banner.

An information screen appears.

9 Touch **Street View**.

The Street view of the location appears, showing photos of the road.

10 Touch the screen and drag your finger in the direction opposite that in which you want the map to move. For example, drag to the left to move the view to the right.

The view shifts to follow your finger.

11 Touch **Back** (◀) to exit Street view.

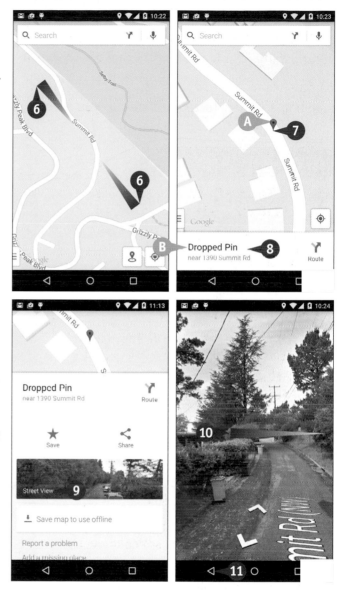

TIPS

What is the difference between swiping and dragging?
Swiping is a more expansive gesture than dragging. You swipe to move from one screen to another, whereas you drag to move within a screen. In some cases, you can either swipe or drag to get the same effect.

Are there other gestures I can use with my phone or tablet?
Yes. Android supports other gestures that you can use within particular apps or features. You will learn about such gestures later in this book.

Work with Notifications

Your phone or tablet can receive many notifications: missed calls, text messages, reminders, meetings, and so on. Android integrates all these notifications into the Notification shade, an area you can pull down from the top of the screen. You can quickly open the Notification shade from the Home screen or almost any other screen. From the Notification shade, you can go to the app that raised a particular notification, dismiss a notification, dismiss all notifications, or simply close the Notification shade again.

Work with Notifications

Open the Notification Shade

1 Touch **Home** (◉).

The Home screen appears.

Note: You can open the Notification shade from almost any Android app. A few apps, such as the Camera app, are exceptions.

2 Touch the status bar at the top of the screen and drag downward.

The Notification shade opens.

Note: On a phone, the Notification shade takes up the whole screen. On a tablet, the Notification shade takes up the center area at the top of the screen.

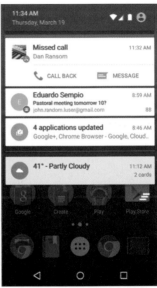

View the Details for a Notification

A The details for the topmost notification normally appear, including any action buttons.

B The details for other notifications are hidden to save space.

1 Drag your finger down the notification whose details you want to view.

C The notification details and any action buttons appear.

Note: Only some notifications have action buttons.

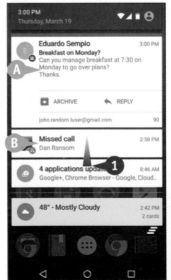
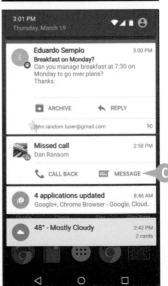

Respond Directly to a Notification

1 In the Notification shade, touch the action button you want to use. For example, for a missed call, touch **Call Back** (📞).

The appropriate app appears, and the action begins. For example, the Phone app appears and starts placing the return call.

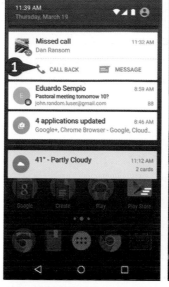

Go to the App That Raised a Notification

1 Touch the appropriate notification.

The app opens and displays the source of the notification.

You can now work in that app.

Note: Drag or swipe open the Notification shade again when you want to work with other notifications.

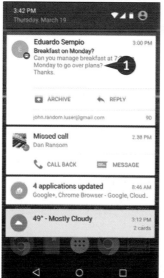

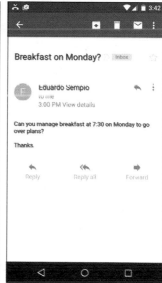

continued ▶

TIP

Do I drag or swipe down to open the Notification shade?
You can either drag or swipe. Dragging the status bar down lets you peek at the contents of the Notification shade without opening it fully. Swiping opens the Notification shade fully at once.

Android also enables you to display your notifications on the lock screen and access them from there. Displaying notifications on the lock screen can be helpful when you need to stay up to date without unlocking your device, but it may mean that others can also see your notifications. To alleviate any security concerns this may raise, you can choose which notifications to display on the lock screen; see Chapter 2 for details.

Work with Notifications (continued)

Dismiss a Notification

1. To dismiss a notification, swipe the notification to the left or right.

   The notification disappears from the list.

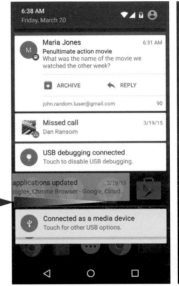

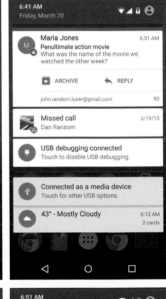

Dismiss All Notifications

1. If Dismiss All (⊟) is not visible, drag your finger up the list of notifications until Dismiss All (⊟) appears.

2. Touch **Dismiss all** (⊟).

   Android dismisses all the alerts that do not require your attention.

   Android closes the Notification shade.

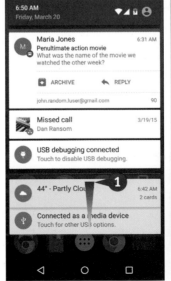

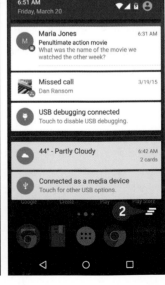

Close the Notification Shade

1 If you do not dismiss all alerts, touch the bar at the bottom of the Notification shade and drag up to close the shade.

Note: You can also swipe up the screen from the bottom to close the Notification shade.

The Notification shade closes, and the Home screen or whichever app was underneath the shade appears.

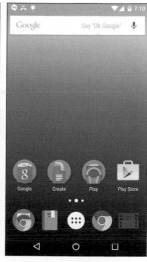

Work with Notifications on the Lock Screen

1 Touch a notification.

D The *Touch again to open* prompt appears.

Note: You can drag your finger down a notification on the lock screen to display any details and action buttons.

Note: You can swipe a notification off the screen to the left or right.

2 Touch the same notification again.

3 Provide your unlocking method if prompted.

Your device unlocks and displays the app that raised the notification.

TIPS

Why do notifications on the lock screen not show details or action buttons?

Notifications on the lock screen are collapsed by default, but you can drag your finger down a notification to display its details and any action buttons available.

Why does my device sometimes require unlocking and sometimes not?

You can set up the Smart Lock feature to unlock your device automatically under specific conditions, such as when the device's camera detects your face, the device detects your smart watch nearby, or the device is in a trusted location, such as your workplace. See Chapter 2 for details.

Using Google Now

Google Now is a feature built into Android that provides information relevant to what you are doing. Google Now uses cards to provide chunks of information, such as weather forecasts and driving directions, that you can quickly browse, act upon, and dismiss. You can customize the types of information that Google Now provides in order to make the information useful. You can access Google Now quickly from your device's Home screen.

Turn Google Now On or Off

When you set up your Android device, the Get Google Now screen appears after you specify your Google account and choose settings for Google Services. If you touch **Yes, I'm in** (⚪ changes to ⦿) and then touch **Next** on the Get Google Now screen, Android enables Google Now on your device.

If you touch **No, thanks** (⚪ changes to ⦿) instead, you can turn on Google Now at any point afterward. Touch **Home** (⬤) to display the Home screen, touch the **Google** search box, and then touch **Get Now Cards**. On the Google screen that appears, shown here, touch **Set Up**, and then touch **Yes, I'm In** on the Set Up Now Cards? screen.

Display the Google Now Screen

When Google Now is turned on for your Android device, you can quickly access the Google Now screen. Touch **Home** (⬤) to display the Home screen, and then swipe right to display the Google Now screen.

At the top of the Google Now screen is the Google search box. You can search by touching this box and then typing or dictating text. You can also start a search by saying "OK Google" when the *Say "Ok Google"* prompt appears.

Other items, such as your location's current and forecast weather and news stories recommended for you, appear further down the screen. Scroll down to see more items.

Navigate Google Now

To navigate Google Now, touch **Menu** (☰). On the menu panel, shown here, you can perform four actions. First, you can touch **Reminders** to display your current reminders or to add new reminders. Second, you can touch **Customize** to display the Customize Google Now screen, which enables you to specify your usual means of transport; select sports and stocks that interest you; define important places, such as your home and your workplace; and choose whether to receive weather updates. Third, you can touch **Settings** to access Google Now's configuration options. Fourth, you can touch **Help & feedback** to get help or provide your feedback.

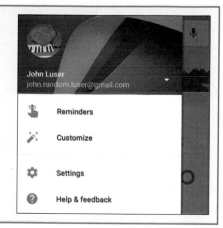

Choose Now Cards Settings

To choose settings for the Now cards you receive, touch Menu (☰), touch **Settings**, and then touch **Now cards** on the Settings screen. On the Now Cards screen, shown here, you can turn Google Now off entirely by setting the **Show cards** switch to Off (⬤ changes to ⬤). Normally, you will want to leave the **Show cards** switch set to On (⬤) and choose other settings. You can set the **Show notifications for card updates** switch to On (⬤ changes to ⬤) to receive notifications for updates. You can touch **Ringtone** to set a ringtone for urgent updates. If your device has a vibration motor, you can set the **Vibrate** switch to On (⬤ changes to ⬤) to receive vibration alerts for urgent reminders. Touch **Back** (◁) twice when you finish choosing settings.

Set Reminders

Google Now enables you to create reminders for tasks you need to perform. To work with reminders, touch **Menu** (☰) and then touch **Reminders**. On the Reminders screen, touch **Add** (⬤) to display the Add a Reminder screen, and then specify the details of the reminder. You can link the reminder to either a time or a place, and you can choose repetition if necessary. Touch **Done** (✔) when you finish.

You can also create reminders by voice. For example, from the Home screen, say "OK Google" and then, at the prompt, say "Remind me" and the details, such as "Remind me to wash the car tomorrow morning." Touch **Done** (✔) if the reminder that your device displays is correct.

CHAPTER 2

Customizing Your Phone or Tablet

To make your phone or tablet work the way you prefer, you can configure its many settings. This chapter shows you how to access the most important settings and use them to personalize the phone or tablet. You learn how to control notifications, audio preferences, screen brightness, and other key aspects of the device's behavior.

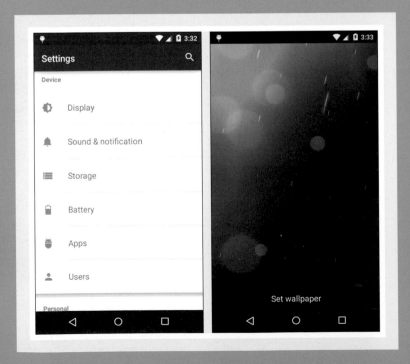

Find the Settings You Need

To configure your phone or tablet, you use the Settings app. This app contains settings for the Android operating system and the features your phone or tablet includes. To reach the settings, you display the Settings screen and then display the appropriate category of settings. Some apps provide access to settings through the apps themselves. If you cannot find the settings for an app on the Settings screen, look within the app.

Find the Settings You Need

Display the Settings Screen Using the Apps Screen

1. Touch **Home** (⬤).

   The Home screen appears.

2. Touch **All Apps** (⊞).

   The Apps screen appears.

Note: If Settings (⚙) is not on the Apps screen that appears first, scroll left or right until you find Settings (⚙).

3. Touch **Settings** (⚙).

   The Settings screen appears.

Display the Settings Screen Using the Quick Settings Panel

1. Pull down with two fingers from the top of the screen.

   The Quick Settings panel opens.

2. Touch **Settings** (⚙).

   The Settings screen appears.

Note: On the Settings screen, you can scroll up or down to see other categories of settings.

Display a Settings Screen

1 On the Settings screen, touch the button for the settings you want to display. For example, touch **Sound & notification** to display the Sound & Notification screen.

2 Touch **Back** (◄) when you are ready to return to the Settings screen.

Ⓐ You can also touch **Back** (←) in the upper-left corner of the screen to go back to the Settings screen.

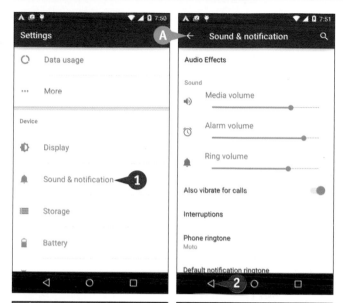

Display the Settings for an App

1 With the app running, touch the **Menu** button. The look of the Menu button varies depending on the app — for example, ⋮, ⋮, or ☰.

The menu opens.

2 Touch **Settings**.

The Settings screen appears.

3 Touch the setting you want to change. For example, ☐ changes to ☑.

4 When you finish changing the settings, touch **Back** (◄) to return to the app.

Ⓑ You can also touch the **Back** button (←) in the upper-left corner of the screen.

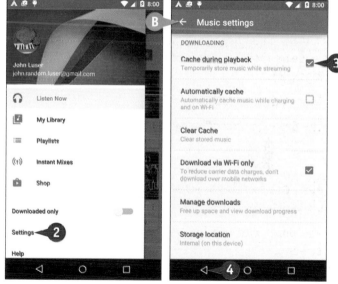

TIP

How can I access key settings quickly?

You can access key settings directly from the Quick Settings panel. Pull down with two fingers from the top of the screen to display the Quick Settings panel. You can then touch the setting you want to change.

You can also open the Quick Settings panel by opening the Notification shade and then touching open space in the bar at the top.

Choose Which Notifications to Receive

Some apps can display notifications to alert you when an event has occurred. For example, Calendar can remind you of upcoming appointments, and Settings can let you know when a software update is available. Notifications are great for keeping track of vital information, but you will probably want to choose which notifications you receive rather than receive all notifications. You can choose which apps give notifications. If your device has a notification light, you can choose whether to have the light pulse to alert you to notifications.

Choose Which Notifications to Receive

1 Touch **Home** (⬤).

The Home screen appears.

2 Touch **All Apps** (⊞).

The Apps screen appears.

3 Touch **Settings** (⚙).

Note: If Settings (⚙) is not on the Apps screen that appears at first, swipe left or right until you find Settings (⚙).

Note: You can also open the Settings app by opening the Quick Settings panel and then touching **Settings** (⚙).

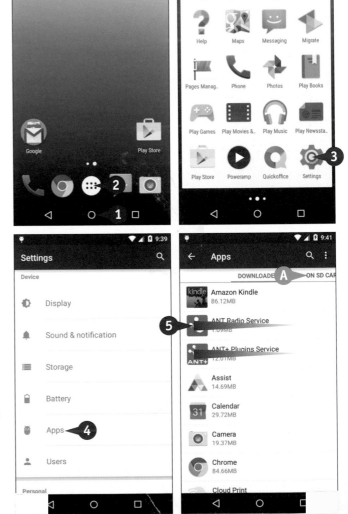

The Settings screen appears.

4 Touch **Apps**.

The Apps screen appears, showing the Downloaded tab at first. This tab shows apps you have added to your device from Google Play.

5 Swipe left two or three times until the All tab appears. This tab shows all the apps.

A The On SD Card tab appears only if your device contains an SD card.

6 Touch the app you want to affect.

The App Info screen for the app appears.

7 Touch **Show notifications** to select (☐ changes to ☑) or deselect (☑ changes to ☐) the check box, controlling whether Android displays notifications from this app.

8 Touch **Back** (◀).

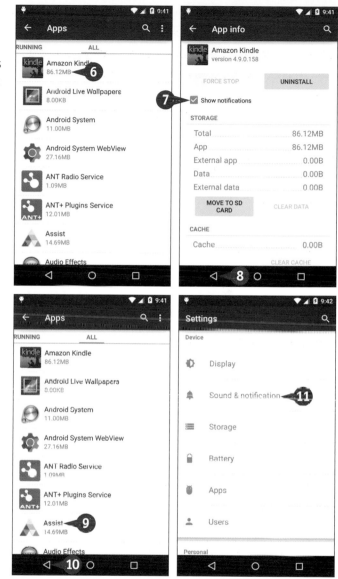

The Apps screen appears.

9 Repeat steps **6** to **8** to choose settings for other apps as needed.

10 Touch **Back** (◀) on the Apps screen.

The Settings screen appears.

11 Touch **Sound & notification**.

TIP

What other actions can I take on the App Info screen for an app?

You can take several other actions on the App Info screen for an app:

- Touch **Force stop** to force the app to stop if it has ceased to respond to your touches.

- Touch **Uninstall** to begin the process of uninstalling the app from your phone or tablet.

- Touch **Clear data** to delete the app's data files, including account details you have entered and settings you have chosen.

- Touch **Clear cache** to clear any data the app has stored in its cache for future use.

continued ▶

Your device can display notifications on the lock screen, enabling you to view them without unlocking your phone, as well as in the Notification shade. This handy feature can raise security concerns, so Android offers you three options: You can choose to display notifications and their content on the lock screen, show that apps have raised notifications but hide notification content that may be sensitive, or simply not display any notifications on the lock screen. Android also enables you to allow some apps to read notifications on your behalf.

Choose Which Notifications to Receive (continued)

The Sound & Notification screen appears.

12 Touch **Default notification ringtone**.

The Default Notification Ringtone dialog box opens.

13 Touch the ringtone you want to hear.

14 Touch **OK** when you have chosen a ringtone.

The Sound & Notification screen appears.

15 Touch **When device is locked**.

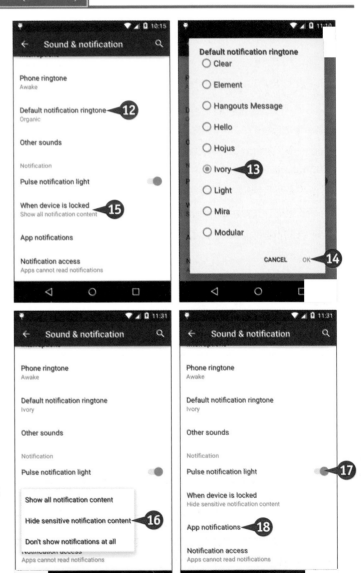

The When Device Is Locked pop-up menu opens.

16 Touch **Show all notification content**, **Hide sensitive notification content**, or **Don't show notifications at all**, depending on what you want the lock screen to show.

17 Set the **Pulse notification light** switch to On (changes to) if you want the phone or tablet's notification light to pulse when you have a notification. Otherwise, set the switch to Off (changes to).

18 Touch **App notifications**.

The App Notifications screen appears.

19 Touch the app you want to affect.

The App Notifications screen for the app appears.

Ⓑ You can touch **Search** (🔍) to search for an app by name.

Ⓒ You can set the **Block** switch to On (⬜ changes to 🔵) to prevent Android from showing notifications from this app.

20 Set the **Priority** switch to On (⬜ changes to 🔵) if you want to give this app's notifications priority. See the following tip for details on priority.

21 Touch **Back** (◀).

The App Notifications screen appears again.

22 Touch **Back** (◀) again.

The Sound & Notification screen appears.

23 Touch **Notification access** if you want to give an app access to notifications.

The Notification Access screen appears.

24 Touch the appropriate app.

The Enable? dialog box opens.

25 Touch **OK**.

Android enables notification access for the app (⬜ changes to ✅).

26 Touch **Back** (◀).

The Sound & Notification screen appears.

27 Touch **Back** (◀) again.

The Settings screen appears.

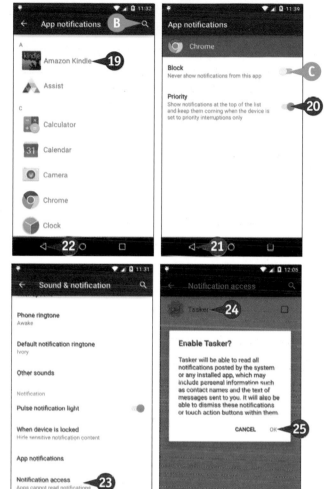

Configure Interruptions and Downtime

Android's Interruptions feature enables you to configure your phone or tablet to disturb you only with the notifications you want and at the appropriate times. You can choose among receiving all interruptions, receiving only priority interruptions, and receiving no interruptions; and you can choose which apps and which people can interrupt you. You can configure the Downtime feature to block off hours when you want to receive no interruptions, such as at night. You can also turn Downtime on and off as needed.

Configure Interruptions and Downtime

1 Touch **Home** (⬤).

The Home screen appears.

2 Touch **All Apps** (⬤).

The Apps screen appears.

3 Touch **Settings** (⚙).

Note: If Settings (⚙) is not on the Apps screen that appears at first, swipe left or right until you find Settings (⚙).

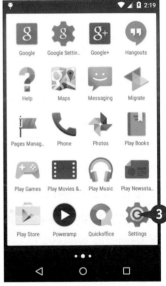

The Settings screen appears.

4 Touch **Sound & notification**.

The Sound & Notification screen appears.

5 Touch **Interruptions**.

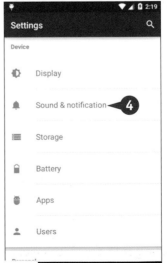

The Interruptions screen appears.

6 Touch **When calls and notifications arrive** and then touch **Always interrupt**, **Allow only priority interruptions**, or **Don't interrupt**, as appropriate.

7 Define your Priority Interruptions list by setting the **Events and reminders** switch, the **Calls** switch, and the **Messages** switch to On (⬜ changes to 🔵) or Off (🔵 changes to ⬜), as needed.

8 Touch **Calls/messages from**.

A pop-up menu opens.

9 Touch **Anyone**, **Starred contacts only**, or **Contacts only**, as appropriate.

10 Touch **Days**.

The Days dialog box opens.

11 Touch each day to select (⬜ changes to ✓) or deselect (✓ changes to ⬜) its check box.

12 Touch **Done**.

13 Touch **Start time**.

The time controls appear.

14 Touch the controls to set the time.

15 Touch **OK**.

16 Touch **End time** and use the time controls to set the end time.

17 Touch **Back** (◁).

The Sound & Notification screen appears.

18 Touch **Back** (◁) again.

The Settings screen appears.

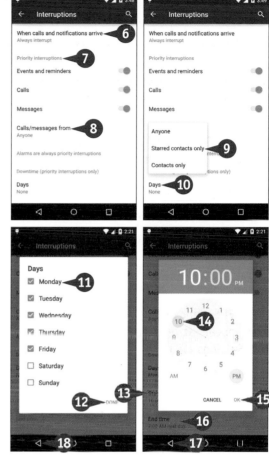

TIP

Can I turn off interruptions temporarily other than by using Downtime?

Yes. You can control interruptions quickly and easily by pressing the Volume Up button or the Volume Down button and then working on the Interruptions panel. Touch **None** to turn off interruptions, touch **Priority** to receive only priority notifications, or touch **All** to receive all notifications. For None or Priority, touch the **Indefinitely** pop-up button to display an extra part of the panel, and then touch **Indefinitely** (🔘 changes to 🔘) or **For one hour** (🔘 changes to 🔘). Touch **More** (➕) or **Less** (➖) to change the number of hours.

Choose Volume and Sound Settings

To control the playback volume of sounds and music on your phone or tablet, you can use either the hardware volume controls or the on-screen controls. To control your phone or tablet's audio feedback, choose settings on the Sound screen. Here, you can control the ringtone and vibration for a phone, set the default notification sound, and choose whether to play sounds to give feedback on touching the screen, locking the screen, or docking the phone or tablet.

Choose Volume and Sound Settings

1 Touch **Home** (⬤).

The Home screen appears.

2 Touch **All Apps** (⊞).

The Apps screen appears.

3 Touch **Settings** (⚙).

Note: If Settings (⚙) is not on the Apps screen that appears first, scroll left or right until you find Settings (⚙).

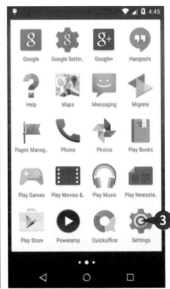

The Settings screen appears.

4 Touch **Sound & notification**.

The Sound & Notification screen appears.

5 Drag the **Media volume** slider to set the playback volume for music and video.

6 Drag the **Alarm volume** slider to set the alarm volume.

7 Drag the **Ring volume** slider to set the ring volume.

8 Set the **Also vibrate for calls** switch to On (⬤ changes to ⬤) or Off (⬤ changes to ⬤), as needed.

9 On a phone, touch **Phone ringtone**.

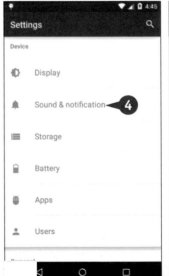

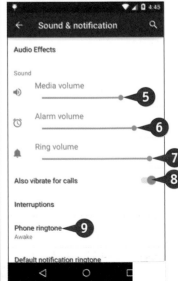

The Phone Ringtone dialog box opens.

10 Touch the ringtone you want to hear
(○ changes to ⦿).

11 When you have chosen a suitable ringtone,
touch **OK**.

The Phone Ringtone dialog box closes.

12 Touch **Other sounds**.

The Other Sounds screen appears.

13 Set the **Dial pad tones** switch, the **Screen
locking sounds** switch, the **Touch sounds**
switch, and the **Vibrate on touch** switch to On
( ) or Off ( ), as needed.

14 Touch **Back** ( ).

The Sound & Notification screen appears.

A You can investigate other sound options your
device offers, such as equalization.

15 Touch **Back** ( ).

The Settings screen appears.

TIP

Is there a quick way to change the volume?
If your phone or tablet has a physical Volume control, press the upper side of the control to increase the
volume, or press the lower side to decrease the volume. A volume control appears on the screen, showing
the volume setting.

From the Volume panel, you can also turn interruptions on and off quickly.

Set Display Brightness and Wallpaper

To make the display easy to view, you can change its brightness. You can also have your device's Adaptive Brightness feature automatically set the display brightness to a level suitable for the ambient brightness that the light sensor detects. You can also choose which picture to use as the wallpaper that appears in the background of the Home screen and lock screen. You can choose a picture of your own, select one of the built-in static wallpapers, or pick a live wallpaper that gradually changes.

Set Display Brightness and Wallpaper

1 Touch **Home** (⬤).

The Home screen appears.

2 Touch **All Apps** (⬚).

The Apps screen appears.

3 Touch **Settings** (⚙).

Note: If Settings (⚙) is not on the Apps screen that appears first, scroll left or right until you find Settings (⚙).

The Settings screen appears.

4 Touch **Display**.

The Display screen appears.

5 Touch **Brightness Level**.

Note: You can quickly change the wallpaper from any Home screen. Touch and hold the wallpaper until the Home screen opens for customization, touch **Wallpapers**, and then choose the wallpaper you want to apply.

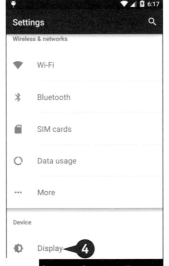

The Brightness panel appears.

6 Drag the **Brightness** slider (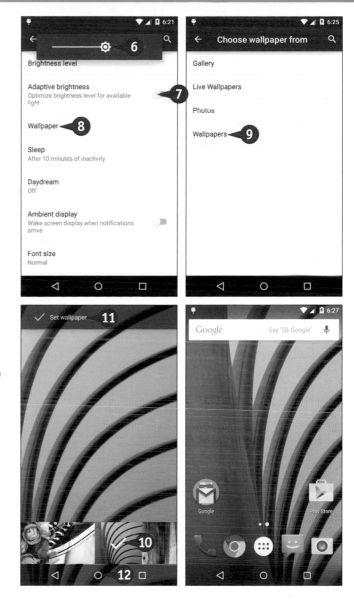) to set the brightness.

7 If you want your device to optimize the brightness to suit the available light, set the **Adaptive brightness** switch to On (changes to).

8 Touch **Wallpaper**.

The Choose Wallpaper From screen appears.

9 Touch the wallpaper source: **Live Wallpapers**, **Photos**, or **Wallpapers**, or another source your device offers. This example uses **Wallpapers**.

10 On the screen that appears, touch the picture, live wallpaper, or wallpaper you want.

Note: Live wallpaper can be attractive to look at, but it requires more power than static wallpaper, so it reduces battery runtime.

11 Touch **Set wallpaper**.

12 Touch **Home** ().

The wallpaper appears on the Home screen.

TIP

Is there a quick way to change the display brightness?
You can quickly change the display brightness from the Quick Settings panel. Pull down with two fingers from the top of the screen to open the Quick Settings panel, and then drag the **Brightness** slider () to the left or right.

Choose Location Access Settings

Your Android phone or tablet can determine your location using satellites in the Global Positioning System, or GPS, known wireless networks, and cell phone towers. Android and your apps can use your location information to tag your photos, customize your searches, and provide local information. In Android, you can choose whether to allow location access and — if you allow it — which means of determining location to use. You can also turn the Location Reporting feature and the Location History feature on and off as needed.

Choose Location Access Settings

1 Touch **Home** (⬤).

The Home screen appears.

2 Touch **All Apps** (▦).

The Apps screen appears.

3 Touch **Settings** (⚙).

Note: If Settings (⚙) is not on the Apps screen that appears first, scroll left or right until you find Settings (⚙).

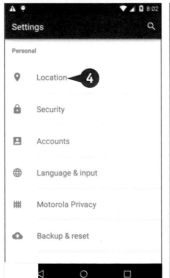

The Settings screen appears.

4 Touch **Location**.

The Location screen appears.

5 Set the **Location** switch to On (◯▭ changes to ▭◯).

Note: If the Use Enhanced Location Service dialog box opens, read the notice and touch **Agree** or **Disagree**, as appropriate.

Ⓐ The Recent Location Requests list shows which apps have recently requested the device's location.

6 Touch **Mode**.

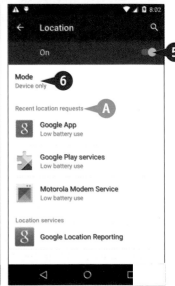

The Location Mode screen appears.

7 Touch **High accuracy**, **Battery saving**, or **Device only** (○ changes to ◉), as appropriate.

8 Touch **Back** (◁).

The Location screen appears.

9 Touch **Google Location Reporting**.

The Google Location Settings screen appears.

10 Touch **Location Reporting**.

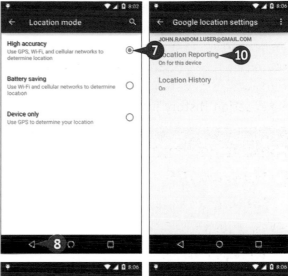

The Location Reporting screen appears.

11 Set the **Location Reporting** switch to On (○■ changes to ■●) or Off (■● changes to ○■), as needed.

12 Touch **Back** (◁).

The Google Location Settings screen appears.

13 Touch **Location History**.

The Location History screen appears.

14 Set the **Location History** switch to On (○■ changes to ■●) or Off (■● changes to ○■), as needed.

B You can touch **Delete Location History** to delete all your stored location data.

TIP

Should I grant location access when apps request it?

This is entirely up to you. Each time an app requests location access, make sure it has a good reason for using location access and is not just snooping on your movements.

Granting location access to apps can help you to get more out of your phone or tablet, but it also raises privacy concerns. For example, allowing social-media apps to access your location lets your friends keep up with your movements, but it can also enable people to stalk you. Similarly, adding location information to your photos enables you to sort them by location, which is helpful. But if you post photos containing location information online, other people can tell exactly where you took them.

Secure Your Phone or Tablet with a PIN

To prevent anyone who picks up your phone or tablet from accessing your data, you can lock the device with a Personal Identification Number, or PIN. This is a numeric code that takes effect when you lock your phone or tablet or it locks itself. To unlock the device, you must provide the PIN. If you need tighter security than a PIN can provide, you can use a password, which is harder to crack.

Secure Your Phone or Tablet with a PIN

1 Touch **Home** (⬤).

The Home screen appears.

2 Touch **All Apps** (⬛).

The Apps screen appears.

3 Touch **Settings** (⬤).

Note: If Settings (⚙) is not on the Apps screen that appears first, scroll left or right until you find Settings (⚙).

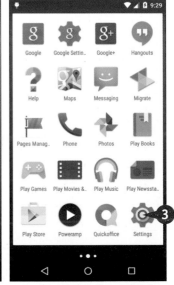

The Settings screen appears.

4 Touch **Security**.

The Security screen appears.

5 Touch **Screen lock**.

Note: Apart from a PIN, most Android devices offer three other locking options. For Swipe, you swipe your finger across the screen; this provides no security. For Pattern, you draw a pattern on a grid of nine dots. For Password, you type a password. The None option disables locking.

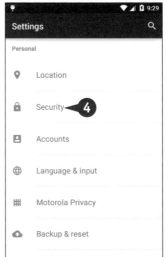

The Choose Screen Lock screen appears.

6 Touch **PIN**.

Note: At this point, you can choose a different means of security by touching **Swipe**, **Pattern**, or **Password**.

The Choose Your PIN screen appears.

7 Type a pin of four digits or more.

8 Touch **Continue**.

A second Choose Your PIN screen appears, prompting you to confirm your PIN.

9 Type the same PIN.

10 Touch **OK**.

The Security screen appears, now showing other options.

11 Set the **Power button instantly locks** switch to On (changes to) if you need tight security.

12 Touch **Automatically lock**.

The Automatically Lock dialog box opens.

13 Touch the appropriate time button — for example, **Immediately**.

The Security screen appears.

14 Touch **Back** (◀).

The Settings screen appears.

What is Smart Lock, and how do I use it?
Smart Lock is a feature that enables you to turn off the screen lock when your device is near a trusted device, is in a trusted place, or can detect a trusted face. For example, a trusted device might be your Android Wear watch; a trusted place could be your workplace, your home, or another location you visit regularly; and your trusted face would normally be the one you see in the mirror. To set up Smart Lock, touch **Smart Lock** on the Security screen. On the Smart Lock screen, touch **Trusted devices**, **Trusted places**, or **Trusted face**, and then follow the prompts.

Encrypt Your Phone or Tablet for Security

After you secure your phone or tablet with a PIN or password, you can protect your valuable data by also encrypting all the data on your device. Encryption scrambles the data so that it can be read only by someone who enters the PIN or password. Before encrypting your device, you must charge its battery fully. During encryption, the device must also be connected to a power source. Android requires both a charged battery and a power source to ensure that encryption can finish even if the power is cut.

Encrypt Your Phone or Tablet for Security

1 Plug your phone or tablet into a power source — either a power adapter or the USB port on a computer or powered USB hub — and charge it fully. Leave the phone or tablet connected to the power.

2 Touch **Home** (⬤).

The Home screen appears.

3 Touch **All Apps** (⬚).

The Apps screen appears.

4 Touch **Settings** (⚙).

Note: If Settings (⚙) is not on the Apps screen that appears first, scroll left or right until you find Settings (⚙).

The Settings screen appears.

5 Touch **Security**.

The Security screen appears.

6 Touch **Encrypt phone** or **Encrypt tablet**. This example uses **Encrypt tablet**.

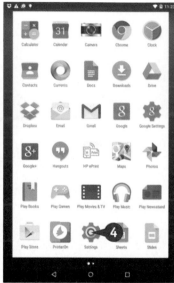

The Encrypt Phone screen or the Encrypt Tablet screen appears.

Note: If your phone or tablet is not plugged in to a power source, the Encrypt Phone button or the Encrypt Tablet button is dimmed and unavailable.

7 Touch **Encrypt phone** or **Encrypt tablet**.

The Confirm Your PIN screen appears.

Note: If your device uses a password rather than a PIN, the Confirm Your Password screen appears.

8 Type your PIN.

9 Touch **Continue**.

The Encrypt? screen appears, warning you that encryption is irreversible and that you must not interrupt it.

10 Touch **Encrypt phone** or **Encrypt tablet**.

Android begins encrypting the phone or tablet, displaying a progress readout on-screen as it does so.

The To Start Android, Enter Your PIN screen appears.

11 Type your PIN.

12 Touch **Done**.

The lock screen appears.

13 Type your PIN.

14 Touch ↲.

The Home screen appears, and you can start using your device normally.

How do I remove encryption from my phone or tablet?
After encrypting your phone or tablet, you cannot remove the encryption and leave the data in place. Instead, you must perform a factory data reset, which wipes the data from the device and restores factory settings. See Chapter 12 for instructions on performing a factory data reset. After the factory data reset, you can restore your apps, settings, and data to the device.

Choose Language and Input Settings

To be able to use your phone or tablet easily, you will want its user interface to use your language. Android supports many languages, and you can quickly switch among them. Android also provides various ways of entering text, ranging from assorted keyboard layouts to speech to typing via the Google voice feature. You can configure your input methods, the spell-checker, and other language options in Language & Input settings.

Choose Language and Input Settings

1 Touch **Home** (⬤).

The Home screen appears.

2 Touch **All Apps** (⊞).

The Apps screen appears.

3 Touch **Settings** (⚙).

Note: If Settings (⚙) is not on the Apps screen that appears first, scroll left or right until you find Settings (⚙).

The Settings screen appears.

4 Touch **Language & input**.

The Language & Input screen appears.

5 To change the language, touch **Language**, touch the appropriate language on the Language screen, and then touch **Settings** (⚙).

6 To use the spell-checker, touch **Spell checker**.

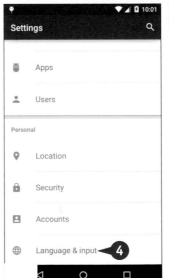

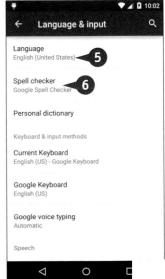

The Spell Checker screen appears.

7 Set the **Spell checker** switch to On (changes to).

8 Touch **Language** to open the Language dialog box, and then touch the language you want to use.

9 Touch **Options** ().

10 Set the **Look up contact names** switch to On (changes to) to look up contact names.

11 Touch **Back** ().

12 Touch **Back** () again.

The Language & Input screen appears.

13 Touch **Voice input** and use the Voice screen options to configure Voice Input.

14 Touch **Back** ().

15 Touch **Text-to-speech output** and use the Text-to-Speech Output screen options to configure the Text-to-Speech feature.

16 To change the pointer speed for an attached mouse or trackpad, touch **Pointer speed** and drag the slider in the Pointer Speed dialog box that opens.

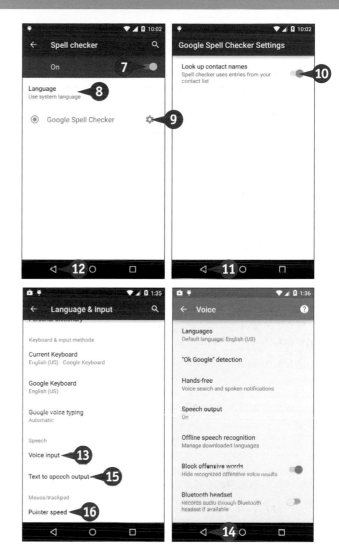

TIP

What is a personal dictionary, and how do I use it?

Your personal dictionary is a list containing terms you can enter quickly by typing a shortcut. For example, if you add the term "Vice President for Sales & Marketing" with the shortcut "vpsm," you can quickly enter the term by typing **vpsm** and touching the term on the spelling suggestions bar.

Touch **Personal dictionary** on the Language & Input screen to display the Personal Dictionary screen. Touch **Add** (), type the word, and then type the shortcut. You can omit the shortcut to add the word to the dictionary to prevent the spell-checker from querying it.

Customize the Home Screens

To make your phone or tablet easy to use, you can customize your Home screens by adding the apps and widgets you find most useful and removing any apps or widgets you do not need. You can reposition the apps and widgets on each Home screen as best suits you, and you can customize the Favorites tray at the bottom of the Home screen with essential apps. You can also resize the widgets to their optimum sizes.

Customize the Home Screens

Put an App on a Home Screen

1 Touch **Home** (⬤).

The Home screen appears.

2 Navigate to the Home screen panel on which you want to put the app.

3 Touch **All Apps** (⊞).

The Apps screen appears.

4 Touch and hold the app you want to add to the Home screen.

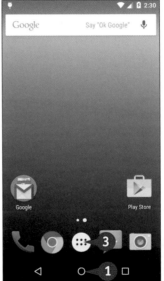

The Home screen appears with the app at the top.

5 Drag the app to where you want it.

Note: You can drag left or right to display a different Home screen panel if necessary.

6 Release the app.

Customize the Favorites Tray

1 Touch **Home** ().

The Home screen appears.

Note: If the Favorites tray is full of apps, you must remove an app before you can add another app.

2 Touch and hold the app you want to remove from the Favorites tray.

A The Remove button appears.

3 Drag the app out of the Favorites tray onto the main part of the Home screen and release it.

4 Touch and hold the app you want to add to the Favorites tray.

The Remove button appears.

5 Drag the app to the Favorites tray and release it.

Put a Widget on the Home Screen

1 Touch **Home** ().

The Home screen appears.

2 Navigate to the Home screen to which you want to add the widget.

3 Touch and hold open space on the Home screen.

The Home screen opens for customization.

B The Home screen panel thumbnails appear.

C The Wallpapers icon, Widgets icon, and Settings icon appear.

4 Touch **Widgets**.

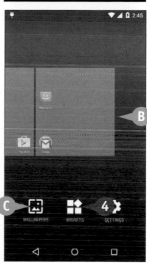

TIP

What are widgets?

Widgets are miniature apps that display useful information or give you quick access to frequently used apps. For example, the Analog Clock widget and Digital Clock widget simply display the time on the Home screen at an easy-to-see size. The Gmail widget displays the contents of a folder, and you can touch a message to open it in the Gmail app. Android comes with a wide range of built-in widgets, but you can also download other widgets from the Play Store and other online sources.

continued ▶

Customize the Home Screens (continued)

To organize the Home screens, you can arrange the apps into folders. You create a folder by dragging one icon onto another icon. Doing this creates a folder containing both items. You can then name the folder. You can create folders both on the main part of the Home screen and in the Favorites tray. After creating a folder, you can populate it with as many apps as needed. You can quickly open an app from within the folder, and you can remove an app from the folder if necessary.

Customize the Home Screens (continued)

The Widgets screen appears.

5 Touch and hold the widget you want to add.

The current Home screen thumbnail appears with the widget at the top.

6 Drag the widget to where you want it.

7 Release the widget.

Note: After you add the widget, you may need to choose options for it — for example, the Photo Gallery widget prompts you to choose which photos to display.

Resize a Widget

1 Touch **Home** (◉).

The Home screen appears.

2 Touch and hold the widget.

Ⓓ A box and adjustment handles appear around the widget.

3 Drag a handle to resize the widget.

4 Touch outside the widget to deselect it.

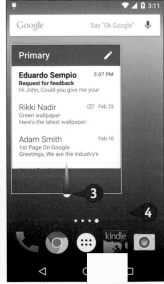

Create a Folder

1 Touch **Home** (⬤).

The Home screen appears.

2 Touch and hold an app you want to put in the new folder.

The Remove button appears.

3 Drag the app to another app destined for the folder.

Android creates an unnamed folder containing the two apps.

4 Touch the folder.

The folder opens.

5 Touch **Unnamed Folder**.

6 Type the folder name.

7 Touch outside the folder.

Note: You can now drag other apps to the folder.

Note: To launch an app from the folder, touch the folder, and then touch the app.

TIP

How do I remove an app or a widget from the Home screen?

Touch and hold the app or widget until the Remove button appears at the top of the screen. Drag the app or widget to the Remove button, and then drop it.

Removing an app from the Home screen removes only the icon for the app. The app itself remains on your device, and you can run it from the Apps screen as usual. If you want to remove the app from your device, follow the instructions in the section "Remove Apps You No Longer Need" in Chapter 8.

Set Up Sleep and Daydream

Android includes Daydream, a feature similar to screen savers on computers. By turning on Daydream and choosing settings, you can make your phone or tablet display information or graphics on-screen while it sleeps or charges. For example, you can display a clock or a photo frame that shows a selection of photos. Whether you choose to use Daydream or not, you can control how long your phone or tablet stays awake before going to sleep automatically.

Set Up Sleep and Daydream

1 Touch **Home** (⬤).

The Home screen appears.

2 Touch **All Apps** (⬚).

The Apps screen appears.

3 Touch **Settings** (⚙).

Note: If Settings (⚙) is not on the Apps screen that appears first, scroll left or right until you find Settings (⚙).

The Settings screen appears.

4 Touch **Display**.

The Display screen appears.

5 Touch **Sleep**.

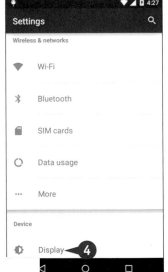

The Sleep dialog box opens.

6 Touch the time to wait before sleep
(◯ changes to ◉).

The Sleep dialog box closes.

7 Touch **Daydream**.

The Daydream screen appears.

8 Set the **Daydream** switch to On
(⬜ changes to 🔵).

9 In the list, touch the Daydream type to use,
such as **Photo Table**.

10 Touch **Settings** (⚙) if the button appears
on your choice. Choose options on the
resulting screen, and then touch **Back** (◀).

11 Touch **Menu** (⋮).

The menu opens.

12 Touch **When to daydream**.

The When to Daydream dialog box opens.

13 Touch **While docked**, **While charging**, or
Either, as appropriate (◯ changes to ◉).

14 Touch the **Menu** button (⋮).

The menu opens.

15 Touch **Start now**.

Daydream starts.

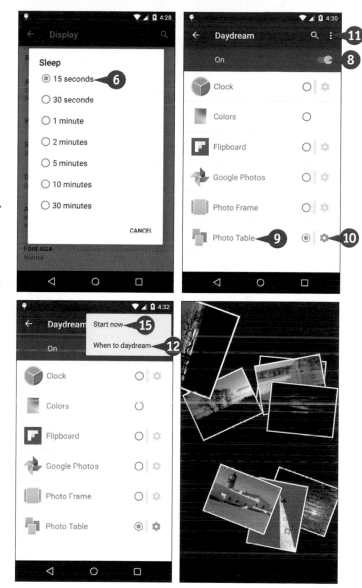

What is the difference between the Photo Frame theme and the Photo Table theme?
Photo Frame shows one photo at a time and is good for enjoying your photos. Photo Table gradually
arranges miniature versions of your photos on a table-like surface and is more of a decorative effect.
In Photo Table, you can rearrange the photos by dragging.

Install Credentials

To connect your phone or tablet to the network or e-mail servers in a company or organization, you may need to use credentials. These are digital certificates, encrypted chunks of code that uniquely identify a computer and are protected against tampering. Before you can use a digital certificate, you must install it on your phone or tablet. You can install it easily from the device's Download folder. If the certificate is not already in the Download folder, you will need to put it there, as explained in the tip.

Install Credentials

Note: If you have not already protected your phone or tablet with a PIN or password, do so now. The device must have a PIN or password before you can install a certificate.

1. Touch **Home** (⬤).

   The Home screen appears.

2. Touch **All Apps** (▦).

   The Apps screen appears.

3. Touch **Settings** (⚙).

Note: If Settings (⚙) is not on the Apps screen that appears first, scroll left or right until you find Settings (⚙).

The Settings screen appears.

4. Touch **Security**.

   The Security screen appears.

5. Touch **Install from storage** or **Install from SD card**, depending on which command your device shows.

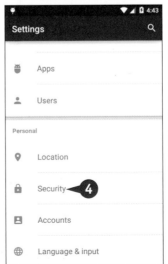

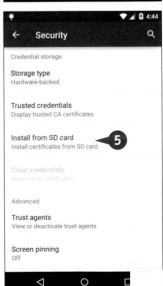

The Downloads screen appears.

Note: If the Recent Files screen appears, touch **Downloads** to display the Downloads screen.

6 Touch the certificate you want to install.

The Confirm Your PIN screen appears.

Note: If your device uses a password rather than a PIN, the Confirm Your Password screen appears. Type your password.

Note: If your device uses Smart Lock, Smart Lock may bypass the Confirm Your PIN screen or the Confirm Your Password screen.

7 Type your PIN.

8 Touch **Next**.

The Name the Certificate dialog box opens.

9 Edit the name as needed.

10 Touch the **Credential use** pop-up menu and then touch **VPN and apps** or **Wi-Fi** to specify how you will use the certificate.

11 Touch **OK**.

Ⓐ Android installs the certificate and displays a message saying it has done so.

12 Touch **Back** (◁).

The Security screen appears.

Note: To remove all the certificates from your phone or tablet, open the Security screen in Settings, and then touch **Clear credentials**.

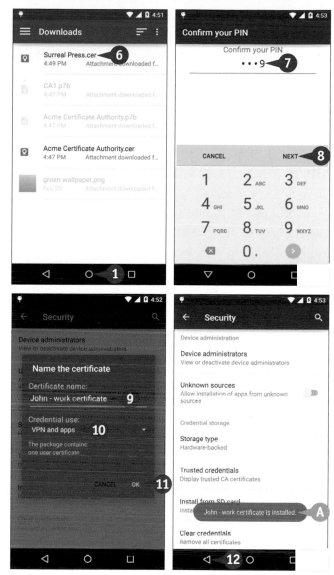

TIP

How do I put a certificate file in my device's storage?

E-mail is the easiest way to install a digital certificate on your phone or tablet. Send the digital certificate as an attachment to a message, and then open the message on the device. In the Attachments area, touch **Menu** (⋮) for the attachment, and then touch **Save**.

If you cannot use e-mail to install a certificate, use an app such as File Explorer, Windows Explorer, or Android File Transfer to copy the certificate file to the Download folder.

CHAPTER 3

Sharing Your Device with Others

Android enables you to share your device with others without compromising your security. You can share by pinning an app to the screen or using Guest mode, add users or restricted profiles, and switch quickly from user to user.

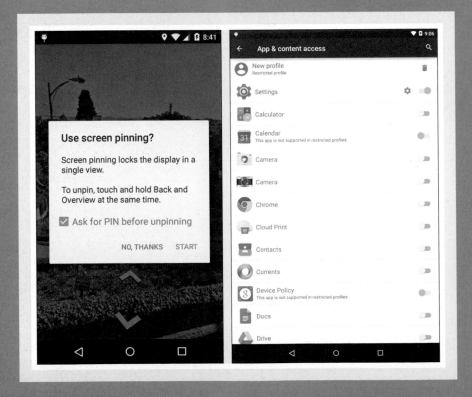

Using Screen Pinning

Sometimes you may want to hand your phone or tablet to someone else so that she can view what is on the screen — but without her being able to access other information on the device. Android enables you to share your device like this by fixing an app to the screen. This feature is called *screen pinning*. Before you can pin an app, you must turn on screen pinning as explained in the tip. You can then pin an app by using the Overview screen.

Using Screen Pinning

Pin an App

1 Touch **Home** (⬤).

The Home screen appears.

2 Touch **All Apps** (▦).

The Apps screen appears.

3 Touch the app you want to open. This example uses **Maps** (🗺).

Note: If the app is already running, you can touch **Overview** (■) and then touch the app's thumbnail to switch to it.

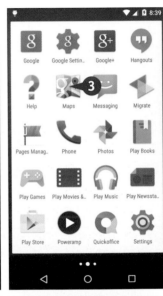

The app opens.

4 Display the content you want to share. For example, in Maps, navigate to the appropriate place.

Note: You can pin only the front app — the app you used last.

5 Touch **Overview** (■).

The Overview screen appears.

6 Touch the bottom thumbnail and pull up.

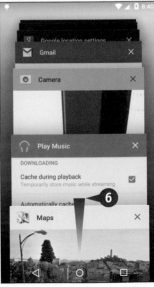

The entire thumbnail appears.

7 Touch **Screen pinning** (⬤).

The app appears.

The Use Screen Pinning? dialog box opens.

8 Touch **Ask for PIN before unpinning**
(☐ changes to ☑).

9 Touch **Start**.

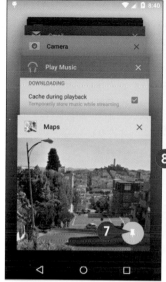

The Use Screen Pinning? dialog box closes.

A The *Screen pinned* message appears briefly.

10 Hand your device to the other person. She can use only the app you have pinned.

11 When you are ready to stop pinning, touch and hold **Back** (◁) and **Overview** (■) together.

The screen locks.

12 Unlock the screen as usual.

Note: If you did not require a PIN to unlock, the *Screen unpinned* message appears briefly. You can then resume normal use.

TIP

How do I turn on screen pinning in the Settings app?

1 Touch **Home** (⬤).

2 Touch **All Apps** (⊞).

3 Touch **Settings** (⚙).

4 Touch **Security**.

5 Touch **Screen pinning**.

6 Set the **Screen pinning** switch to On (⬤ changes to ⬤).

Using Guest Mode

When you need to allow someone else to use your phone or tablet, you can switch to Guest mode. Guest mode enables someone else to use your device without being able to access your data. For example, you might use Guest mode to enable someone to make a phone call using your phone. Guest mode is enabled by default, and you can switch to it quickly. After the other person finishes using your device, you can switch back to your own account swiftly and easily.

Using Guest Mode

Switch to Guest Mode

1 Touch **Home** (◉).

The Home screen appears.

2 Pull down from the top of the screen with two fingers.

The Quick Settings panel opens.

3 Touch **User** (👤).

The User screen appears.

4 Touch **Add guest**.

The lock screen appears.

Note: When you switch to Guest mode, Android displays a different wallpaper as a visual cue to indicate the change.

5 Hand the device to your guest.

6 Your guest can now swipe the **lock icon** (🔒) up to unlock the device.

Remove the Guest Session and Return to Your Account

1 When your guest returns your device, touch **Home** (⬤).

The Home screen appears.

2 Pull down from the top of the screen with two fingers.

The Quick Settings panel opens.

3 Touch **User** (👤).

The User screen appears.

4 Touch **Remove guest**.

A If you do not want to end the Guest session yet, touch **Owner** (👤) to switch to your account.

The Remove Guest? dialog box opens.

5 Touch **Remove**.

Android removes the Guest session.

The lock screen appears, showing your regular wallpaper.

6 Unlock the device as usual.

TIP

How can I keep the files I create in a Guest session?
To keep the files you create in a Guest session on someone else's device, you must copy or move the files before you end the Guest session. For example, you can copy the files to another device via Bluetooth or Near Field Communications; you can upload the files to an online storage site, such as Google Drive or Dropbox; or you can simply use the Gmail app to e-mail the files to yourself.

Add a User to Your Phone or Tablet

If you need to share your device with one or more other people, you can set up a separate user account for each person. Having separate user accounts enables you to keep each person's files, messages, and settings separate. You can switch quickly from one account to another. On a tablet, you have another option: You can create a restricted profile, which is like a user account but which has restrictions applied. See the next section, "Create a Restricted Profile on a Tablet," for details.

Add a User to Your Phone or Tablet

1 Touch **Home** (⬤).

The Home screen appears.

2 Pull down from the top of the screen with two fingers.

The Quick Settings panel opens.

3 Touch **User** (👤).

The User screen appears.

4 Touch **Add User**.

The Add New User? dialog box opens.

5 Touch **OK**.

The lock screen appears.

Note: When you add a new user, Android displays a different wallpaper as a visual cue to indicate the change.

⑥ Hand the device to the person who will be the new user.

⑦ The new user should swipe the **lock icon** (🔒) upward.

The screen unlocks.

The Welcome screen appears.

⑧ The new user should touch **Next** (→).

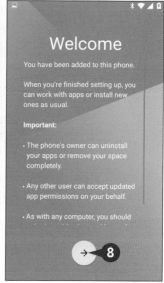

⑨ On the Add Your Account screen, the new user should touch **Enter your email** and follow the prompts to add a Google account.

⑩ On the Google Services screen, the user should touch **More** to see the remaining options, and then touch **Next** to proceed with the setup.

When the setup finishes, the Home screen appears, and the new user can start using the device.

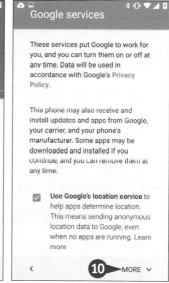

TIP

How do I secure another user's account?
You cannot directly secure another user's account, but it is important that you persuade all other users to secure their accounts. By default, each new user account uses the Swipe screen lock, which provides no security at all. Explain to other users that security is vital and convince them to set a PIN or password to protect their accounts.

Create a Restricted Profile on a Tablet

If you have a tablet, you can create not only extra user accounts, but also restricted profiles. A restricted profile is similar to a user account, but you can set restrictions on what the person who uses it can do. To set up a restricted profile, you start from your owner account, the account you used to set up the tablet. After choosing which apps and features to make available to the profile, you can hand the tablet to the person who will use the profile.

Create a Restricted Profile on a Tablet

1. Touch **Home** (⬤).

   The Home screen appears.

2. Pull down from the top of the screen with two fingers.

   The Quick Settings panel opens.

3. Touch **Settings** (⚙).

   The Settings screen appears.

4. Touch **Users**.

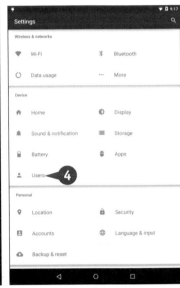

   The Users screen appears.

5. Touch **Add user or profile**.

   The Add dialog box opens.

6. Touch **Restricted profile**.

   The App & Content Access screen appears.

7. Touch **New profile**.

   The Profile Info dialog box opens.

8. Type the name for the profile user.

   A. You can touch **User** (🧑) and then touch **Take photo** or **Choose photo from Gallery** to add a photo.

9. Touch **OK**.

10 Touch **Settings**.

The Location button appears.

11 Touch **Location** (☐ changes to ☑) if you want to allow apps to use location information.

12 Set the switches to On (⬤ changes to ⬤) or Off (⬤ changes to ⬤) to control which features are available in the profile.

13 Touch **Back** (◀).

The Users screen appears.

14 Touch the button for the new profile.

The lock screen for the new profile appears, showing a different wallpaper.

15 Hand the tablet to the person who will use the profile.

16 The person should swipe the **lock icon** (🔒) up to unlock the screen. She can then start using the tablet.

B You can switch to another account by touching **User** (☻) and then touching the appropriate account in the list that appears.

TIP

When should I create a restricted profile instead of a user account?
Normally, you would create a user account for each responsible adult user who will use your tablet regularly. You would create a restricted profile for any child or any adult user whom you wish to allow to use only some of the tablet's features. For example, you could create a restricted profile to allow the user to read books, newspapers, and magazines, but not to browse the Internet or communicate via e-mail.

Switch Users on a Multiuser Device

When you have set up multiple users on a device, you and other users can switch among your accounts quickly via the User screen. You can access the User screen either from the lock screen or from inside your account. On a tablet, you can also switch users quickly via the Users pop-up menu that appears directly on the lock screen.

Switch Users on a Multiuser Device

Switch Users on a Phone or Tablet

1 Pull down from the top of the screen with two fingers.

The Quick Settings panel opens.

Note: You can open the Quick Settings panel either from the lock screen or from within your user account.

2 Touch **User** ().

The User screen appears.

A The circle indicates the active user account.

3 Touch the user account to which you want to switch.

The lock screen for that user account appears.

4 Swipe the **lock icon** (🔒) upward.

If Android prompts you to unlock the device, perform your unlocking action, such as drawing your pattern or entering your PIN or password.

Switch Users on a Tablet

1 Touch **User** ().

The Users list appears.

B The white circle shows the active user account.

2 Touch the user account to which you want to switch.

The lock screen for that user account appears.

3 Swipe the **lock icon** (🔒) upward.

Your unlock method appears — for example, the PIN entry screen.

4 Perform your unlock action. For example, type your PIN and touch the **check mark** (☑).

The tablet unlocks, and you can start using your account.

TIP

How do I share my apps with other users?

You cannot share your apps with other users. Each user must install apps on his own user account — for example, buying the apps from the Play Store. The good news is that when a user buys an app that is already installed on the tablet, Android uses the copy on the tablet rather than installing it again and taking up twice the space. But even in this case, Android simulates the download, as if the user was installing a new app.

Configure or Remove a User Account

After creating a user account, you may need to configure it. At this writing, you can configure a user account only on a phone, not on a tablet; and the only setting you can change is permitting or not permitting phone calls and SMS messaging. However, future versions of Android may add other configurable features. When you no longer need a certain user account on your device, you can remove that account. To remove an account, you must log in with the owner account for the device.

Configure or Remove a User Account

1 Touch **Home** (⬤).

The Home screen appears.

2 Pull down from the top of the screen with two fingers.

The Quick Settings panel opens.

3 Touch **User** (👤).

The User screen appears.

4 Touch **More settings**.

The Users screen appears.

Ⓐ Your account shows you are the owner.

5 Touch **Settings** (⚙) for the account you want to configure or remove.

The settings screen for the user account opens. This example shows the user's name as Maria.

⑥ Set the **Allow phone calls and SMS** switch On (⬤ changes to ⬤) or Off (⬤ changes to ⬤), as needed.

⑦ If you want to remove the user account from your device, touch **Remove user**.

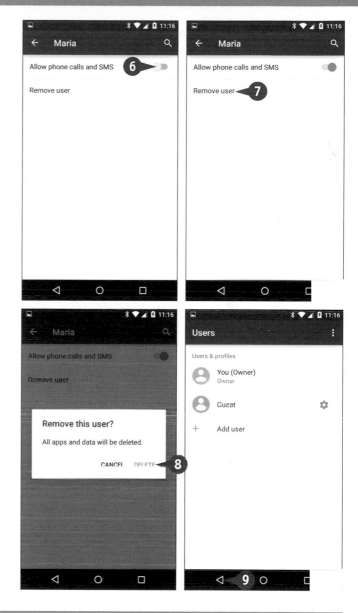

The Remove This User? dialog box opens.

⑧ Touch **Delete**.

Android removes the user account and deletes all its apps and data from the device.

The Users screen appears.

⑨ Touch **Back** (◁).

The Home screen appears.

TIP

What other actions can I take from the Users screen?

When logged in with the owner account, you can touch **Menu** (⋮) to open the menu, and then touch **Add users when device is locked** (☐ changes to ☑) if you want to be able to add users to your device straight from the lock screen.

When logged in with a nonowner account, you can touch **Menu** (⋮) to open the menu, and then touch **Delete** *account* **from this device** to start deleting your account. In the distressingly existential Delete Yourself? dialog box that opens, touch **Delete**.

CHAPTER 4

Working with Text, Voice, and Accessibility

You can input text using the on-screen keyboard, the Gesture Typing feature, and dictation. Android also provides Cut, Copy, and Paste; Voice Actions; Voice Search; and helpful accessibility options.

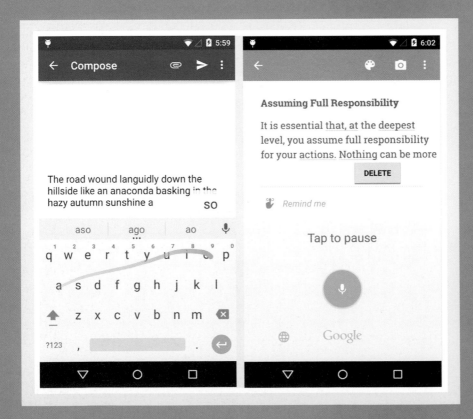

Using the On-Screen Keyboard and Gesture Typing

The most straightforward way to enter text in an app is by touching the keys on the on-screen keyboard. Android automatically displays this keyboard when you touch an input field. The Android keyboard also provides a feature called Gesture Typing. In Gesture Typing, you touch the first letter of a word, and then slide your finger to each of the other letters in turn. When you stop, Android automatically inserts the most likely matching word.

Using the On-Screen Keyboard and Gesture Typing

Open an App That Allows Text Input

Note: This example uses the Gmail app, but you can use any other app that allows text input.

1 Touch **Home** (⬤).

The Home screen appears.

2 Touch **All Apps** (▦).

The Apps screen appears.

3 Touch **Gmail** (M).

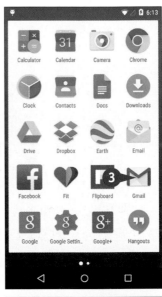

Gmail opens.

4 Touch **Compose** (✎).

A new message opens.

Ⓐ The on-screen keyboard appears automatically.

Note: Android automatically switches Shift on (⬆ changes to ⬆) at the beginning of a paragraph or sentence. After you type the first letter of a sentence or paragraph, Android turns Shift off (⬆ changes to ⬆), so the keyboard types lowercase letters unless you touch **Shift** (⬆). You can turn on Caps Lock by double-tapping **Shift** (⬆ changes to ⬆).

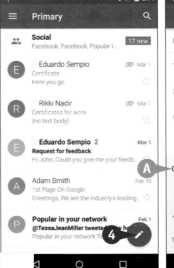

Type on the On-Screen Keyboard

1 Touch the **Compose email** field in the new message.

B Android turns on Shift (⬆ changes to ⬆) at the beginning of the paragraph.

2 Start typing the words you want.

C As you type, the suggestions bar shows words you may be typing.

3 If a suggestion is correct, touch it. Otherwise, keep typing.

D The word appears in the document.

4 If three dots appear under the middle suggestion in the suggestions bar, you can touch and hold the middle button.

The suggestions panel opens.

5 Touch the word you want to insert.

TIP

How can I speed up my typing on my phone or tablet?

Here are three ways in which you can enter text faster:

- Use Gesture Typing, which is usually faster than touching individual keys.
- Use the Personal Dictionary feature to enter standard terms faster by using abbreviations.
- When you need to enter serious amounts of text, connect a hardware keyboard to your phone or tablet. Bluetooth is usually the easiest means of connecting a keyboard, but you can also connect some keyboards directly to the micro-USB port on some devices.

continued ▶

Using the On-Screen Keyboard and Gesture Typing (continued)

To help you enter text quickly, the Android keyboard provides a feature called Gesture Typing. In Gesture Typing, you touch the first letter of a word, and then slide your finger to each of the other letters in turn. When you stop, Android automatically inserts the most likely matching word. Gesture Typing can be impressively accurate. If you turn on the Phrase Gesture feature, you can slide your finger over the spacebar to indicate the end of a word, and continue gesturing without lifting your finger.

Using the On-Screen Keyboard and Gesture Typing (continued)

E The word appears in the document.

Note: You can type a period by touching the spacebar twice in quick succession.

6 Touch **?123**.

The numeric keyboard appears, and you can type numbers and some symbols.

7 Touch **=\<**.

The symbols keyboard appears, and you can type other symbols.

8 Touch **ABC**.

The letter keyboard appears again.

9 If you need to enter an alternative character or related character, touch and hold the base character. In this example, touch and hold the **a** key.

The pop-up panel appears.

10 Touch the character you want to insert.

F The character with the darker gray background is the default. You can enter it by lifting your finger after the pop-up panel appears.

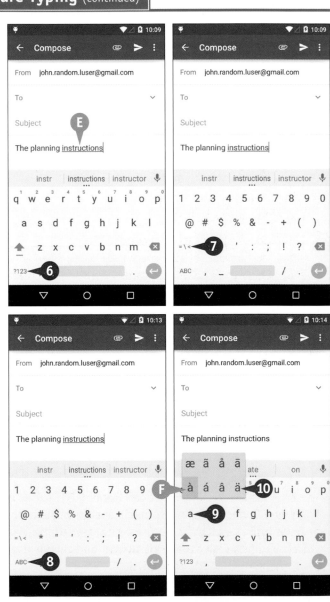

11 Touch and hold the period (**.**) key on the letter keyboard. The punctuation pop-up panel appears.

12 Slide your finger to the character you want to enter, and then lift your finger.

The character appears in the document.

13 Touch **Enter** (⏎) when you want to create a new paragraph.

Use Gesture Typing

1 Touch the first letter of the word.

2 Without raising your finger, slide to each successive letter in turn.

3 If the pop-up suggestion is correct, lift your finger to accept it. Otherwise, continue to the end of the word.

Note: You can also slide your finger over the spacebar to indicate the end of a word, and then continue sliding your finger on the keyboard to start the next word.

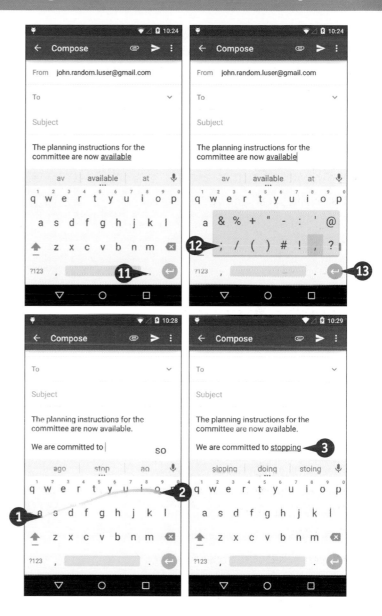

TIP

Why does Gesture Typing not work on my device?

You may need to turn it on. Touch **Home** (◉), touch **All Apps** (⣿), and then touch **Settings** (⚙). Touch **Language & input**, and then touch **Google Keyboard**. Touch **Gesture Typing**, and then set the **Enable gesture typing** switch to On (⬜ changes to ⬤). You can also set the **Dynamic floating preview** switch, the **Show gesture trail** switch, and the **Phrase gesture switch** to On (⬜ changes to ⬤) or Off (⬤ changes to ⬜), as needed.

Edit Text and Use Cut, Copy, and Paste

When you work with text, you often need to edit what you have written. Android makes it easy to edit existing text and select part or all of your text. After selecting text, you can cut it or copy it to the clipboard and then paste it elsewhere. Cutting text removes it from the document, whereas copying text leaves it in the document. You can paste text from the clipboard multiple times if necessary until you copy or cut other text.

Edit Text and Use Cut, Copy, and Paste

Open Gmail and Edit Text

1 Open Gmail and begin a new message by following the first steps in the previous section.

2 Type some text.

3 Touch where you want to position the insertion point.

The arrow for moving the insertion point (●) appears.

4 If necessary, drag the arrow (●) to move the insertion point.

5 Edit the text as needed.

Select Text and Use Cut, Copy, and Paste

1 Touch and hold a word.

Android highlights the word and displays selection handles around it.

2 Drag the start handle (●) or the end handle (●) to change the selection as needed.

A You can touch **Select All** (▦) to select all the text.

3 Touch **Copy** (▣) to copy the text.

B You can touch **Cut** (✄) to cut the text.

Note: After selecting text, you can touch **Delete** (✕) on the keyboard to delete it without placing it on the clipboard.

C You can touch **End Selection** (◄) to turn off selection mode.

④ Touch and hold where you want to paste the copied or cut text.

Note: If you want the text you paste to replace an existing word, double-tap that word, and then touch **Paste**. To replace multiple words, select them, and then touch **Paste** (📋) on the toolbar.

The Paste button appears.

⑤ Touch **Paste**.

The copied or cut text appears in the document.

Replace a Word

① Touch and hold the word.

Android selects the word.

A toolbar appears.

② Touch **Replace**.

A list of suggested replacements appears.

③ Touch the appropriate word.

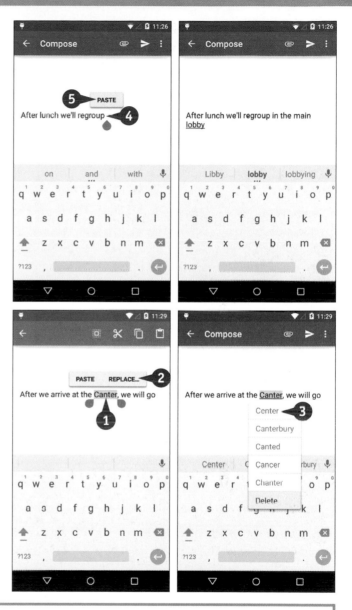

TIPS

How many items can I put on the clipboard?

The clipboard contains only a single item. Each time you cut or copy text, it replaces the current contents of the clipboard. But you can continue to paste the contents of the clipboard as many times as needed until you place another item on the clipboard.

Can I transfer the contents of the clipboard to my computer?

You cannot access the clipboard directly from your computer, but you can easily transfer the contents of the clipboard using workarounds. For example, begin a new message in the Gmail app and address it to yourself. You can then paste in the contents of the clipboard and send the message.

Give Commands with Voice Actions

Android's powerful Voice Actions feature enables you to take essential actions by using your voice to tell your phone or tablet what you want. Voice Actions requires an Internet connection, because the speech recognition runs on Google's servers. You can use Voice Actions either with your device's built-in microphone or with the microphone on a headset or another hands-free device. Unless you are in a quiet environment, or you hold your phone or tablet close to your face, a headset microphone gives much better results than the built-in microphone.

Open Voice Actions

Before you can start using Voice Actions to control your phone or tablet, you must open Voice Actions. You can do this in several ways. In most cases, the easiest way is to touch **Home** (⬤) to display the Home screen, and then either say "OK Google" or touch the Google box at the top.

When you are using the Chrome app, touch the omnibox at the top of the screen and then touch the **microphone** icon (🎤).

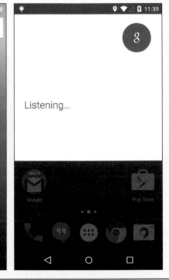

Open a Web Page

One of the most useful Voice Actions is to open a web page using only your voice. You can use this feature to browse the web more easily on your phone or tablet.

To open a web page using your voice, first open Voice Actions. You can then say "Go to" and the web page's address. Android launches your default browser — for example, Chrome — and displays the web page. For example, say "Go to capitalone.com."

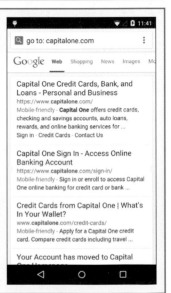

Send an E-Mail Message

You can use Voice Actions to send an e-mail message to a contact. This feature is great for composing and sending messages quickly. To send an e-mail message, open Voice Actions. You can then say "Send e-mail" and the contact's name, then "subject" and the subject, followed by "message" and the message. Android creates an e-mail message to the contact and enters the text. Review the message, and then touch **Send** (➤) to send it.

Send a Text Message

You can use Voice Actions to send a text message to a contact. This feature is especially helpful when you do not have time to type a message. To send a text message, open Voice Actions. Say "Send text to" and the contact's name, then say "message" and the message. Android creates a text message to the contact, enters the text, and presents it for your review. Touch **Send** (➤) to send it.

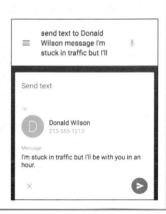

Send Yourself a Reminder

Another helpful use of Voice Actions is to send yourself a reminder. Open Voice Actions, then say "Note to self" and the reminder. Android listens to what you say and creates a text note in your chosen app, such as the Keep app. If the note is correct, touch **Done** (✓); if not, touch **Cancel** (✕) to cancel the note.

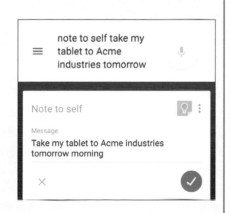

Set an Alarm

You can use Voice Actions to set an alarm without needing to open the Clock app. To set an alarm, open Voice Actions, then say "Set an alarm" followed by the time; optionally, add "label" and a name for the alarm. Verify the time as Android sets the alarm. If it is correct, touch **Done** (✓) or simply allow Android to finish setting the alarm, which takes a few seconds. If not, touch **Cancel** (✕) to cancel the alarm.

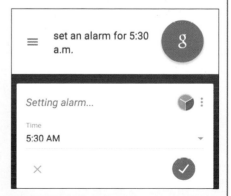

Dictate Text into Apps

Android can transcribe your speech quickly and accurately into correctly spelled and punctuated text. Using your phone or tablet, you can dictate into any app that supports the keyboard, enabling you to dictate e-mail messages, notes, documents, and more. To get the most out of dictation, it is helpful to know the standard terms for dictating punctuation and layout.

Dictate Text into Apps

Open an App That Allows Text Input

Note: This example uses the Gmail app, but you can use another app that allows text input.

1 Touch **Home** (⬤).

The Home screen appears.

2 Touch **All Apps** (⬚).

The Apps screen appears.

3 Touch **Gmail** (M).

Gmail opens.

4 Touch **New Message** (✎).

A new message opens.

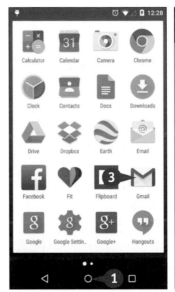

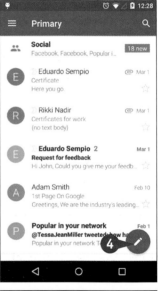

Dictate Text

1 Touch the **Compose email** field in the new message.

2 Touch the **microphone** icon (🎤) on the suggestions bar.

The speech-recognition panel replaces the keyboard.

Ⓐ The microphone icon (🎤) and *Speak now* prompt indicate that Android is listening for voice input.

3 Speak the text you want to dictate.

Ⓑ The text appears as you speak.

Note: After a few seconds of silence, Android stops listening (🎤 changes to).

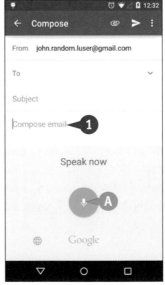

When you pause, a Delete button appears for a few seconds.

C You can touch **Delete** to delete the last section of text you dictated.

4 If Android has incorrectly transcribed part of the text, touch the appropriate underlined word or phrase.

A list of suggestions appears.

5 Touch the word or phrase you want to insert.

6 Touch the **microphone** icon (🎤) when you are ready to begin dictating again.

7 Touch the **microphone** icon (⬤) if you need to pause dictation.

Note: You can say standard punctuation terms including "comma," "period," "colon," "exclamation point" or "exclamation mark," and "question mark."

Note: Say "new paragraph" to end the current paragraph and create a new one.

8 Touch **Keyboard** (⌨) when you want to display the keyboard again.

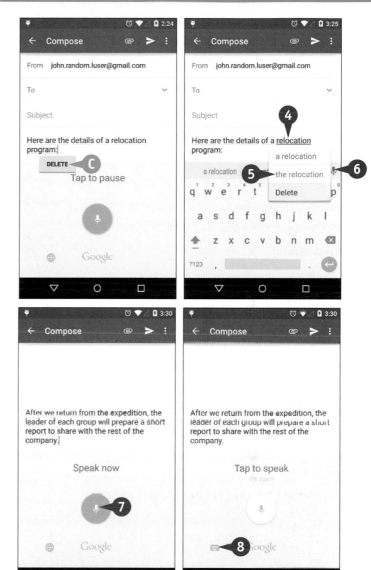

TIP

How can I make sure dictation is as accurate as possible?

Follow these suggestions to get accurate results when dictating text:

- Use a headset microphone rather than your phone or tablet's built-in microphone. When you must use the built-in microphone, hold the device close to your face to deliver a strong signal and minimize ambient noise.
- Speak clearly.
- Pause at the end of each sentence so that Android can catch up with you.

Gather Information with Voice Search

Android's capability to accept voice input enables you to use your voice to research a wide variety of information online. By using Voice Search, you can quickly and easily request information about sports, find showtimes for movies, and identify the location of ZIP codes. You can also locate restaurants, get flight information, and learn the time in another place. Voice Search works with natural-language queries, so you do not have to structure your questions and requests in a set format. However, you can get more accurate search results by using suitable keywords.

Find Information About Sports

You can use Voice Search to find information about sports, such as the result of a recent game by a particular team or the date of a future event. To find information about sports, first activate Google Search by touching **Home** (◉) and then saying "OK Google" or touching the **microphone icon** (🎤) in the Google box. You can then ask a question such as "Did the Lakers win their last game?" or "When is the next White Sox game?"

Find Showtimes for Movies

You can use Voice Search to find out the current showtimes for a movie in a particular city or location. To find out movie showtimes, first activate Google Search by touching **Home** (◉) and then saying "OK Google" or touching the **microphone** icon (🎤) in the Google box. You can then say "Movie" followed by the movie's name and the city or location. For example, say "Movie *American Sniper* Chicago."

Identify the Location of Area Codes and ZIP Codes

You can use Voice Search to identify the location for a particular telephone area code or a ZIP code. To find out this information, first activate Google Search by touching **Home** (◉) and then saying "OK Google" or touching the **microphone** icon (🎤) in the Google box. You can then say "area code" followed by the area code — for example, "area code 707" — or "ZIP code" followed by the ZIP code.

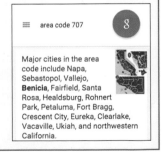

Get Flight Information

You can use Voice Search to get information about flights. This capability is useful when you need to check whether the flight you are hoping to take or meet is on time or has been delayed. To get flight information, first activate Google Search by touching **Home** (⬤) and then saying "OK Google" or touching the **microphone** icon (🎤) in the Google box. You can then say the airline's name, the word "flight," and then the flight number. For example, say "Air Canada flight AC794."

Locate a Restaurant

You can use Voice Search to get information about restaurants in a specified location. This capability is useful when you want to find a particular type of food. To get restaurant information, first activate Google Search by touching **Home** (⬤) and then saying "OK Google" or touching the **microphone icon** (🎤) in the Google box. Say the type of food you want and the keyword "food," and then give the location. For example, say "Japanese food in Phoenix, Arizona."

Find Out the Time in Another Location

You can use Voice Search to find out the time in another location. This capability is useful for making sure you place phone calls or set appointments during waking hours rather than sleeping hours. To find out the time in another location, first activate Google Search by touching **Home** (⬤) and then saying "OK Google" or touching the **microphone** icon (🎤) in the Google box. Then say "Time" followed by the location. For example, say "Time Tokyo" to find out the time in Tokyo, Japan.

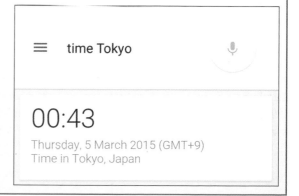

Set Up Accessibility Features

To make your phone or tablet easier and more convenient to use, Android offers a set of accessibility features. You can reach these features through the Settings app. If you have difficulty reading the text on-screen, you can turn on the Large Text feature to enlarge the text, and you can make the screen easy to magnify. You can also turn on text-to-speech conversion to enable you to listen to the text on-screen. Another option is to have your device speak passwords aloud to you.

Set Up Accessibility Features

1 Touch **Home** (⬤).

The Home screen appears.

2 Touch **All Apps** (▦).

The Apps screen appears.

3 Touch **Settings** (⚙).

Note: If Settings (⚙) is not on the Apps screen that appears first, scroll left or right until you find Settings (⚙).

The Settings screen appears.

4 Touch **Accessibility**.

The Accessibility screen appears.

5 To use magnification, touch **Magnification gestures**.

Note: With magnification gestures on, triple-tap to magnify what is on-screen. Drag two or more fingers across the screen to pan. To magnify temporarily, triple-tap and hold; while holding, you can pan by dragging. Pinch in or out with two fingers to adjust the zoom level.

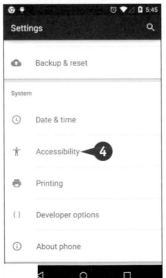

The Magnification Gestures screen appears.

6 Set the **Magnification gestures** switch to On (changes to).

7 Touch **Back** ( ).

8 To use large text, touch **Large Text** (changes to).

9 Touch **Power button ends call** (changes to) if you want to end calls by pressing the Power button.

10 Touch **Auto-rotate screen** (changes to) to enable automatic rotation.

11 Touch **Speak passwords** (changes to) to have Android speak passwords you type.

12 Touch **Accessibility shortcut**.

The Accessibility Shortcut screen appears.

13 Set the **Accessibility shortcut** switch to On (changes to).

14 Touch **Back** ( ).

15 Touch **Touch & hold delay**.

The Touch & Hold Delay dialog box opens.

16 Touch **Short**, **Medium**, or **Long** (changes to), as needed.

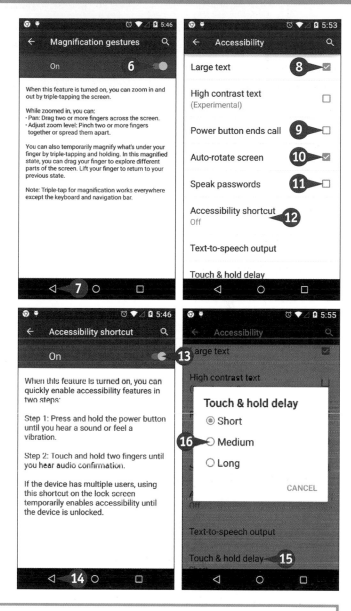

TIPS

How do I use the Accessibility shortcut?

Hold down the Power button until your device beeps or vibrates, then touch and hold with two fingers until your device beeps.

How do I configure the Text-to-speech feature?

On the Accessibility screen in Settings, touch **Text-to-speech output** to display the Text-to-Speech Output screen. In the Preferred Engine list, select the text-to-speech engine to use (changes to) if there is a choice, then touch **Settings** ( ) and choose settings. In the General area, touch **Speech rate** and then touch the appropriate speed, such as **Slow** or **Normal**, in the Speech Rate dialog box.

Using TalkBack and Explore by Touch

If you find it hard to see items on your phone or tablet's screen, you can use the TalkBack feature to read the screen to you. TalkBack says the name of the current screen or dialog box and announces the items you touch on-screen, enabling you to navigate your device by listening. If you turn on TalkBack, you can also use the Explore by Touch feature, which announces what is under your finger on the screen.

Using TalkBack and Explore by Touch

1 Touch **Home** (⬤).

The Home screen appears.

2 Touch **All Apps** (⬚).

The Apps screen appears.

3 Touch **Settings** (⚙).

Note: If Settings (⚙) is not on the Apps screen that appears first, scroll left or right until you find Settings (⚙).

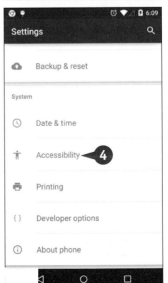

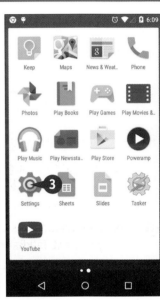

The Settings screen appears.

Note: On a phone, you may need to scroll down to display the Accessibility button.

4 Touch **Accessibility**.

The Accessibility screen appears.

5 Touch **TalkBack** to display the TalkBack screen.

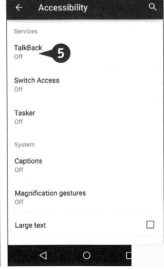

6 Set the **TalkBack** switch to On (changes to).

The Use TalkBack? dialog box opens.

7 Touch **OK**.

The TalkBack tutorial starts.

8 Touch **Next** to select the button, touch again to activate it, and follow through the tutorial.

9 When the tutorial ends, touch **Settings**.

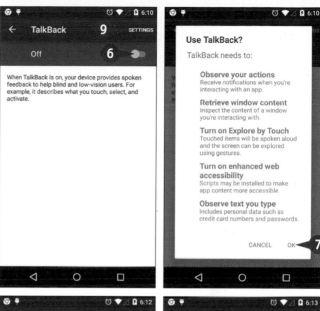

The TalkBack Settings screen appears.

10 Touch **Use pitch changes** (changes to) if you want keyboard feedback to use a lower-pitched voice.

11 Touch **Use proximity sensor** (changes to) if you want TalkBack to stop when you bring your phone to your face.

12 Touch **Explore by touch** (changes to) if you want to use Explore by Touch.

13 Touch **Launch "Explore by touch" tutorial** to view the tutorial.

14 Touch **Manage gestures** and choose gestures on the Manage Gestures screen.

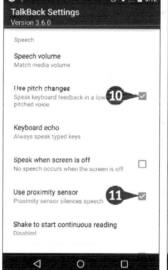

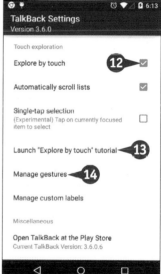

TIPS

What other TalkBack settings can I configure?

Touch **Speech volume** to open the Speech Volume dialog box, and then touch the appropriate option, such as **Match media volume** (changes to). Touch **Speak caller ID** (changes to) if you want TalkBack to announce incoming call numbers.

What settings can I choose on the Manage Gestures screen?

You can choose how Android interprets gestures. For example, you can map the gesture of swiping down and then right to the Back button or to opening the Notification shade. Touch the gesture you want to change, then touch the button or action in the dialog box that opens (changes to).

CHAPTER 5

Setting Up Communications

In this chapter, you learn how to add your e-mail accounts to your phone or tablet. You also learn to choose options for your contacts and calendars.

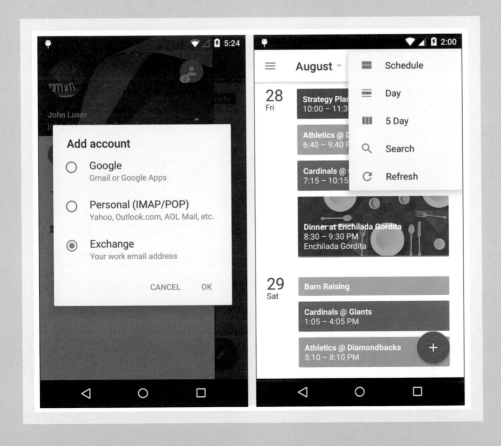

Set Up Your E-Mail Accounts

The Gmail app included with your device enables you to access e-mail accounts on both Google's Gmail service and most other e-mail services. Normally, you set up your main Gmail account during initial setup of your device. You can subsequently add your other e-mail accounts to the Gmail app. To set up an account, you need your e-mail address and your password. For some accounts, you may need to know the details of the mail servers involved.

Set Up Your E-Mail Accounts

Open Gmail and Display the Add Account Dialog Box

1 Touch **Home** (⬤).

The Home screen appears.

A If the Google folder appears on the Home screen, touch **Google** and then touch **Gmail** (M).

2 Touch **All Apps** (⊞).

The Apps screen appears.

3 Touch **Gmail** (M).

Note: If Gmail (M) is not on the Apps screen that appears first, scroll left or right until you find Gmail (M).

Gmail opens.

4 Touch **Menu** (☰).

The menu panel opens.

5 Touch the account name.

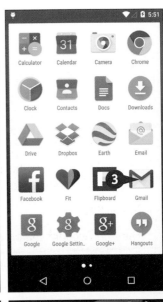

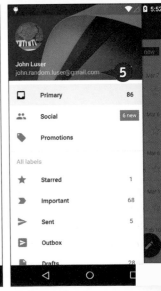

The account-management panel opens.

6 Touch **Add account**.

The Add Account dialog box opens.

7 Touch **Google**, **Personal (IMAP/POP)**, or **Exchange** (○ changes to ◉), as needed, and then follow the instructions in the appropriate following subsection.

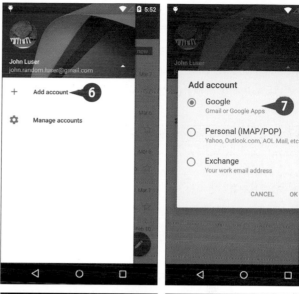

Add a Google Account

1 In the Add Account dialog box, touch **Google** (○ changes to ◉).

2 Touch **OK**.

The Add Account dialog box closes.

The Add Your Account screen appears.

3 Touch **Enter your email** and type your account name.

4 Touch **Next**.

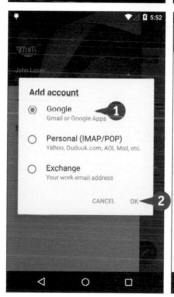

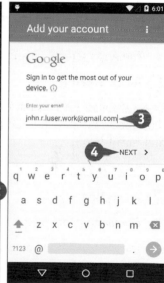

TIP

Which items should I sync with my Gmail account?

To get the most out of your phone and tablet, it is usually a good idea to sync most, if not all, of the items that appear on the Sync Your Account screen. Touch **Sync App Data** (☐ changes to ✓) to sync data about the apps you use. Touch **Sync Calendar** (☐ changes to ✓) to sync your calendar information. Touch **Sync Contacts** (☐ changes to ✓) to sync contact information and streamline your communications. Touch **Sync Docs** (☐ changes to ✓) to sync your Google Docs.

continued ▶

When setting up a POP3 account or IMAP account, you may need to provide the hostnames of the incoming mail server and the outgoing mail server. You may also need to select the correct security type, the port number for the incoming server and outgoing server, and whether your e-mail app needs to sign in to the outgoing server. It is a good idea to ask your e-mail provider for this information before trying to set up your account.

Set Up Your E-Mail Accounts (continued)

The Password screen appears.

5 Touch **Password** and type your password.

6 Touch **Next**.

The Terms of Service and Privacy Policy screen appears.

7 Touch **Accept**.

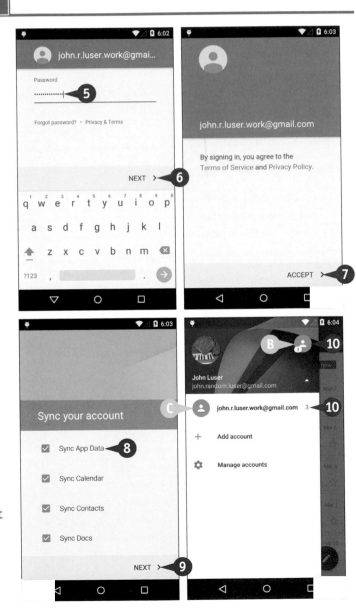

The Sync Your Account screen appears.

8 Touch any item (☑ changes to ☐) you do not want to sync.

9 Touch **Next**.

The account-management panel appears.

B An icon appears for the account you just added.

C The account also appears by name.

10 Touch either the account icon or the account name.

Gmail switches to the account.

Add an IMAP or POP Account

1 In the Add Account dialog box, touch **Personal (IMAP/POP)** (◯ changes to ◉).

2 Touch **OK**.

The Add Account dialog box closes.

The Email Account screen appears.

3 Touch **Email address** and type your e-mail address.

4 Touch **Next**.

The Account Type screen appears.

5 Touch **Personal (POP3)** for a POP3 account, or touch **Personal (IMAP)** for an IMAP account. See the tip for information about POP3 and IMAP.

The Sign In screen appears.

6 Touch **Password** and type your password.

7 Touch **Next**.

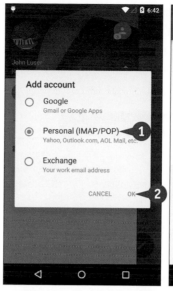

TIP

Should I choose Personal (POP3) or Personal (IMAP) for my e-mail account?
Ask your e-mail provider whether your account uses POP3 or IMAP. POP3 and IMAP are different technologies for incoming mail servers: POP3 is the Post Office Protocol, and IMAP is Internet Mail Access Protocol.

Some e-mail providers let you use either POP3 or IMAP for e-mail accounts. If your ISP gives you this choice, it is best to use IMAP for an account that you access from multiple computers and devices.

continued ▶

The Gmail app can set up some accounts automatically after you provide the e-mail address and password: Gmail detects or looks up the servers for the address and applies suitable settings. If Gmail is unable to find the server names, it prompts you to provide them. Automatic setup is usually helpful, but for some accounts you may need to specify the servers manually. In such cases, you can touch the Manual Setup button instead of the Next button on the Email Account screen.

Set Up Your E-Mail Accounts (continued)

The Incoming Server Settings screen appears.

8 If necessary, touch **Server** and edit the server name.

9 Touch **Security Type** and then touch the required security type.

10 Verify that the port number is correct. If not, change it.

Note: Select the security type before you change the port number, because Gmail automatically applies the default port for the security type you select.

11 Touch **Next**.

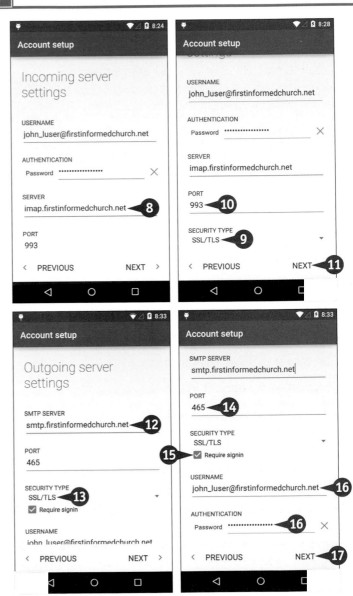

The Outgoing Server Settings screen appears.

12 If necessary, touch **SMTP server** and edit the name.

13 Touch **Security Type** and then touch the required security type.

14 Verify that the port number is correct. If not, change it.

15 Touch **Require signin** (☐ changes to ☑) if your e-mail provider requires you to sign in to the outgoing server.

16 Edit your username and password if necessary.

17 Touch **Next**.

The Account Options screen appears.

Note: The options on the Account Options screen vary depending on the account type.

18 Touch **Sync frequency** and then touch the frequency, such as **Every 5 minutes**.

19 Touch **Notify me when email arrives** (☐ changes to ✓) to receive notifications.

20 Touch **Sync email from this account** (☐ changes to ✓) to sync this account.

21 Touch **Automatically download attachments when connected to Wi-Fi** (☐ changes to ✓) to download attachments via Wi-Fi.

22 Touch **Next**.

The Your Account Is Set Up and Email Is on Its Way! screen appears.

23 Type the descriptive name you want to see for this account.

24 Type your name as you want it to appear on messages you send.

25 Touch **Next**.

The account-management panel appears.

ⓓ An icon appears for the account you just added.

ⓔ The account also appears by name.

26 Touch either the account icon or the account name.

Gmail switches to the account.

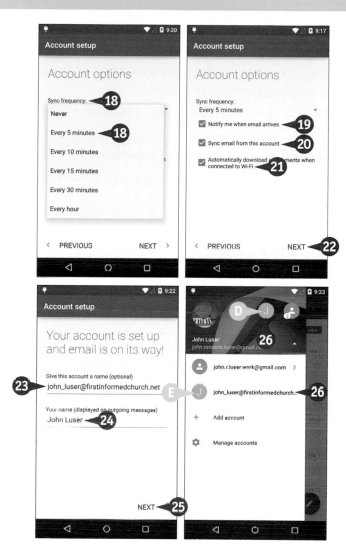

TIPS

Is there a disadvantage to choosing Automatic for the Inbox checking frequency?
The Automatic setting causes the Gmail app to use a technology called Push, in which the server notifies your device whenever new mail is available. Using Push, you receive your messages more quickly, but your device uses more battery power.

Is it a good idea to automatically download attachments when connected to Wi-Fi?
Yes. Downloading automatically when your device has a Wi-Fi connection helps you avoid downloading attachments over a cellular connection, which can quickly consume your data plan.

continued ▶

Microsoft Exchange Server is widely used server software that provides e-mail, contact management, and scheduling. If your company or organization uses Microsoft Exchange Server, you can connect your Android phone or tablet and work with your e-mail messages, contacts, and calendars. To connect to Exchange Server, you set up an account in the Gmail app. Before you start, ask your Exchange Server administrator or systems administrator for your e-mail address, password, the Exchange domain name, and the name of the Exchange server to use.

Set Up Your E-Mail Accounts (continued)

Add an Exchange Account

1 In the Add Account dialog box, touch **Exchange** (○ changes to ◉).

2 Touch **OK**.

The Add Account dialog box closes.

The Email Account screen appears.

3 Touch the **Email address** prompt and type your e-mail address.

4 Touch **Next**.

The Sign In screen appears.

5 Touch **Password** and type your password.

6 Touch **Next**.

The Incoming Server Settings screen appears.

7 If necessary, edit your username.

8 If necessary, edit your password.

F If the Exchange system uses digital certificates for security, touch **Select** and then select your certificate.

9 If necessary, edit the server name.

10 Touch **Security Type** and then touch the required security type.

11 Verify that the port number is correct. If not, change it.

12 Touch **Next**.

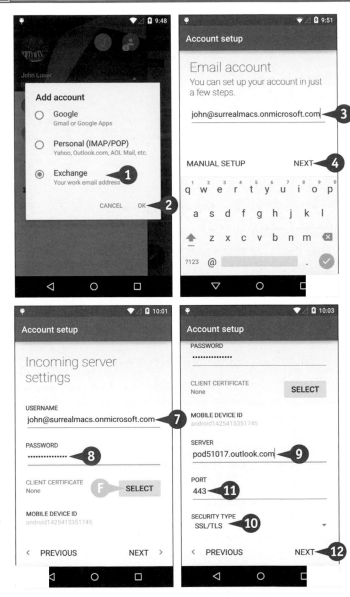

The Remote Security Administration dialog box opens.

13 Touch **OK**.

The Remote Security dialog box closes.

The Account Options screen appears.

14 Touch **Sync frequency** and then touch **Automatic (Push)**.

15 Touch **Sync emails from** and then touch the time period, such as **Last week**.

16 Touch the check boxes to turn options on (☑) or off (☐), as needed.

17 Touch **Next**.

The Activate Device Administrator? screen appears.

18 Touch **Activate**.

The Your Account Is Set Up and Email Is on Its Way screen appears.

19 Type the descriptive name you want to see for this account.

20 Touch **Next**.

The account-management panel appears, with your Exchange account listed on it.

21 Touch the account name when you want to switch to the Exchange account.

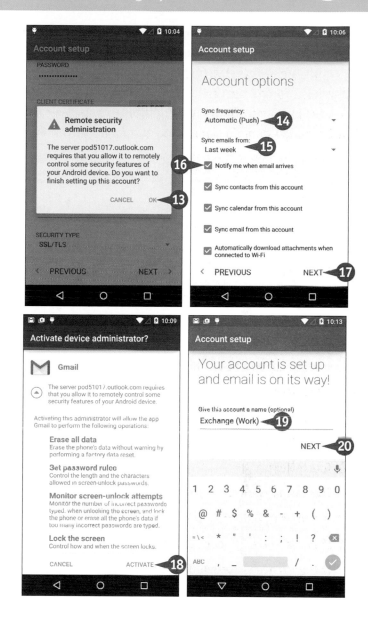

What security type should I choose for Exchange?

Most likely you should choose **SSL/TLS** in the Security Type pop-up menu, but ask your Exchange Server administrator to confirm this.

What is a digital certificate and where do I get one?

A digital certificate is a section of encrypted computer code used to identify a computer or device. Normally, if you need to use a digital certificate to secure the connection between your phone or tablet and an Exchange server, an administrator will provide it and install it on your device.

Choose Settings in Gmail

The Gmail app offers many settings that enable you to make it work the way you prefer. To get the most out of Gmail on your phone or tablet, it is a good idea to spend a few minutes exploring the settings that you can change and choosing options that suit you. When customizing the Gmail app, you can start with the General settings category, which contains settings that apply to all your accounts. You can then choose account-specific settings for each of your Gmail accounts.

Choose Settings in Gmail

Display the Settings Screen

1 Touch **Home** (⬤).

The Home screen appears.

2 Touch **All Apps** (⬚).

The Apps screen appears.

3 Touch **Gmail** (M).

Note: If Gmail (M) is not on the Apps screen that appears first, scroll left or right until you find Gmail (M).

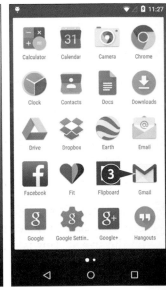

Your Inbox appears.

4 Touch **Menu** (☰).

The menu opens.

5 Touch **Settings**.

The Settings screen appears.

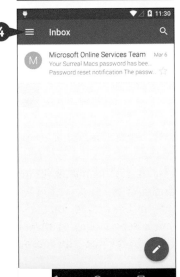

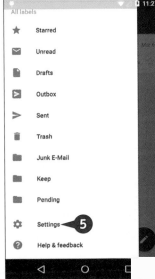

Choose General Settings

1 On the Settings screen, touch **General settings**.

The General Settings screen appears.

2 Touch **Swipe actions** (☐ changes to ✓) to enable swipe actions in the conversation list.

3 Touch **Sender image** (☐ changes to ✓) to display sender images in mailboxes.

4 Touch **Reply all** (☐ changes to ✓) if you want to use the Reply All action by default.

5 Touch **Gmail default action**.

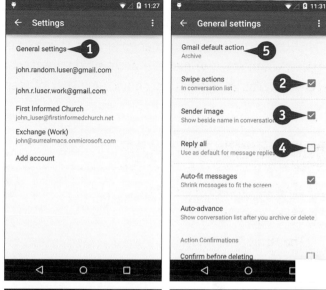

The Default Action dialog box opens.

6 Touch **Archive** or **Delete** (○ changes to ◉), as needed.

The Default Action dialog box closes.

7 Touch **Auto-fit messages** (☐ changes to ✓) to have Gmail shrink messages so that they fit on the screen. This is usually helpful.

8 Touch **Auto-advance**.

Should I turn on the Reply All option on the General Settings screen?

Not unless your company or organization mandates it. Turning on this option makes Gmail use Reply All as the default action for any message on which you were not the only recipient. The result is that you are much more likely to send a reply to all recipients when you intended to send it only to the message's sender.

How do I create a signature for messages I send?

Open the settings screen for the appropriate account, touch **Signature**, type the text in the Signature dialog box, and then touch **OK**. Touch **Enter** (⏎) if you want to create multiple lines in the signature.

continued ▶

Y ou can choose to have the Gmail app confirm any or all of three actions: deleting messages, archiving messages, and sending messages. These confirmations are useful if you use your device anywhere you may get bumped or jostled, such as on public transit, or if your touch is unsure. The settings you can configure for an individual e-mail account depend on the account type, but most account types enable you to choose whether to receive notifications, download attachments via Wi-Fi, and show all images in messages.

Choose Settings in Gmail (continued)

The Advance To dialog box opens.

9 Touch **Newer**, **Older**, or **Conversation list** (○ changes to ◉), as needed.

The Advance To dialog box closes.

10 Touch **Confirm before deleting** (☐ changes to ☑) if you want confirmation before deleting messages.

11 Touch **Confirm before archiving** (☐ changes to ☑) if you want confirmation before archiving.

12 Touch **Confirm before sending** (☐ changes to ☑) if you want confirmation before sending.

13 Touch **Back** (◀).

The Settings screen appears.

Choose Account-Specific Settings

1 Touch the account you want to configure.

The account's settings screen opens.

Note: The settings available depend on the account type. This section shows the settings for a Gmail account.

2 Touch **Inbox type**.

The Inbox Type dialog box opens.

3 Touch **Default Inbox** (○ changes to ◉).

Note: Gmail offers two inbox types: Default Inbox and Priority Inbox. See the section "Set Up and Use Priority Inbox" later in this chapter for coverage of Priority Inbox.

4 Touch **Notifications** (☐ changes to ✓) to receive notifications from this account in the status bar.

Ⓐ You can touch **Signature** to create a signature for outgoing messages.

5 Touch **Inbox categories**.

The Inbox Categories screen appears.

6 Touch each category (☐ changes to ✓) you want to use in a Gmail account.

7 At the bottom of the screen, touch **Include starred in Primary** (☐ changes to ✓) to include starred messages in the Primary category.

8 Touch **Back** (◁).

The account's settings screen appears.

Ⓑ You can touch **Inbox sound & vibrate** and then choose sync, notification, and vibration settings on the Sync & Notify screen.

9 Touch **Download attachment**s (☐ changes to ✓) to download attachments automatically via Wi-Fi.

10 Touch **Images**.

The Images dialog box opens.

11 Touch **Always show** or **Ask before showing** (◯ changes to ◉).

12 Touch **Back** (◁).

The Settings screen appears.

13 Touch **Back** (◁).

Your Inbox appears.

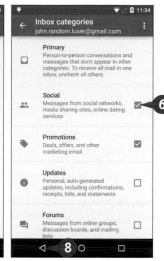

Why might I want to hide pictures in messages?

A picture in a message can deliberately compromise your privacy. In such an attack, the sender includes in the message a reference to an image on a remote server. When you open the message and image, the e-mail app downloads the image from the remote server. In doing this, marketers can learn information about you and track your surfing habits across the Internet.

If you hide pictures in messages, the picture areas appear as placeholder boxes. When you establish a message is harmless and want to see a picture, touch the placeholder to download the picture.

Remove an E-Mail Account

Sometimes you may need to remove an e-mail account from your phone or tablet — for example, because you no longer use the account. You can remove an account easily by using the Settings app. You can also start the process of removing the account directly from the account-management panel in the Gmail app. But because this approach also takes you to the Settings app, it is usually easier to go directly to the Settings app.

Remove an E-Mail Account

1 Touch **Home** (⬤).

The Home screen appears.

2 Touch **All Apps** (⠿).

The Apps screen appears.

3 Touch **Settings** (⚙).

Note: If Settings (⚙) is not on the Apps screen that appears first, scroll left or right until you find Settings (⚙).

The Settings app opens.

4 In the Personal section, touch **Accounts**.

The Accounts screen appears.

5 Touch the account you want to remove.

Ⓐ You can also start adding a new account by touching **Add account** on the Accounts screen.

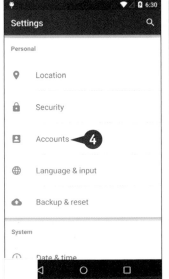

The account's screen appears.

6 Touch the account name.

The Sync screen appears, showing the account's sync information.

7 Touch **Menu** (⋮).

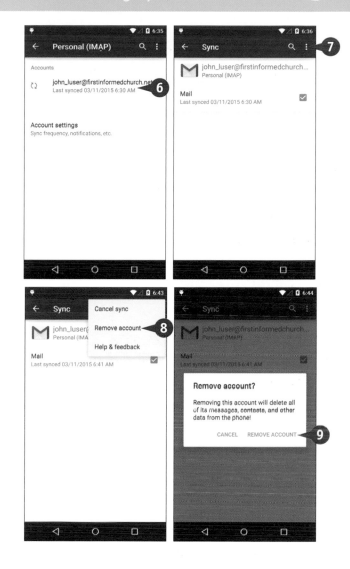

The menu opens.

8 Touch **Remove account**.

The Remove Account? dialog box opens.

9 Touch **Remove Account**.

The Settings app removes the account.

The Settings screen appears.

How can I stop an account from syncing without removing it from my device?

1 Touch **Home** (◯).

2 Touch **All Apps** (⊞).

3 Touch **Settings** (⚙).

4 Touch **Accounts**.

5 Touch the account you want to affect.

6 Touch the account's name to display the Sync screen.

7 Touch each item, such as **Contacts** or **Mail**, that you want to stop syncing (☑ changes to ☐).

Set Up and Use Priority Inbox

If your Gmail account receives many e-mail messages, you can use Gmail's Priority Inbox feature to identify the messages that urgently need your attention. Priority Inbox tries to identify your important messages so it can present them to you separately from your less important messages. To use Priority Inbox, you turn the feature on in Gmail's settings. You can then display Priority Inbox in Gmail and work through its contents.

Set Up and Use Priority Inbox

Turn On the Priority Inbox Feature

1 Touch **Home** (⬤).

The Home screen appears.

2 Touch **All Apps** (⊞).

The Apps screen appears.

3 Touch **Gmail** (M).

Note: If Gmail (M) is not on the Apps screen that appears first, scroll left or right until you find Gmail (M).

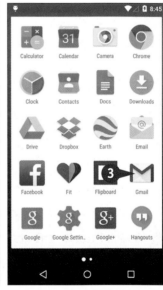

Your Inbox appears.

4 Touch **Menu** (☰).

The menu opens.

5 Touch **Settings**.

The Settings screen appears.

6 Touch the Gmail account for which you want to set up Priority Inbox.

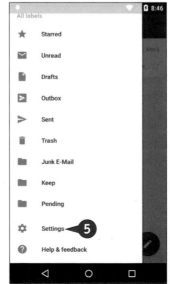

The account's settings screen appears.

7 Touch **Inbox type**.

The Inbox Type dialog box opens.

8 Touch **Priority Inbox** (○ changes to ◉).

9 Touch **Back** (◀).

The Settings screen appears.

Note: You can touch another Gmail account to set up Priority Inbox for it.

10 Touch **Back** (◀).

Your Inbox appears.

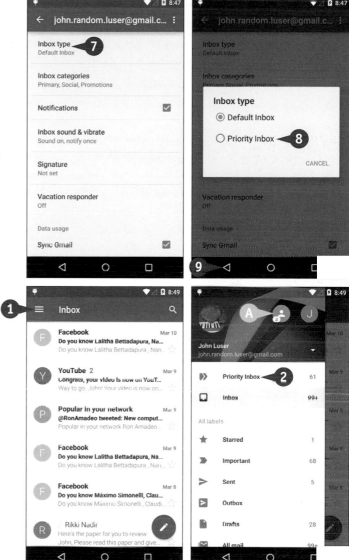

View Your Priority Inbox

1 In Gmail, touch the pop-up menu at the top of the screen.

The pop-up menu opens.

A If necessary, touch a different account.

2 Touch **Priority Inbox**.

Priority Inbox appears, and you can work with the messages it contains.

TIP

How does Priority Inbox work?

Priority Inbox collects any messages in conversations you and Gmail have labeled as important. You can mark a message as important by selecting it, touching **Menu** (⋮), and then touching **Mark important**. Gmail automatically labels messages as important for various reasons, such as messages that come from people you contact frequently or messages that are part of a conversation you have labeled as important.

Priority Inbox is a clever and helpful feature, but it is not foolproof. Even if Priority Inbox seems to be catching all your important messages, be sure to check your other messages in case any vital ones have ended up with your less important messages.

Choose Which Contacts to Display

 ndroid provides the Contacts app to manage your contacts. The Contacts app syncs contacts from your Google account, so your Google Contacts automatically show up in the Contacts app. You can also sync contacts from other e-mail accounts or import contacts manually. If you have many contacts, you may want to display only one group of them — for example, only your Facebook contacts or only your Corporate contacts. You can do this easily, but you can also create a custom display group that contains exactly the contacts you want to see.

Choose Which Contacts to Display

1 Touch **Home** (⬤).

The Home screen appears.

2 Touch **All Apps** (▦).

The Apps screen appears.

3 Touch **Contacts** (▣).

Note: If Contacts (▣) is not on the Apps screen that appears first, scroll left or right until you find Contacts (▣).

4 Touch **Menu** (⋮).

The menu opens.

5 Touch **Contacts to display**.

The Contacts to Display screen appears.

6 To use an existing group, touch it (◯ changes to ◉) and skip the remaining steps in this list.

7 To create a custom group, touch **Customize** (◯ changes to ◉).

The Define Custom View screen appears.

8 Touch an account's heading.

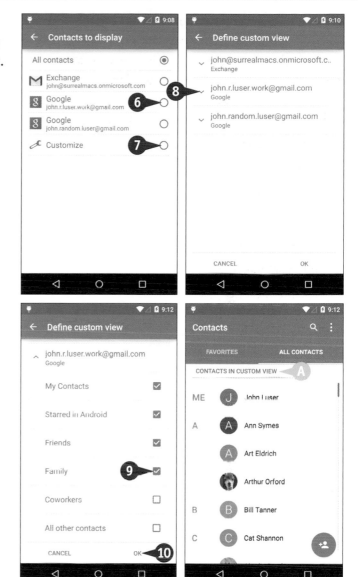

The account's contact groups appear.

9 Touch each group you want to include (☐ changes to ☑).

10 Touch **OK**.

The Contacts in Custom View screen appears, showing the contacts in the groups you chose.

A The bar at the top of the contacts shows *Contacts in Custom View* or the name of the account you chose.

What is the Favorites tab at the top of the Contacts screen for?

Touch the **Favorites** tab to display your list of favorite contacts — those you like best or contact most frequently. You can make a contact a favorite by touching the contact to display the details screen and then touching **Favorite** (☆ changes to ★).

How do I display all my contacts again?

In the Contacts app, touch the bar at the top of the contacts to go straight to the Contacts to Display screen. You can then touch **All contacts** (◯ changes to ◉) to display the full list of contacts.

Import Your Contacts into the Contacts App

Your phone or tablet can sync contacts with your Google account or with other e-mail accounts that you set up, such as Exchange Server. But if you have contact data stored elsewhere, you will need to import it into your device. You can import contact information from vCard files, a widely used format, by sending the files to your device or placing the files on it. If your device takes a SIM card, you can import contacts stored on a compatible SIM card — for example, from your old phone.

Import Your Contacts into the Contacts App

Import Contacts Attached to an E-Mail Message

1 Touch the vCard file attached to the message. Touch the main part of the button, not the Menu button (⋮) at its right end.

Note: If the Complete Action Using dialog box opens, touch **Contacts** and **Always**.

Ⓐ The Contacts app caches the file to temporary local storage.

The Create Contact Under Account dialog box opens.

2 Touch the account into which you want to import the contact data.

Ⓑ Android displays an acknowledgment and then imports the contact data.

Note: If your contact data is stored in a spreadsheet such as Microsoft Excel, save it as a comma-separated values, or CSV, file. You can then import that file into Google Contacts online and sync the contacts to your phone or tablet.

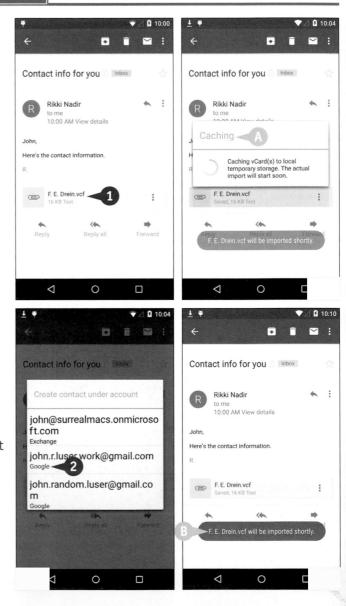

Import Contacts from a File

1 Copy the file to the Download folder on your phone or tablet using an app such as Windows Explorer or Android File Transfer.

2 In the Contacts app, touch **Menu** (⋮).

The menu opens.

3 Touch **Import/export**.

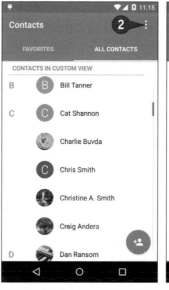
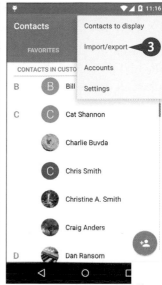

The Import/Export Contacts dialog box opens.

4 Touch **Import from storage**.

Note: To import contacts from a SIM card you have inserted in your device, touch **Import from SIM card**.

The Create Contact Under Account dialog box opens.

5 Touch the account in which you want to store the contact data.

The Contacts app imports the contact data.

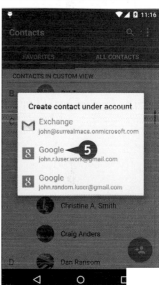

TIP

How do I avoid getting duplicate contacts when I import contacts from a file?
After importing the data from the vCard file, delete it from the Download folder so that you can import further files from there without importing the contact data again. You can delete the file using File Explorer or Windows Explorer on your PC, Android File Transfer on your Mac, or an app such as ES File Explorer on your device.

A ndroid's Calendar app enables you to track your time commitments on your device. You can easily add your appointments to the calendar, send invitations to other people for meetings and shared appointments, and accept invitations to events other people have created. The Calendar app can notify you of upcoming appointments by playing sounds or by vibrating, if your device has a vibration motor. You can choose your notifications and control when they appear from the Settings screen in the Calendar app.

Choose Calendar Notifications and Reminders

1 Touch **Home** (⬤).

The Home screen appears.

2 Touch **All Apps** (▦).

The Apps screen appears.

3 Touch **Calendar** (📅).

Note: If Calendar (📅) is not on the Apps screen that appears first, scroll left or right until you find Calendar (📅).

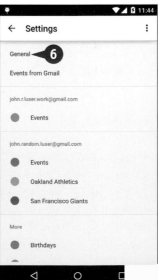

The Calendar app opens.

4 Touch **Menu** (☰).

The menu panel opens.

5 Touch **Settings**.

The Settings screen appears.

6 Touch **General** to display the General screen.

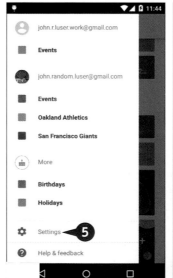
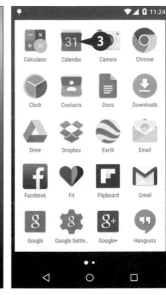

7 Set the **Notify on this device** switch to On (changes to) to receive notifications.

8 Set the **Vibrate** switch to On (changes to) if you want the device to vibrate for reminders.

9 Touch **Tone**.

The Ringtones dialog box opens.

10 Touch a sound (○ changes to ◉) to hear it.

11 Touch **OK**.

12 Touch **Back** (◁).

The Settings screen appears.

13 Touch the calendar for which you want to configure reminders, such as **Events**.

The calendar's settings screen appears.

Ⓐ You can touch **Color** and choose the color to use for the calendar.

14 Touch the current time setting in the Default Notifications section.

A pop-up panel appears.

15 Touch the timing for default notifications.

Ⓑ You can touch **Custom** to set custom timing.

16 Touch **Back** (◁).

The calendar appears.

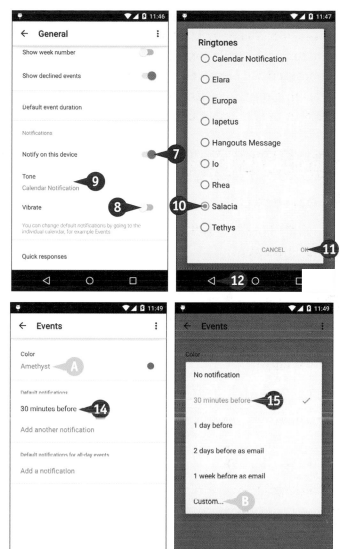

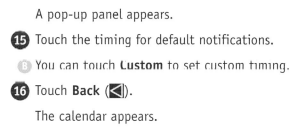

TIP

What are quick responses in the Calendar?
Quick responses are pieces of boilerplate text you can insert quickly in your replies to calendar invitations. To set up your quick responses, touch **Quick responses** on the General screen, and then work on the Quick Responses screen. The default quick responses are "Be there in about 10 minutes"; "Go ahead and start without me"; "Running just a couple of minutes late"; and "Sorry, I can't make it. We'll have to reschedule." Touch a quick response to open it for editing, type the text you want, and then touch **OK**. As of this writing, you cannot create new quick responses.

Choose Week and Time Zone Settings

The Calendar app lets you choose whether to display the week number in the year from Week 1 to Week 52. You can also choose which day to use as the start of the week: Saturday, Sunday, or Monday. If you travel to different time zones, you may need to specify in which time zone to show event dates and times. Otherwise, Calendar uses the time zone for your current location.

Choose Week and Time Zone Settings

1 Touch **Home** (⬤).

The Home screen appears.

2 Touch **All Apps** (▦).

The Apps screen appears.

3 Touch **Calendar** (31).

Note: If Calendar (31) is not on the Apps screen that appears first, scroll left or right until you find Calendar (31).

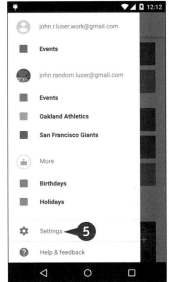

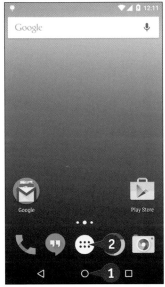

The Calendar app opens.

4 Touch **Menu** (▤).

The menu panel opens.

5 Touch **Settings**.

The Settings screen appears.

6 Touch **General**.

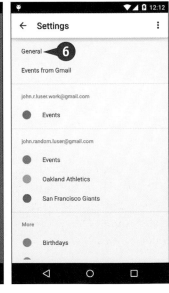

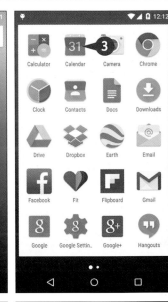

The General screen appears.

7 Set the **Show week number** switch to On (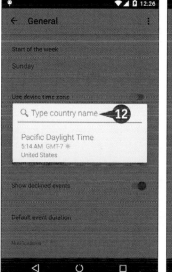 changes to) if you want to show week numbers.

8 Touch **Start of the week**.

The Start of the Week dialog box opens.

9 Touch the day on which you want your week to start (✓ appears).

The Start of the Week dialog box closes.

10 Set the **Use device time zone** switch to On (changes to) if you want to use time zones.

11 Touch **Time zone**.

The Time Zone dialog box opens.

12 Touch **Type country name** and type the country name.

A list of matches appears.

13 Touch the time zone to use.

The Time Zone dialog box closes.

14 Touch **Back** ().

The calendar appears.

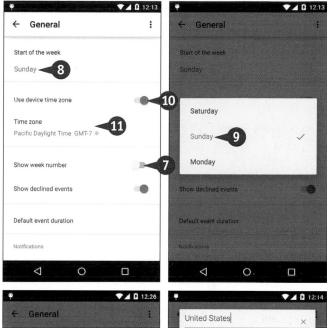

What does the Show Declined Events switch do?

Set the **Show declined events** switch to On (changes to) if you want events to which you have been invited but which you have declined to appear in your calendar. Depending on your business life and social life, you may find it helpful to see events you have declined as well as those you have accepted, so you know what you are missing and you remember who you might be snubbing.

CHAPTER 6

Networking and Communicating

In this chapter, you learn to control your Android device's cellular, Bluetooth, and wireless connections; share your device's Internet connection; and transfer data and make purchases wirelessly.

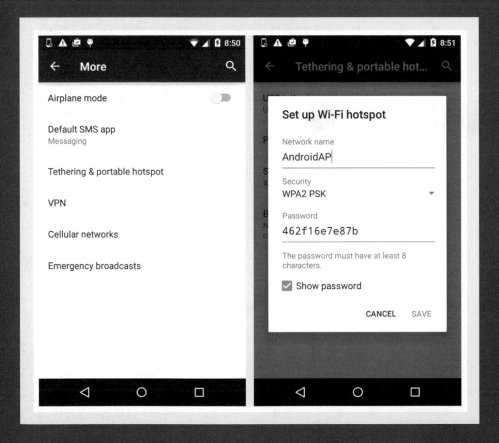

Control Wi-Fi, Bluetooth, and Cellular Access

If your Android device has cellular capability, you will normally want to keep it connected to the cellular network so that you can make or receive calls and access the Internet when no Wi-Fi connection is available. But when you do not need or may not use the cellular network, you can turn on Airplane mode to cut off all connections. Turning on Airplane mode turns off Wi-Fi and Bluetooth connections as well. But you can also turn Wi-Fi and Bluetooth on and off separately when you need to.

Control Wi-Fi, Bluetooth, and Cellular Access

Open the Quick Settings Panel

1 Touch **Home** (◉).

The Home screen appears.

Ⓐ The Wi-Fi icon (▽) shows the strength of the Wi-Fi signal.

Ⓑ The Cellular icon (◢) shows the strength of the cellular signal.

2 Pull down from the top of the screen with two fingers.

The Quick Settings panel opens.

Ⓒ The Wi-Fi icon (▽) shows the strength of the Wi-Fi signal.

Ⓓ The Cellular icon (◢) shows the strength of the cellular signal.

Ⓔ The example phone has two SIM slots. Here, the second slot contains no SIM.

Turn On Airplane Mode

1 In the Quick Settings panel, touch **Airplane Mode** (✈ changes to ✈).

Android turns on Airplane mode.

Ⓕ Android turns off Wi-Fi (▽ changes to ◣).

Ⓖ Android turns off cellular service (◢ changes to ◢).

Ⓗ Android turns off Bluetooth if it was on (✳ changes to ◣).

Note: To turn off Airplane mode, open the Quick Settings panel and touch **Airplane Mode** (✈ changes to ◣).

Turn On Wi-Fi

1 In the Quick Settings panel, touch **Wi-Fi** ( changes to) to turn Wi-Fi back on when Airplane mode is on.

Your phone or tablet connects to a known Wi-Fi network if one is available.

I Arrows to the right of the Wi-Fi icon (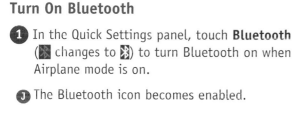) indicate data transfer. The up arrow indicates that the device is sending data, and the down arrow indicates that the device is receiving data.

Turn On Bluetooth

1 In the Quick Settings panel, touch **Bluetooth** (changes to) to turn Bluetooth on when Airplane mode is on.

J The Bluetooth icon becomes enabled.

TIPS

When should I use Airplane mode?
Airplane mode is designed for use on airplanes, but you can also use it any other time you want to take your device offline. For example, you may want to use Airplane mode while in the movie theater or in important meetings.

Should I turn Bluetooth on or leave it off?
Turn Bluetooth on if you want to use Bluetooth devices with your phone or tablet. When you are not using Bluetooth, turn it off to save battery power.

Connect Bluetooth Devices

To extend the functionality of your phone or tablet, you can connect devices to it that communicate using the wireless Bluetooth technology. Bluetooth is a networking protocol that is limited to short distances, typically up to about 30 feet. For example, you can connect a Bluetooth headset and microphone so that you can listen to music and make and take phone calls. Or you can connect a Bluetooth keyboard so that you can quickly type e-mail messages, notes, or documents.

Connect Bluetooth Devices

1 Touch **Home** (⬤).

The Home screen appears.

2 Touch **All Apps** (▦).

The Apps screen appears.

3 Touch **Settings** (⚙).

Note: If Settings (⚙) is not on the Apps screen that appears first, scroll left or right until you find Settings (⚙).

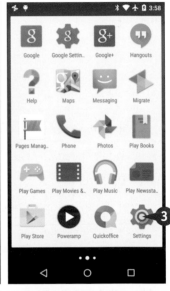

The Settings screen appears.

4 Touch **Bluetooth**.

The Bluetooth screen appears.

5 If the **Bluetooth** switch is Off (◯▬), set it to On (◯▬ changes to ▬◯).

Note: By default, Android makes your device visible to other Bluetooth devices while Bluetooth Settings is open. At other times, it is not visible to other devices.

6 Turn on the Bluetooth device and make it visible.

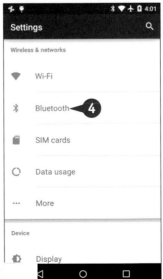

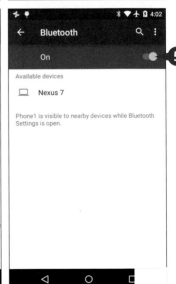

7 If the device does not appear in the Available Devices list, touch **Menu** (▤) and then touch **Refresh**.

Your phone or tablet searches for Bluetooth devices and displays a list of those it finds.

8 Touch the button for the device you want to connect.

9 When connecting a keyboard, type the code shown in the Bluetooth Pairing Request dialog box.

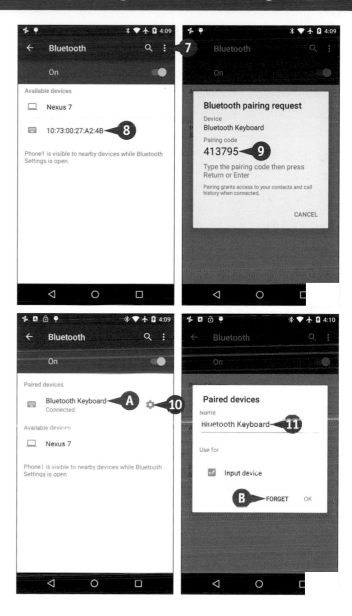

Android pairs the device.

Ⓐ The device appears in the Paired Devices list.

10 Touch **Options** (⚙).

The Paired Devices dialog box opens.

11 Optionally, touch the **Name** field and then type a new name for the device.

Note: Renaming lets you give a device a descriptive name rather than a make or model number.

Ⓑ When you no longer need to use the paired device, touch **Forget** to remove the pairing.

TIPS

What else can I do with Bluetooth?
You can connect your phone or tablet to your Bluetooth-enabled computer or another Bluetooth-enabled device via Bluetooth and transfer files back and forth. File transfer is slow compared to Wi-Fi, but it can be highly convenient.

Where do I find the files I receive via Bluetooth?
From the Bluetooth screen in the Settings app, touch **Menu** (▤) to open the menu, then touch **Show received files**. The Bluetooth Received screen appears, showing a list of the files your device has received.

Control Data Roaming and Cellular Usage

When you need to use your phone or cellular-capable tablet in a location where your carrier does not provide Internet service, you can turn on the Data Roaming feature and access the Internet using other carriers' networks. You may incur extra charges when using data roaming, especially when you use it in another country. For this reason, it is best to turn data roaming on only when you need it. Normally, you will want to use data roaming only when no wireless network connection is available.

Control Data Roaming and Cellular Usage

1 Touch **Home** (◉).

The Home screen appears.

2 Touch **All Apps** (▦).

The Apps screen appears.

3 Touch **Settings** (⚙).

Note: If Settings (⚙) is not on the Apps screen that appears first, scroll left or right until you find Settings (⚙).

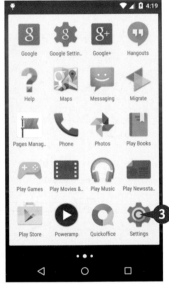

The Settings screen appears.

4 Touch **More**.

The More screen appears.

5 Touch **Cellular networks**.

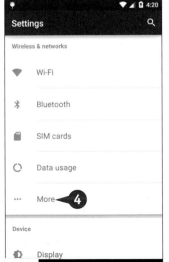

The Cellular Network Settings screen appears.

6 To enable data, touch **Data enabled** (☐ changes to ☑).

7 To use data roaming, touch **Data roaming** (☐ changes to ☑).

The Attention dialog box opens.

8 Touch **OK**.

The Attention dialog box closes.

9 Touch **Back** (◀).

The More screen appears.

10 Touch **Back** (◀) again.

The Settings screen appears.

11 Touch **Data usage**.

The Data Usage screen appears.

12 Set the **Set cellular data limit** switch to On (⬜ changes to ⬤).

13 Touch **Data usage cycle** and set the cycle's dates.

Ⓐ The readout shows how much data you have used.

14 Drag the **Limit bar** (⬤) up or down to set the data limit.

15 Drag the **Warning bar** (⬤) up or down to set the warning level.

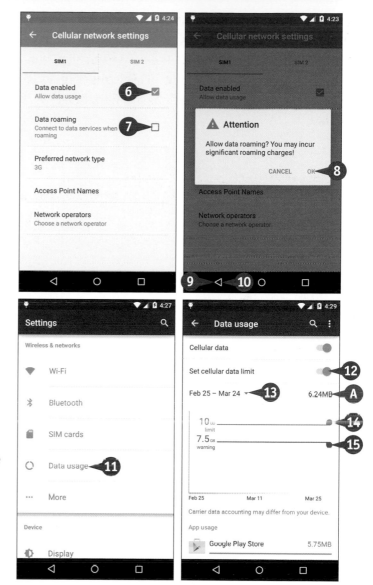

TIPS

How can I see which apps have used the most cellular data?

Look at the App Usage list on the Data Usage screen. This list shows the apps that have used cellular data sorted in descending order, so the top of the list shows the app that has used the most data.

How can I prevent an app from using so much cellular data?

You can prevent the app from transferring data in the background. On the Data Usage screen, touch the app's button in the App Usage list to display the App Data Usage screen. You can then set the **Restrict app background data** switch to On (⬜ changes to ⬤).

Connect Your Device to a Different Carrier

The SIM card makes your phone or cellular-capable tablet connect automatically to a particular carrier's network, such as the AT&T network or the Verizon network. When you go outside your carrier's network, you can connect the phone or tablet manually to a different carrier — for example, when you travel abroad. To connect to a different carrier, you may need to set up an account with that carrier or pay extra charges to your standard carrier.

Connect Your Device to a Different Carrier

1 Touch **Home** (◯).

The Home screen appears.

2 Touch **All Apps** (⊞).

The Apps screen appears.

3 Touch **Settings** (⚙).

Note: If Settings (⚙) is not on the Apps screen that appears first, scroll left or right until you find Settings (⚙).

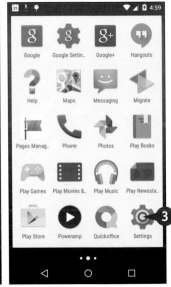

The Settings screen appears.

4 Touch **More**.

The More screen appears.

5 Touch **Cellular networks**.

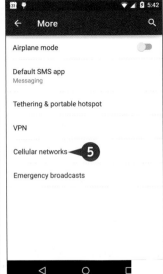

The Cellular Network Settings screen appears.

6 Touch **Network operators**.

The Available Networks screen appears.

Android displays the Searching bar while it searches for available networks.

7 Touch the network you want to use.

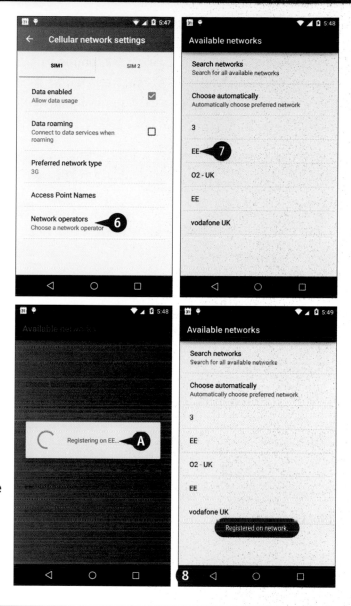

A Android registers your device with the carrier.

8 Touch **Back** (◄).

The Cellular Network Settings screen appears.

9 Touch **Back** (◄) again.

The More screen appears.

10 Touch **Back** (◄) a third time.

The Settings screen appears.

Note: To return to your regular carrier, touch **Choose automatically** on the Available Networks screen.

TIP

Is there another way to change carriers?

If your phone or cellular-capable tablet has an easily accessible SIM card and your device is not locked to a particular carrier, you can remove the existing SIM card and replace it with one for the carrier to which you want to switch.

If you need to be able to change carriers easily, consider getting a dual-SIM phone. Once you have loaded two SIM cards from suitable carriers into the phone, you can quickly switch from one SIM to another. Use the SIM Cards screen in the Settings app to configure the SIM cards.

Connect to Your Work Network via VPN

I̲f you use your phone or tablet for work, you may need to connect it to your work network. By using the settings, username, and password that the network's administrator provides, you can connect via *virtual private networking*, or VPN, across the Internet. VPN uses encryption to create a secure connection across the Internet. By using VPN, you can connect securely from anywhere you have an Internet connection. Before you create a VPN connection, you must set a lock screen pattern, PIN, or password on your device for security.

Connect to Your Work Network via VPN

1 Touch **Home** (⬤).

The Home screen appears.

2 Touch **All Apps** (⦂⦂⦂).

The Apps screen appears.

3 Touch **Settings** (⚙).

Note: If Settings (⚙) is not on the Apps screen that appears first, scroll left or right until you find Settings (⚙).

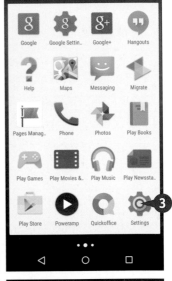

The Settings screen appears.

4 Touch **More**.

The More screen appears.

5 Touch **VPN**.

Note: If you have not yet set a lock screen pattern, PIN, or password, an Attention dialog box opens when you touch **VPN**. Touch **OK** to display the Unlock Selection screen; then touch **Pattern**, **PIN**, or **Password**, as needed; and set up the security mechanism. For effective security, use PIN or Password rather than Pattern.

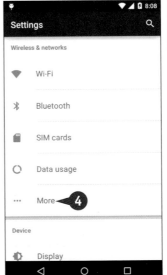

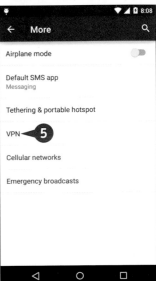

The VPN screen appears.

6 Touch **Add** (➕).

The Edit VPN Profile dialog box opens.

7 Type a descriptive name for the connection.

8 Choose the VPN type. See the first tip for more information.

9 Type the server address.

10 Type the security information.

11 Touch **Save**.

12 Touch the VPN's name.

13 In the Connect To dialog box, type your username.

14 Type your password.

15 Touch the **Save account information** check box (☐ changes to ☑) if you want to save your details.

16 Touch **Connect**.

Ⓐ The *Connected* readout appears. You can now work with network resources such as e-mail and network folders.

17 When you are ready to disconnect, touch the VPN's name.

18 In the VPN Is Connected dialog box, touch **Disconnect**.

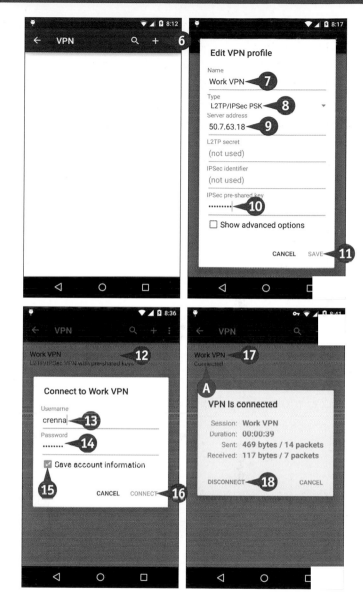

TIPS

What VPN type should I choose?

You must use the type of connection the VPN server uses. Ask the VPN's administrator which VPN type this is. PPTP, the Point-to-Point Tunneling Protocol, and L2TP, the Layer 2 Tunneling Protocol, are the most widely used VPN types, but it is hard to guess what type you need.

What is the pre-shared key?

The pre-shared key, also called a *shared secret*, is a group password for the VPN. The pre-shared key, or PSK, is shared among a group of users rather than being dedicated to a single user.

Using the Tethering Feature

Your phone or cellular-capable tablet can share its cellular connection with your computer or other devices. This feature enables you to connect your computer or Wi-Fi–only devices to the Internet through the cellular connection your phone or tablet has established. You can share the Internet access in two ways. The first way is tethering, in which you connect your Android device to your computer via USB and share the connection across the USB cable. The second way is by turning your Android device into a portable Wi-Fi hotspot, as explained in the following section.

Using the Tethering Feature

Turn Tethering On or Off

1 Connect your phone or tablet to your computer via the USB cable.

2 Touch **Home** (⊙).

The Home screen appears.

3 Touch **All Apps** (⊞).

The Apps screen appears.

4 Touch **Settings** (⚙).

Note: If Settings (⚙) is not on the Apps screen that appears first, scroll left or right until you find Settings (⚙).

The Settings screen appears.

5 Touch **More**.

The More screen appears.

6 Touch **Tethering & portable hotspot**.

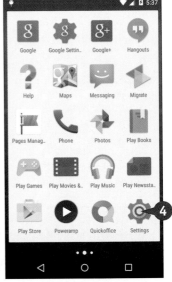

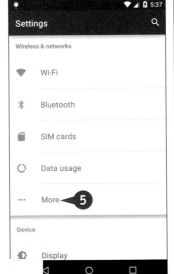

The Tethering & Portable Hotspot screen appears.

7 Set the **USB tethering** switch to On (⬜ changes to 🔵).

A The USB tethering button shows the readout *Tethered*.

Your computer starts using the phone or tablet's Internet connection across the USB cable.

8 When you finish using the connection, set the **USB tethering** switch to Off (🔵 changes to ⬜).

Set Your Mac to Use the Tethered Connection

1 On your Mac, press **Control**+click **System Preferences** (🔘) on the Dock.

The System Preferences contextual menu opens.

2 Click **Network**.

The Network preferences pane appears.

3 In the left pane, click the entry for your Android device.

4 Click **Apply** if the button has dark text rather than grayed-out text.

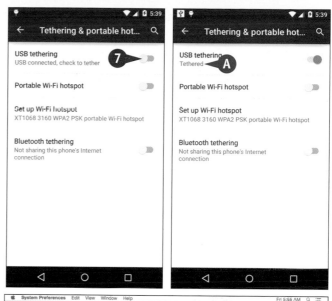

TIP

Why does my Android device not appear in my Mac's Network preferences?

You may need to install a driver, a piece of software that enables the Mac to use the Android device's USB connection. The HoRNDIS driver available at http://joshuawise.com/horndis enables OS X to use many Android devices this way.

To install HoRNDIS, you must allow applications downloaded from identified developers. Click **System Preferences** (🔘) on the Dock, click **Security & Privacy**, click **General**, and then click **Mac App Store and identified developers** in the Allow Applications Downloaded From area. You may need to click the lock icon and type your password to make these changes.

Using the Portable Hotspot Feature

Your Android phone or cellular-capable tablet can act as a Wi-Fi hotspot to share its cellular Internet access with your computer and other devices. This feature is called Portable Hotspot. For you to use Portable Hotspot, your cellular carrier must permit you to use it. Many carriers charge an extra fee per month for using Portable Hotspot. Verify your carrier's policy for Portable Hotspot and be careful not to exceed your cellular data allowance.

Using the Portable Hotspot Feature

Set Up Portable Hotspot

1 Touch **Home** (⬤).

The Home screen appears.

2 Touch **All Apps** (⊞).

The Apps screen appears.

3 Touch **Settings** (⚙).

Note: If Settings (⚙) is not on the Apps screen that appears first, scroll left or right until you find Settings (⚙).

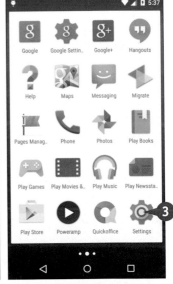

The Settings screen appears.

4 Touch **More**.

The More screen appears.

5 Touch **Tethering & portable hotspot**.

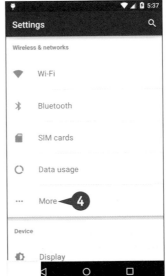

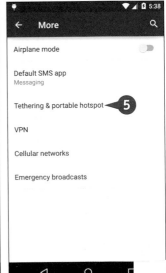

The Tethering & Portable Hotspot screen appears.

6 Touch **Set up Wi-Fi hotspot**.

The Set Up Wi-Fi Hotspot dialog box opens.

7 Type the name for the hotspot.

8 Touch **Security** and choose the security type. See the first tip for a recommendation.

9 Touch **Password** and type a password of eight characters or more.

A Touch **Show password** (☐ changes to ☑) if you need to verify the password.

10 Touch **Save**.

The Set Up Wi-Fi Hotspot dialog box closes.

B The hotspot's details appear on the Set Up Wi-Fi Hotspot button.

11 Set the **Portable Wi-Fi hotspot** switch to On (⬤ changes to ⬤).

C The Portable Hotspot icon (◉) appears in the status bar to indicate the Portable Hotspot feature is active.

You can now connect your computers or devices to the portable hotspot's Wi-Fi network.

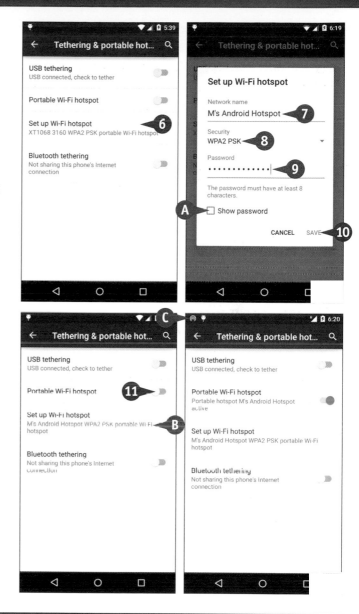

TIPS

What security type should I choose for my Wi-Fi hotspot?

WPA2 PSK is the most secure type. Use WPA2 PSK unless any of the devices you need to connect to the hotspot does not support this security method. Do not use Open, because any device within Wi-Fi range will be able to connect freely to your hotspot.

Are there disadvantages to using Portable Hotspot?

Because the devices share the Internet connection, the more devices you use, the slower the connection speed will appear to be on each device. You must also be careful not to exceed your cellular data allowance, which could run up extra costs.

Manage Your Wireless Networks

Your Android phone or tablet can connect to both infrastructure wireless networks and ad hoc wireless networks. An infrastructure network uses a wireless access point, whereas an ad hoc network is hosted by a device. The first time you connect to a Wi-Fi network, you provide the network's password. After that, your phone or tablet stores the password for future connections. You can make the device forget a network you no longer use.

Manage Your Wireless Networks

Connect to an Infrastructure Wireless Network

1 Touch **Home** (⬤).

The Home screen appears.

2 Touch **All Apps** (⬚).

The Apps screen appears.

3 Touch **Settings** (⚙).

Note: If Settings (⚙) is not on the Apps screen that appears first, scroll left or right until you find Settings (⚙).

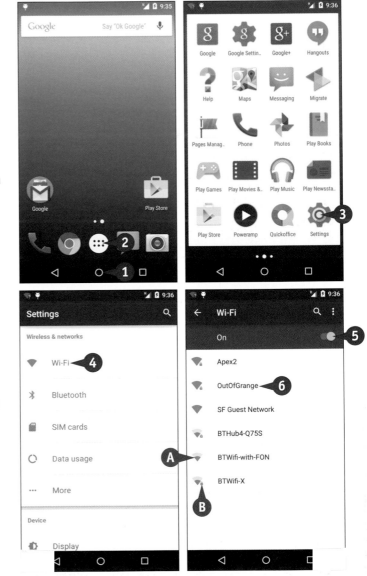

The Settings screen appears.

4 Touch **Wi-Fi**.

The Wi-Fi screen appears.

5 Make sure the **Wi-Fi** switch is set to On (⚫▬).

Ⓐ The Wi-Fi symbol (📶) shows the network's signal strength.

Ⓑ The lock icon (🔒) indicates the network uses security.

6 Touch the network to which you want to connect.

Note: If the network has no password, your phone or tablet connects to it without prompting you for a password.

138

A dialog box for connecting to the network opens.

7 Type the password.

C You can touch **Show password** (☐ changes to ☑) to display the password characters.

8 Touch **Connect**.

Your device connects to the network.

D The Wi-Fi signal icon (▼) appears in the status bar.

E The *Connected* readout appears below the network's name.

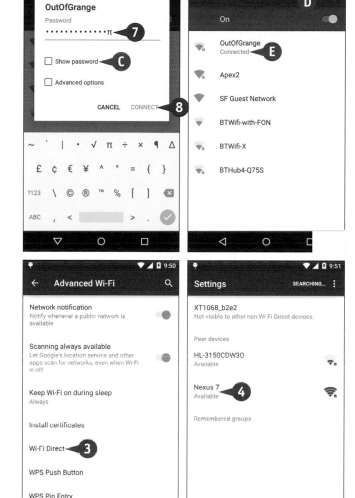

Connect to an Ad Hoc Wireless Network

1 Display the Wi-Fi screen by following steps **1** to **5** in the previous subsection.

2 Touch **Menu** (⋮) and then touch **Advanced**.

The Advanced Wi-Fi screen appears.

3 Touch **Wi-Fi Direct**.

The Wi-Fi Direct screen appears.

4 In the Peer Devices list, touch the device to which you want to connect.

When the peer device accepts the invitation to connect, Android establishes the network.

TIPS

How do I stop my phone or tablet from using a wireless network?

Tell the device to forget the network. On the Wi-Fi screen, touch the network's name, then touch **Forget** in the dialog box for the network.

I get the message *Authentication problem* when I try to connect to a network. How do I solve this?

The *Authentication problem* message usually means you have mistyped the password. On the Wi-Fi screen, touch the network's name, then touch **Forget** in the dialog box for the network. Touch the network's name again and retype the password. Touch the **Show password** check box (☐ changes to ☑) so you can see the characters and make sure they are correct.

Log In to Wi-Fi Hotspots

When you are in town or on the road, you can log in to Wi-Fi hotspots to enjoy fast Internet access without using your phone or cellular tablet's data allowance. You can find Wi-Fi hotspots at many locations, including coffee shops and restaurants, hotels and airports, municipal areas, and even some parks and highway rest stops. Some Wi-Fi hotspots charge for access, whereas others are free. If you travel extensively, consider signing up for a plan that provides long-term access to Wi-Fi hotspots.

Log In to Wi-Fi Hotspots

1 Touch **Home** (⬤).

The Home screen appears.

2 Touch **All Apps** (⬛).

The Apps screen appears.

3 Touch **Settings** (⚙).

Note: If Settings (⚙) is not on the Apps screen that appears first, scroll left or right until you find Settings (⚙).

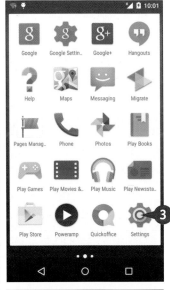

The Settings screen appears.

4 Touch **Wi-Fi**.

The Wi-Fi screen appears.

5 Touch the network to which you want to connect.

Note: If your phone or tablet prompts you to enter a username and password, enter those the hotspot operator has given you.

Your phone or tablet joins the hotspot. The Wi-Fi screen displays *Connected* next to the hotspot.

6 Touch **Home** (⬤).

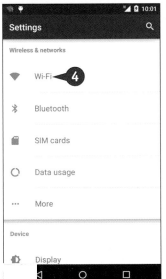

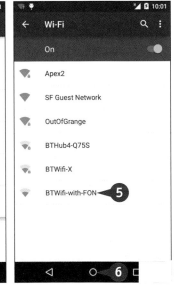

CHAPTER
6

Networking and Communicating

The Home screen appears.

7 Touch **Chrome** ().

The Chrome app opens and displays a login page for the hotspot.

8 Type the login information for the hotspot.

9 Touch the button for logging in.

After connecting to the hotspot, you can use the Internet. For example, you can browse the web using Chrome or send and receive e-mail using the Gmail app or the Email app.

10 When you finish using the hotspot, touch **Overview** (■).

The Overview screen appears.

11 Touch the **Settings** thumbnail for the Wi-Fi screen.

The Wi-Fi screen in the Settings app appears.

12 Touch the Wi-Fi network's name.

The network's dialog box opens.

13 Touch **Forget**.

Your Android device forgets the network.

TIP

What precautions should I take when using Wi-Fi hotspots?

The main danger is that you may connect to a malevolent network. To stay safe, connect only to hotspots provided by reputable establishments — for example, national hotel chains or restaurant chains — instead of hotspots run by unknown operators. Even then, it is best not to transmit any private information that may interest eavesdroppers.

When you finish using a Wi-Fi hotspot that you do not plan to use again, tell your phone or tablet to forget the network. To forget the network, touch the Wi-Fi network's name on the Wi-Fi screen, and then touch **Forget**.

Transfer Data Using Android Beam

Android includes a feature called Android Beam that lets you transfer data wirelessly between Android devices. Android Beam uses a technology called *Near Field Communication*, or NFC, which enables NFC-enabled smartphones and tablets to automatically establish a radio connection when you bring them close together. If your phone or tablet includes an NFC chip, you can transfer data to another NFC-enabled device by bringing them back-to-back briefly. This feature is great for transferring contacts, photos, and other data you want to share quickly and effortlessly.

Transfer Data Using Android Beam

Turn On Android Beam

1 Touch **Home** (◉).

The Home screen appears.

2 Pull down from the top of the screen with two fingers.

The Quick Settings panel opens.

3 Touch **Settings** (⚙).

The Settings screen appears.

4 Touch **More**.

The More screen appears.

5 Set the **NFC** switch to On (⬜ changes to ⬤).

6 If Android Beam shows Off, touch **Android Beam**. Otherwise, skip the remaining steps in this section.

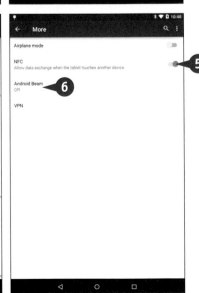

The Android Beam screen appears.

7 Set the **Android Beam** switch to On (⬜ changes to 🔵).

8 Touch **Back** (◁).

The Wireless & Networks screen appears.

A The *Ready to transmit app content via NFC* readout appears.

Transfer Data via Android Beam

1 Open the app that contains the data you want to transfer. For example, touch **Home** (⬤), touch **All Apps** (⠿), and then touch **Contacts** (▣) to open the People app. Then touch a contact to display the record.

2 Bring your device back-to-back with another NFC-enabled device.

When the NFC chips connect, your device vibrates, the screen image shrinks, and the *Touch to Beam* prompt appears.

3 Touch the **Touch to beam** prompt.

Your device beams the data to the other device.

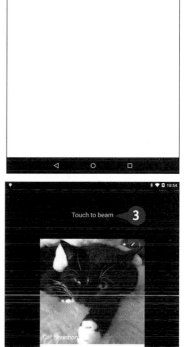

TIPS

Why can't my phone and tablet connect via Android Beam?
If you have turned on NFC and enabled Android Beam on both devices, the problem is most likely that you have not brought the NFC chips close enough to each other. Hold the phone and tablet back-to-back and move the phone around the tablet until the devices vibrate. You will then have found the right location to use for Android Beam connections.

What happens when my device receives data via Android Beam?
Your device accepts the data, but it may prompt you to decide where to place it. For example, if the Contacts app receives a contact, it may prompt you to choose in which account to place the new contact.

Make Payments with NFC

If your Android device contains a Near Field Communication chip, you can use NFC to make payments with contactless payment systems. To make a payment, you bring your phone or tablet to within a few inches of the NFC payment terminal and then confirm the transaction by touching a prompt on the screen. This payment system can be fast, convenient, and practical, eliminating the need to bring your wallet out into the open, take physical money from it, and receive and put away change. Contactless payment systems are currently available in various major chains and major public locations, such as airports and stations. Experts expect contactless payment systems to become widely used in the coming years.

Create a Google Wallet Account

Before you can make an NFC payment, you must set up a Google Wallet account. Google Wallet is a secure digital payment technology developed and promoted by Google. After setting up a Google Wallet account and adding a means of payment, you can use Google Wallet to make payments online or with your Android device. To create a Google Wallet account, type https://www.google.com/wallet/ in the address box in your web browser and then click **Sign up**. With the account created, you can add a means of payment: a credit card, a debit card, or a voucher. You can add multiple means of payment and switch among them as needed. If you lose your Android device, or if someone steals it, you can disable Google Wallet on the device to prevent anyone else from making payments with it.

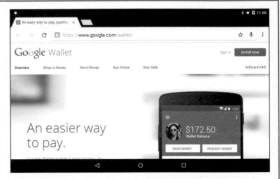

Install Wallet on Your Phone or Tablet

After creating a Google Wallet account, you can set up your phone or tablet to use the account so that you can make payments with the device. To do so, you set up the Wallet app on your device. If your phone or tablet does not have the Wallet app installed, you can install it by touching **Play Store** on the Apps screen, touching **Apps**, and then searching for **Wallet**. After you locate the Wallet app, download and install it, and then sign in to it.

Enable NFC on Your Android Device

To make NFC payments using your Android phone or tablet, you must enable NFC on your device. To do so, touch **Home** (⬤), then touch **All Apps** (⬚) to display the Apps screen. Touch **Settings** (⚙) to open the Settings app, touch **More** to display the More screen, and then set the **NFC** switch to On (changes to).

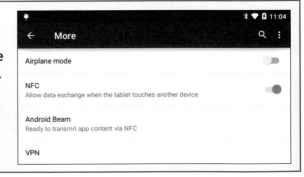

Learn Where You Can Make NFC Payments

At this writing, you can make NFC payments at hundreds of thousands of stores in the United States. Major merchants that accept NFC payments include Banana Republic, Foot Locker, Macy's, OfficeMax, ToysRUs, and Old Navy. The list of stores that

accept NFC payments is increasing rapidly, and Google plans to introduce Google Wallet in other countries in the near future. Most stores that accept NFC payments display signs near their checkout terminals. If you do not see a sign, ask a member of the staff if the store accepts NFC payments.

Make a Payment via NFC

When you have set up your Android phone or tablet with Google Wallet and enabled NFC, you can make payments using NFC at establishments that accept contactless payments. To make a payment with NFC, first unlock your phone or tablet. Touch **Home** (⬤) to display the

Home screen, and then touch **All Apps** (▦) to display the Apps screen. Touch **Wallet** to launch the Wallet app. On the screen of payment options that Wallet displays, touch the card or voucher you want to use. Touch the back of your phone or tablet to the payment terminal.

Take Other Actions with NFC

NFC is a powerful and flexible technology that is currently finding new uses in both business and home settings. As well as making payments, you may be able to use your phone or tablet to authorize you to enter buildings or zones controlled by contactless terminals. If your work or play

involves such areas, find out whether your phone or tablet can substitute for a pass card you would normally carry. If so, you can use your Android device to access controlled areas.

CHAPTER 7

Phoning, Messaging, and Social Networking

With your Android phone, you can make phone calls and conference calls anywhere you go. With either a phone or a tablet, you can also enjoy instant messaging, video calling, and social networking.

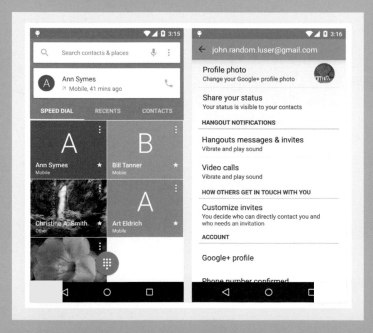

Make Phone Calls

With your Android phone, you can make phone calls anywhere you have a connection to the cellular network. You can make a phone call by dialing the phone number using the keypad, but you can place calls more easily by tapping the appropriate phone number for a contact or by using your Recents, the list of recent calls.

To enable other people near you to hear both ends of the phone call you are making, you can switch on your phone's speaker.

Make Phone Calls

Open the Phone App

1. Touch **Home** (●).

   The Home screen appears.

2. Touch **Phone** (📞).

   The Phone app opens and displays the screen you used last — for example, the Speed Dial screen.

   Note: You can also place a call to a phone number that your phone has identified — for example, by tapping an underlined phone number that represents a link on a web page.

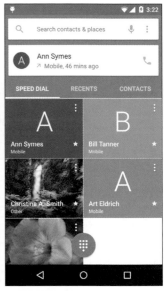

Dial a Call Using the Keypad

1. In the Phone app, touch **Keypad** (⊞) at the bottom of the screen.

   The Keypad screen appears.

2. Touch the number keys to dial the number.

3. Touch **Dial** (📞) at the bottom of the Keypad screen.

   Your phone makes the call.

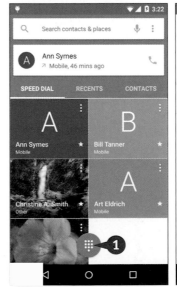

Dial a Call to a Contact

1 In the Phone app, touch **Contacts**.

The Contacts list appears.

2 Touch the contact you want to call.

The contact's information appears.

3 Touch the number to call.

Your phone makes the call.

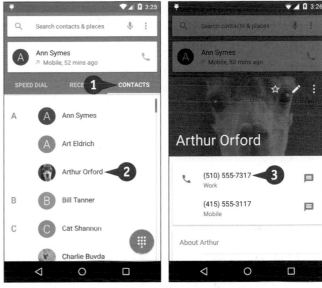

End a Phone Call

1 Touch **End Call** ( ).

Your phone ends the call.

A The *Call ended* message appears for a moment.

Your phone then displays the screen from which you placed the call — for example, the Contacts screen.

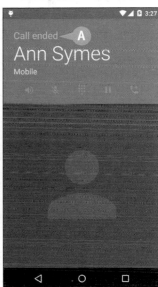

TIP

Can I use my phone as a speakerphone?
Yes, as long as your phone has a speaker, which most do. All you need to do is touch **Speaker** ( ) on the control panel that appears while you are making a phone call. Your phone starts playing the call through the main speaker rather than the ear speaker, turning your phone into a speakerphone. Touch **Speaker** ( ) again when you want to switch off the speaker.

Make Phone Calls with a Headset

I f you have a headset with a microphone and built-in controls, you can use it to listen to music and to make and receive phone calls. Using the headset is convenient both when you are out and about and when you are listening to music, because you can accept an incoming call using the headset controls without even looking at your phone's screen. Your phone automatically pauses the music when you answer a phone call and resumes it after the call ends.

Make Phone Calls with a Headset

Make a Call Using the Headset

1 Connect the headset to your phone if it is not already connected.

Note: You can dial a call by activating Voice Actions and speaking the number or the contact's name. See Chapter 4 for instructions on using Voice Actions.

2 Touch **Home** (⬤).

The Home screen appears.

3 Touch **Phone** (📞).

The Phone app opens.

4 Dial the call.

5 If you need to change the volume, press the Volume Up button or the Volume Down button on either the headset or the phone.

6 Press the clicker button on the headset to mute or unmute the call.

7 Touch **End call** (🔴) to end the call.

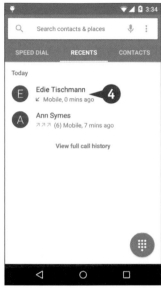

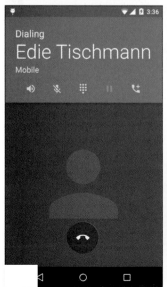

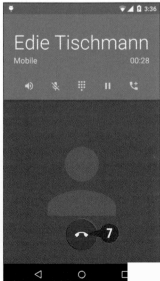

Take a Call Using the Headset

1 Connect the headset to your phone if it is not already connected.

When you receive an incoming call, the phone ringtone plays in the headset and the screen comes on if it is off.

A The lock screen shows the caller's name and phone details — for example, Mobile or the phone number.

Note: If you are listening to music or watching a video when you receive a call, your phone automatically fades and pauses the music.

2 Press the clicker button on the headset to take the call.

B Alternatively, you can drag Call (📞) to **Pick Up** (📞), **Hang Up** (📵), or **Send Text** (🖹).

The lock screen shows the caller's name and the call's duration.

3 If you need to change the volume, press the Volume Up button or the Volume Down button on the headset.

4 Press the clicker button on the headset to mute or unmute the call if necessary.

5 Touch **End Call** (📵) when you are ready to end the call.

The Phone app appears, showing the screen you last used.

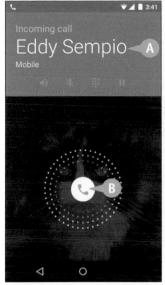
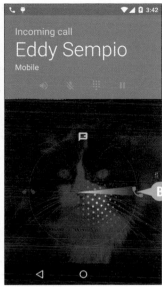

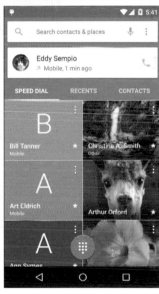

TIP

Can I take further actions using the headset?
This depends on the model of headset and how tightly it is integrated with your phone. Many headsets include volume buttons that you can press to increase or decrease the audio volume during a call. Some headsets have extra functionality — for example, you can press a button to end a call. Explore your headset's controls or read its documentation to find out all it can do.

Make a Conference Call

When you need to talk to more than one person at a time, you can make a conference call using your Android phone. This capability is great for both business and social calls. To make a conference call, you do not need to set it up with an operator in advance; instead, you call the first participant, and then add each other participant in turn. During a conference call, you can talk in private to individual participants. You can also drop a participant from the call without affecting the other participants.

Make a Conference Call

Establish a Conference Call

1 Touch **Home** (⬤).

The Home screen appears.

2 Touch **Phone** (📞).

The Phone app opens.

3 Touch **Contacts**.

The Contacts screen appears.

Note: You can also call a contact by using the keypad or Recents.

4 Touch the phone number for the contact you want to call first.

Your phone makes the call.

5 After the contact answers the call, touch **Add participant** (📞).

The Keypad screen appears.

6 Touch **Back** (◁).

Note: You can also swipe down the Keypad screen to display the other screens.

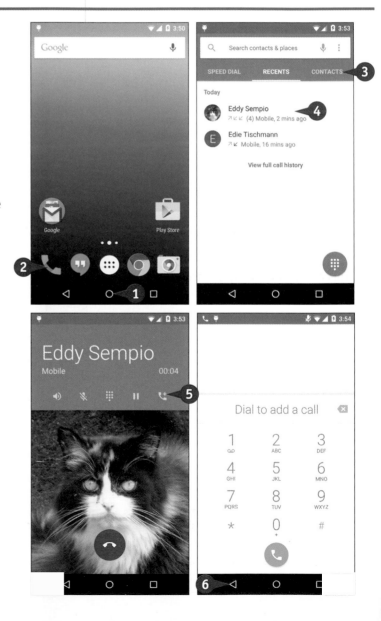

The screen you last used appears — for example, the Recents screen.

7 Locate the contact and touch the phone number to use.

A Your phone places the first call on hold.

B Your phone makes the new call.

8 Touch **Merge calls** ( ).

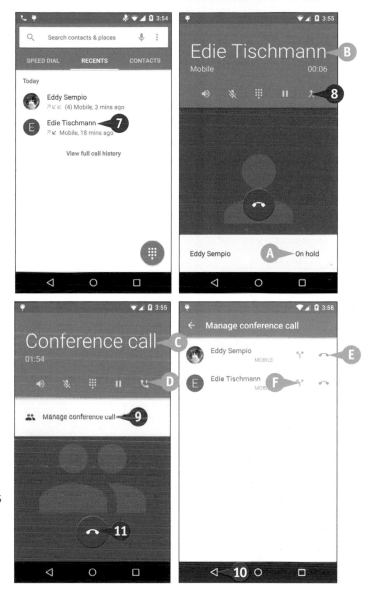

C The Phone app merges the calls.

You can now speak to both participants.

D You can touch **Add participant** ( ) to add someone else to the call.

9 To speak privately to or disconnect one participant, touch **Manage conference call**.

E Touch **End call** ( ) to disconnect a participant.

F Touch **Split calls** ( ) to speak privately to a participant, putting the other participants on hold.

10 Touch **Back** ( ) to return to the call.

11 Touch **End call** ( ) to end the call.

TIPS

How do I get back to my conference call after leaving it?
You can leave the conference call and work with other apps by touching **Home** ( ) or **Overview** ( ) and then touching the app you want. To return to the call, either touch **Overview** ( ) and then touch the Phone thumbnail, or open the Notification shade and touch **Ongoing call**. You can also touch **Hang Up** ( ) in the Notification shade to end the call without returning to the Phone app.

How many participants can I include in a conference call?
The number of participants depends on your cellular carrier rather than on Android. Contact your carrier's support department to find out the limit.

Call with Speed Dial, Recents, and History

The Phone app enables you to make calls quickly by using the Recents list, the Speed Dial screen, and the History screen. The Speed Dial screen shows your Favorites plus your most frequently called contacts who are not Favorites; the Recents list shows the most recent calls you have made and received; and the History screen enables you to view all calls made and received, or just the calls you missed, since you last cleared your call log.

Call with Speed Dial, Recents, and History

Call Using the Speed Dial Screen

1 Touch **Home** (⬤).

The Home screen appears.

2 Touch **Phone** (📞).

The Phone app opens, and the Speed Dial screen appears.

Ⓐ Your last call appears at the top of the Speed Dial screen. You can scroll the screen up to hide the last call and see more Speed Dial buttons.

3 Touch the contact you want to call.

The Choose Number dialog box opens if the contact record contains multiple numbers.

Ⓑ You can touch **Remember this choice** (☐ changes to ☑) to make the Phone app remember your choice.

4 Touch the number to use.

The Phone app places the call.

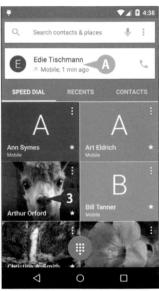

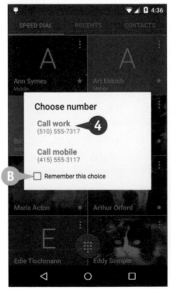

Call Using the Recents List

1 In the Phone app, touch **Recents**.

The Recents list appears.

2 Touch the contact you want to call.

Note: If the Choose Number dialog box opens, touch **Remember this choice** (☐ changes to ☑) if necessary, and then touch the appropriate number.

The Phone app places the call.

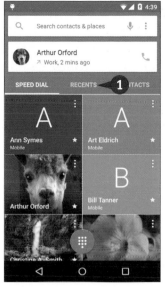

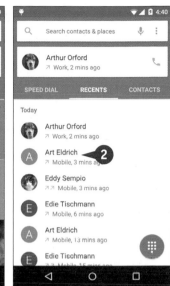

Call Using History

1 In the Phone app, touch **Menu** (⋮).

The menu opens.

2 Touch **Call History**.

The History screen appears.

C You can touch **Missed** to display only the calls you missed.

3 Touch the contact you want to call.

Note: If the Choose Number dialog box opens, touch **Remember this choice** (☐ changes to ☑) if necessary, and then touch the appropriate number.

The Phone app places the call.

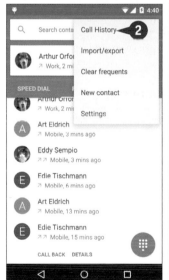

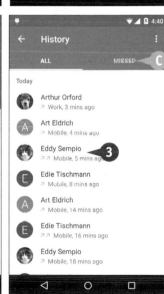

 TIP

How can I remove a contact from the Speed Dial list?

You can remove a single contact by touching and holding the contact on the Speed Dial screen and then dragging to the Remove button that appears at the top.

If the contact is a Favorite, removing the contact from the Speed Dial screen also removes Favorite status from the contact.

You can remove all contacts who are not Favorites from the Speed Dial screen by touching **Menu** (⋮) and then touching **Clear frequents**.

Send and Receive Instant Messages with Hangouts

The Hangouts app included with Android enables you to send instant messages easily. An instant message can use either SMS or MMS. SMS stands for *Short Message Service*; MMS stands for *Multimedia Messaging Service*. An SMS message consists of only text, whereas an MMS message can contain text, videos, photos, sounds, or other data. When you start a message, the Hangouts app creates it as an SMS message. If you add a photo, video, or other content, Hangouts automatically converts the message to an MMS message.

Send and Receive Instant Messages with Hangouts

1 Touch **Home** (◉).

The Home screen appears.

2 Touch **Hangouts** (💬).

Note: If Hangouts (💬) does not appear on the Home screen, touch **All Apps** (⊞), and then touch **Hangouts** (💬).

The Hangouts app opens.

3 Touch **Contacts** (👤).

4 Touch the appropriate contact.

A You can touch **Type a name, email, number, or circle** to contact someone who is not on the Contacts list.

The hangout for the contact opens.

B You can touch **Anyone else?** (👥+) to add another contact.

5 Touch **Attach** (📎).

The Attach dialog box opens.

6 Touch **Take photo**, **Send photo**, **Share your location**, or **Send sticker**, as appropriate. This example uses **Send photo**.

Note: A sticker is a graphic intended to convey a message or feeling.

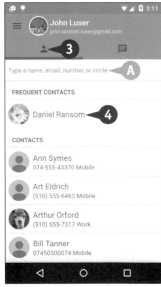

Your photos appear.

Note: To navigate to other photos, touch **Menu** (▤) to display the Open From panel, and then touch the collection or location.

7 Touch the photo you want to send.

C The photo appears in the hangout.

8 Touch the **Photo ready to send** prompt.

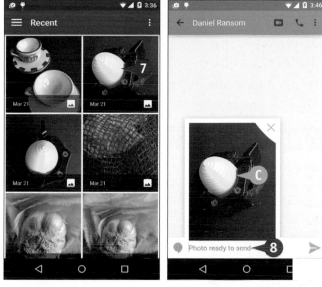

The keyboard appears.

9 Type the message.

10 Touch **Send** (➤).

The Hangouts app sends the message.

D The message appears in the hangout.

E A reply from the contact appears.

F You can continue the conversation.

G You can touch **Anyone else?** to add someone else to the hangout.

TIPS

Can I send Hangouts messages through the cellular network?

Yes. You can send Hangouts messages over the cellular network from an Android phone. The Hangouts app starts each message as an SMS message. If you add a photo or other media, the Hangouts app converts the message to MMS.

How can I tell whether my phone is using the cellular network or Hangouts to send messages?

The Hangouts app displays an icon to the left of the message box to indicate which service it is using. When *SMS* or *MMS* appears, the Hangouts app is using the cellular network directly. When the silhouette of the Hangouts logo appears, the app is using the Hangouts online service.

Manage Your Hangouts and Instant Messages

The Hangouts app enables you to create a separate hangout for each contact or group of contacts with whom you want to be able to communicate. The hangout stores the instant messages you exchange with that contact or group of contacts so you can easily refer to them. When you no longer need a hangout, you can archive or delete it. Archiving removes the hangout from the Hangouts list but keeps the hangout and its contents available for reference. Deleting the hangout removes all content.

Manage Your Hangouts and Instant Messages

Open the Hangouts App and Open a Hangout

1 Touch **Home** (⬤).

The Home screen appears.

2 Touch **Hangouts** (💬).

Note: If Hangouts (💬) does not appear on the Home screen, touch **All Apps** (⬚), and then touch **Hangouts** (💬).

The Hangouts app opens.

3 Touch **Hangouts** (📄).

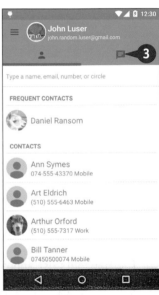

The Hangouts list appears.

4 Touch the hangout you want to open.

The hangout opens, and its contents appear.

Ⓐ You can touch the prompt, such as **Send Hangouts message**, to continue the conversation.

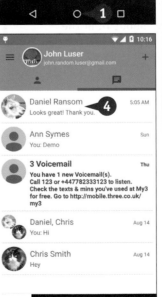

158

Delete a Hangout

1 With the hangout open, touch **Menu** (⋮).

The menu opens.

Ⓑ You can touch **Archive** to archive the hangout. Archiving removes the hangout from the Hangouts list but does not delete it, so you can access it later if necessary. To access an archived hangout, touch **Menu** (☰) and then touch **Archived**.

2 Touch **Delete**.

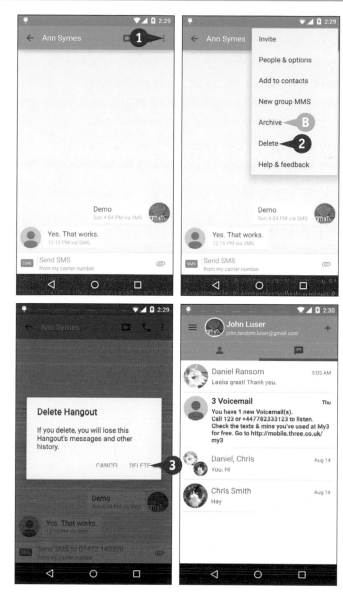

The Delete Hangout dialog box opens, warning you that you will lose the hangout's messages and other history.

3 Touch **Delete** if you are sure you want to delete the hangout.

The Hangouts app deletes the hangout.

The Hangouts list appears.

Note: You can also delete a hangout from the Hangouts screen. Touch and hold the hangout until the Hangouts app switches to selection mode, and then touch **Delete** (🗑). In the Delete Hangout dialog box, touch **Delete**.

TIP

Why does the Delete command not appear on the menu for a hangout?
The Delete command does not appear for a group hangout, one that contains multiple other people. Touch **Leave** on the menu to leave the group hangout. After you leave the hangout, you no longer receive its messages.

continued ▶

SMS hangouts work differently than Hangouts service hangouts. An SMS hangout consists of separate messages that you can manipulate individually, whereas a Hangouts service hangout contains a conversation that you can manipulate only as a single object. You can merge an SMS hangout with a Hangouts service hangout so that you can view the messages from both hangouts together. You can turn history off or on for a Hangouts service hangout. In an SMS hangout, you can delete or forward individual messages as needed, whereas in a Hangouts service hangout, you can only copy text from messages.

Manage Your Hangouts and Instant Messages (continued)

Merge an SMS Hangout with a Hangouts Service Hangout

1 In the Hangouts app, touch **Hangouts** (▤).

The Hangouts list appears.

2 Touch and hold one of the hangouts you want to merge.

The Hangouts app switches to selection mode.

A highlight appears on the hangout.

3 Touch the hangout with which you want to merge the selected hangout.

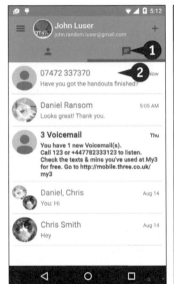

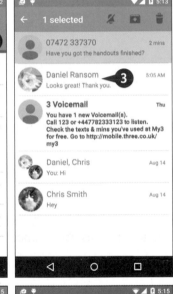

The second highlight becomes selected.

4 Touch **Merge**.

The Hangouts app merges the two hangouts into a single hangout.

Note: To unmerge a merged hangout, open the hangout, touch **Menu** (⋮), and then touch **Un-merge SMS**.

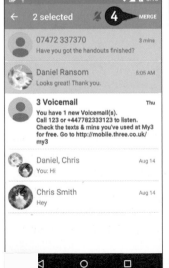

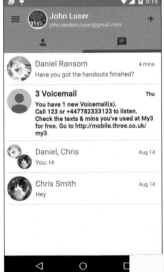

Turn Off History for a Hangout

1 In the Hangouts app, touch **Hangouts** (▤).

The Hangouts list appears.

2 Touch the hangout for which you want to turn off history.

The hangout opens.

3 Touch **Menu** (⋮).

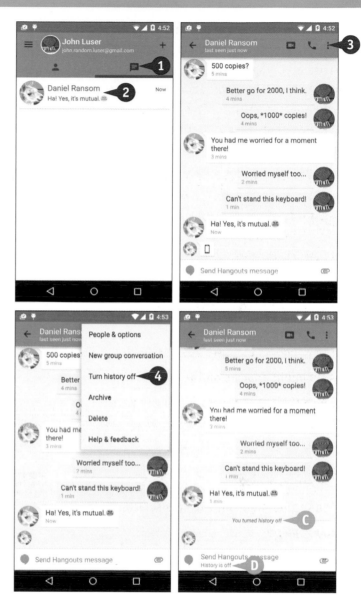

The menu opens.

4 Touch **Turn history off**.

C The message *You turned history off* appears in the hangout.

D The message box shows *History is off*.

Note: Other people in the hangout see a message such as *John turned history off*.

Note: To turn history on again, touch **Menu** (⋮) and then touch **Turn history on**.

 TIP

How do I forward a message to someone else?

In an SMS hangout, touch and hold the message until the Message Options dialog box opens, and then touch **Forward**. In the Select Account dialog box, touch the appropriate account. Then, in the Hangouts dialog box, either touch an existing hangout or touch **New message** and specify the recipient.

In a Hangouts service hangout, you cannot directly forward a message. Touch and hold the message until the Message Options dialog box opens, and then touch **Copy**. Go to the appropriate hangout, or start a new hangout, and then paste the copied text into a message.

Using Video Chat with Hangouts

Hangouts enables you to hold audio and video chats with your contacts. You can start an audio or video chat either directly with the contact or from within a hangout.

To make calls via Hangouts, your phone or tablet must be connected to either a wireless network or the cellular network. Using a wireless network is preferable because you typically get better performance and do not use up your cellular data allowance.

Using Video Chat with Hangouts

1 Touch **Home** (⬤).

The Home screen appears.

2 Touch **Hangouts** (💬).

Note: If Hangouts (💬) does not appear on the Home screen, touch **All Apps** (⦂⦂⦂), and then touch **Hangouts** (💬).

The Hangouts app opens.

3 Touch **Contacts** (👤).

4 Touch the contact with whom you want to chat.

Ⓐ You can touch **Type a name, email, number, or circle** to contact someone who is not on the Contacts list.

A hangout for the contact opens.

Ⓑ You can touch **Anyone Else?** (➕👤) to add someone else to the hangout.

5 Touch **Video Call** (📹).

The Video Call screen appears.

Ⓒ Your video preview appears. You can adjust the camera position as needed.

Ⓓ You can touch **Rear camera** (📷) to switch from the front camera to the rear camera (📷 changes to ⦂⦂). Touch **Front camera** (⦂⦂) when you want to switch back (⦂⦂ changes to 📷).

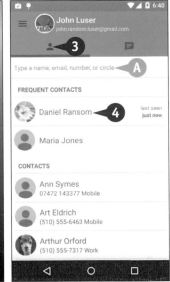

E You can touch **Speaker** (🔊 or 📢) to control whether the audio plays through the main speaker (🔊) or the ear speaker (📢).

F If your contact accepts the call, a message appears saying that the contact joined the call.

Your contact's video feed appears on-screen.

G Your own video appears in an inset window.

6 To control the call, touch the screen.

The on-screen controls appear.

H You can touch **Mute** (🎤) to mute your microphone (🎤 changes to 🎤). Touch **Unmute** (🎤) to unmute the audio (🎤 changes to 🎤).

I You can touch **Video Off** (▢) to turn video off (▢ changes to 📷). Touch **Video On** (📷) when you want to turn video on again (📷 changes to ▢).

7 Touch **Hang Up** (📞).

Hangouts ends the call.

TIP

How do I prevent someone from contacting me in Hangouts?

You can block someone to prevent him from contacting you. In the Hangouts app, touch **Contacts** (👤), and then touch the contact. Touch **Menu** (⋮) and then touch **People & options** to display the People & Options screen. Touch **Block *Contact*** and then touch **Block** in the Block *Contact* dialog box that opens.

To unblock someone you have blocked, touch **Menu** (☰) and then touch **Blocked people**. On the Blocked People screen, touch **Unblock** for the person you want to unblock.

Install and Use Skype

If you want to chat or make either voice or video calls with people who do not use Hangouts, you can install and use Skype. Skype is a service that enables you to chat and make both voice and video calls with other Skype users; you can also make voice calls to telephones. To install Skype on your phone or tablet, you open the Play Store app and download the app. To make calls with Skype, you use a Skype account or a Microsoft account.

Install the Skype App

Touch **Play Store** ( ) on either the Home screen or the Apps screen to open the Play Store app, touch **Apps**, touch **Search** ( ), and then type **skype**. Touch the search result called **Skype – free IM & video calls** from Skype. Touch **Install** to start the installation, then review the many permissions the app requires and touch **Accept** to proceed. After the installation finishes, touch **Open** on the Skype screen in the Play Store app. If you have started using another app, touch **Home** ( ), touch **All Apps** ( ), and then touch **Skype** ( ) on the Apps screen.

Sign In to Skype

You can sign in to Skype with either a Skype account or a Microsoft account. A Skype account is an account set up specifically for Skype. A Microsoft account is an account for a Microsoft service, such as a Hotmail account or an Outlook.com account, that covers Skype as well. On the Sign In screen, touch **Skype Name** to sign in using a Skype account, or touch **Microsoft account** to sign in using your Microsoft account. If you have neither type of account yet, touch **Create account** to start creating a Skype account, and then follow through the screens that appear.

Choose Whether to Add Friends Automatically

After you sign in, the Add Your Friends to Skype screen appears, letting you decide whether to allow Skype to scan your Android address book for people you know on Skype and add them to your people list. If you touch **Add friends**, Skype scans your address book immediately, and then scans it periodically thereafter for new entries. To turn off scanning, touch **Menu** ( ), touch **Settings**, touch **Automatically add friends**, touch **Don't use my address book**, and then touch **OK**. If you do not want to add friends, touch **Cancel** ( ) in the upper-left corner of the Automatically Add Friends screen.

Navigate Skype

With the Skype app open, you can navigate quickly among its three main areas by touching **Recent**, **Favorites**, or **People**. The Recent screen shows recent activity, such as friend requests and details of calls. The Favorites screen shows each contact you designate as a favorite by touching and holding the contact's entry and then touching **Add to favorites** on the pop-up menu. The People screen shows your full list of contacts.

Place and Receive Calls

Skype enables you to place and receive both phone calls and video calls easily. On the Recent screen, the Favorites screen, or the People screen, touch the contact you want to call. On the contact's screen, touch **Phone Call** (▢) or **Video Call** (▢) to place the call.

From the contact's screen, you can also send a text message by touching the *Type a message here* prompt, typing the message, and then touch **Send** (▢).

When someone calls you, touch **Accept** (▢) to accept the call or **Decline** (▢) to decline it.

Change Your Status or Sign Out of Skype

When you sign in, Skype sets your status to Available, enabling other people to see that you are online. If you want to prevent other people from seeing that you are online, touch your profile picture in the upper-right corner and then touch **Invisible** instead of Available.

When you finish using Skype, you can sign out of the app. To do so, touch **Menu** (▢) and then touch **Sign Out**.

Set Up Google+

Google+ is Google's social network. With your Android phone or tablet, you can easily log in to Google+ and stay connected to your social network wherever you go. Before you can use Google+, you must set it up by connecting it to your Google account. Google+ includes a range of social networking features. You can use the Google Circles feature to organize your contacts into different groups for easy communication; share your photos in moments using the Instant Upload feature; and chat with your family, friends, and colleagues using the Hangouts feature.

Set Up Google+

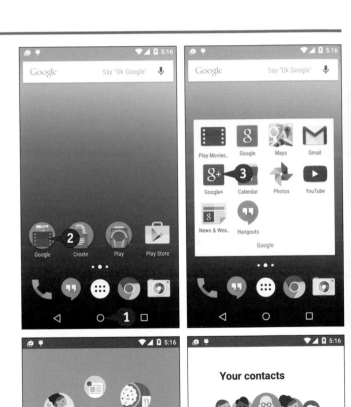

1 Touch **Home** (⬤).

The Home screen appears.

2 Touch **Google** (▦).

The Google folder opens.

3 Touch **Google+** (8+).

Note: If Google (▦) does not appear on the Home screen, touch **All Apps** (⣿) and then touch **Google+** (8+).

The Google+ introductory screen appears.

4 Touch **Next**.

The Your Contacts screen appears.

5 Touch **Keep my address book up to date** (☑ changes to ☐) if you do not want to add your Google+ connections to your Android contacts.

6 Touch **Improve suggestions** (☑ changes to ☐) if you do not want Google to make suggestions based on the people with whom you communicate.

7 Touch **Next**.

166

The Google+ Home screen appears, showing the Suggested Communities list.

Ⓐ You can touch **View all** to view all communities.

❽ Touch a community you want to join.

The first time you touch a community, the Google+ Terms of Service dialog box opens.

Ⓑ You can touch the links to display information on specific items.

❾ Touch **Accept** to continue.

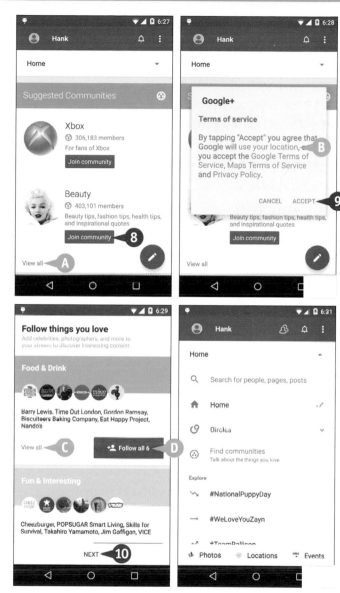

The Follow Things You Love screen appears.

Ⓒ You can touch **View all** to view all items in a category.

Ⓓ You can touch **Follow all** to follow all the suggested items. Following an item adds it to your Following circle.

❿ Touch **Next**.

The Home screen appears with the menu panel open, and you can navigate Google+ as explained in the next section.

What are circles in Google+?

Circles are separate groups within your social network. Google+ provides circles called Friends, Family, Acquaintances, and Following to get you started, so you can associate your contacts with different groups. You can also access the What's Hot circle and the Nearby circle, create your own custom circles, and share data only with particular circles. For example, you may want to share some items with your friends but not with your acquaintances.

What are communities in Google+?

A community is a group of people who share an interest. A community is similar to a discussion forum on other online services. A community can be either private or public.

Navigate Google+

After setting up Google+ on your phone or tablet, you can enjoy social networking on it. From the Home screen that Google+ displays when you launch the app, you can easily navigate to a circle or a community. You can view the posts for one or more circles, comment on posts, or post your own photos. You can write posts, share moods, and even shoot new videos and post them immediately.

Navigate Google+

1 Touch **Home** (◉).

The Home screen appears.

2 Touch **Google** (▣).

The Google folder opens.

3 Touch **Google+** (8+).

Note: If Google (▣) does not appear on the Home screen, touch **All Apps** (⬚) and then touch **Google+** (8+).

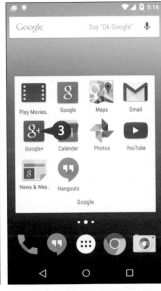

The Google+ app opens, showing your Home screen.

4 Touch **Home**.

The menu panel appears.

5 Touch **Circles**.

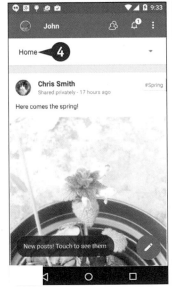

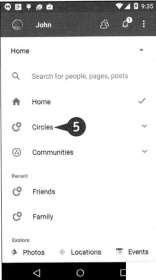

The Circles list expands.

6 Touch the circle you want to view. This example uses **Friends**.

The screen for the circle appears, showing recent posts.

A You can touch the post to open it.

B You can touch **+1** to mark your approval or agreement.

C You can touch **Comment** (🖃) to comment on the post.

7 Touch **Compose** (✏️).

The Compose screen appears.

D You can touch the icon and text, such as **Public** (🌐), to choose the circles or communities for the post.

8 Touch **Write something** and type the content for the post.

E You can touch **Add your location** (📍) to add your location.

9 Touch a displayed photo to add it, or touch **All photos** (🔁) to choose from all your photos. Touch **Camera** (📷) to take a photo or a video.

10 Touch **Post** (➤).

Google+ sends the post to the circles or communities you chose.

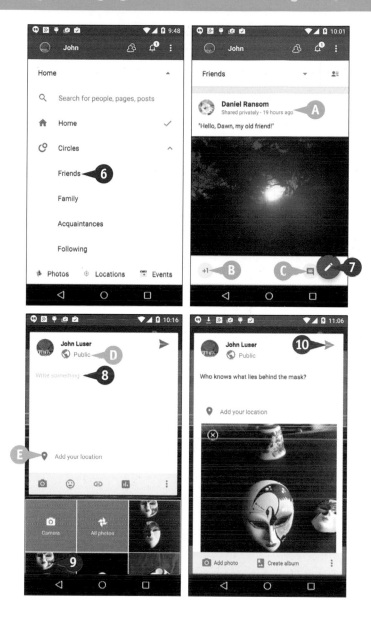

TIPS

How do I control which notifications I receive?

Touch **Menu** (⋮) and then touch **Settings**. On the Settings screen, touch your Google+ account name, then touch **Notifications** to display the Notification shade. You can then turn notifications on and off, choose your ringtone, turn vibration on or off, and choose whether to get notifications for mentions, shares, comments, and other Google+ events that involve you.

How do I get rid of a post?

If you do not want to see a post, you can mute it. Touch the post to open it, touch **Menu** (⋮), and then touch **Mute**. In the Mute dialog box that opens, touch **OK**.

Navigate Facebook

Your Android device enables you to access Facebook from anywhere it has an Internet connection. You can access Facebook through a browser, but for a presentation tailored to your device, you may prefer to use the Facebook app. You will need to install this app if it is not already installed.

Your Facebook home page shows what is new in your social network. You can quickly access other pages and take other actions, such as reviewing friend requests and reading your notifications. You can also easily post updates and submit friend requests.

Navigate Facebook

1 Touch **Home** (◉).

The Home screen appears.

2 Touch **All Apps** (⊞).

The Apps screen appears.

3 Touch **Facebook** (🅵).

Note: If Facebook (🅵) does not appear on the Apps screen, you need to install it. Touch **Play Store** (▶), touch **Apps**, touch **Search** (🔍), and then type **Facebook**. Touch the result called Facebook (🅵), touch **Install**, review the permissions, and then touch **Accept**.

The Facebook app opens.

Your home page appears.

Ⓐ You can touch **Like** (👍) to like an item.

Ⓑ You can touch **Comment** (💬) to comment on an item.

4 Touch a person's name to display the person's profile.

Ⓒ You can touch **Add Friend** (👤₊) to add the person as a friend.

Ⓓ You can touch **Follow** (🗇₊) to follow the person.

Ⓔ You can touch **Message** (💬) to send a message to the person.

5 Touch **Back** (◁).

6 Touch **Friend Requests** (👥).

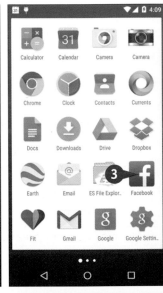

170

Your friend requests appear.

Ⓕ You can touch **Confirm** to confirm a friend.

Ⓖ You can touch **Delete** to delete the friend request.

⑦ Touch **Messages** (💬).

Your messages appear.

Note: If the Messages screen shows the message *Messenger Is a Better Way to Text*, touch **Get Messenger** to go to the Messenger app on Google Play, then touch **Install** to install it.

Ⓗ You can touch **Message** (📝) to write a new message.

⑧ Touch **Notifications** (🌐).

Your notifications appear.

Ⓘ You can touch a notification to open it. You can then take actions such as responding to a poke.

⑨ Touch **Menu** (≡) in the upper-right corner of the screen.

The menu panel appears.

⑩ Touch the area of Facebook you want to display.

TIP

How can I make the Facebook app work my way?

In the Facebook app, touch **Menu** (≡) to display the menu, then touch **App Settings** to display the Settings screen. Here you can choose General settings including whether to turn Facebook chat and sounds on or off, whether to sync your photos, or whether to clear your device's browsing data. You can also choose a wide range of Notification settings, including whether your device vibrates or flashes its phone LED when you receive a notification.

Send Tweets

If you like tweeting on the Twitter microblogging service, reading other people's tweets, or both, you will likely want to use the Twitter app on your Android device. You will need to install this app if it is not already installed.

A tweet can contain text, photos, or both. You can add hashtags, such as #animals or #cute, to help readers locate your tweets. You can also add a location to your tweets when you want to share them with others.

Send Tweets

1 Touch **Home** (⬤).

The Home screen appears.

2 Touch **All Apps** (⬛).

The Apps screen appears.

3 Touch **Twitter** (🐦).

Note: If Twitter (🐦) does not appear on the Apps screen, you need to install it. Touch **Play Store** (▶), touch **Apps**, touch **Search** (🔍), and then type **twitter**. Touch the result called **Twitter** (🐦), touch **Install**, review the permissions, and then touch **Accept**.

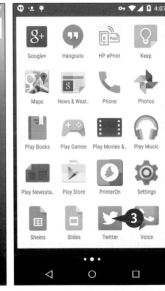

Your Twitter home screen appears, showing the latest posts from the people you are following.

Note: To start a tweet by taking a photo, touch **Add Photo** (📷). To start a tweet with an existing picture, touch **Add Picture** (🖼).

4 Touch **What's happening?**.

The screen for creating a tweet appears.

5 Type the text of your tweet.

6 To add a photo, touch **Add Picture** (🖼).

The Select Media screen appears, showing recent photos.

Ⓐ You can touch **Take Photo** (📷) to take a photo.

Ⓑ You can touch **Photos** (🖼️) to display all your photos.

Note: To add the photo to the tweet without editing it, touch the photo instead of Full Screen (⤢).

⑦ Touch the photo you want to use.

The screen for editing the photo appears.

⑧ Edit the photo as explained in the first tip.

⑨ Touch **Done**.

The Select Media screen appears with the photo selected.

⑩ Touch **Done**.

The photo appears in your tweet.

Ⓒ You can add your location by touching **Location** (📍) and then touching **Enable** in the Tweet Location dialog box.

⑪ Touch **Tweet**.

Twitter posts the tweet.

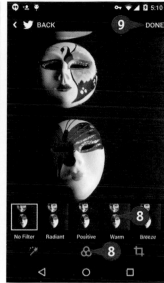

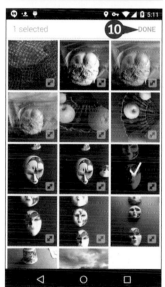

TIPS

What do the three buttons at the bottom of the picture-editing screen do?

Touch **Enhance** (🪄) to enhance the photo's colors. Touch **Filters** (🎨) to view the available filters you can apply to the photo. Touch **Crop** (🔲) to display the cropping tools, and then crop the photo as you want.

Is there another way to start a tweet?

Yes. You can also start a tweet from a photo. In the Photos app, touch the photo you want to use, touch **Share** (📤), and then touch **Twitter** (🐦) to start a tweet.

CHAPTER 8

Working with Apps

Apps are software that provide specific functionality to your phone or tablet. Android comes with some apps built in, and you can install further apps to make your device perform the tasks you need. You can download apps from Google's Play Store or other sources, run them as needed, and switch quickly among them. To keep apps running well, you can update them manually or automatically.

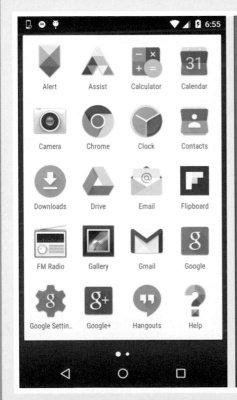

Run Apps and Switch Quickly Among Them

When you need to use an app on your Android device, you run it. You can run any app from the Apps screen, but you can also put apps on the Home screen or on the Favorites bar so that you can run them directly from the Home screen. You can run multiple apps at once. Each app appears full screen, so you work in a single app at a time, but you can switch from one app to another as needed. You can switch apps quickly by using the Overview screen.

Run Apps and Switch Quickly Among Them

Launch Multiple Apps

1 Touch **Home** (⬤).

The Home screen appears.

2 Touch **All Apps** (⊞).

The Apps screen appears.

Note: If necessary, swipe left to display more apps.

3 Touch the first app you want to launch.

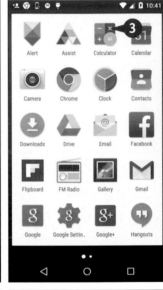

The app opens.

4 Touch **Home** (⬤).

The Home screen appears.

5 Touch **All Apps** (⊞).

The Apps screen appears.

Note: If necessary, swipe left to display more apps.

6 Touch the second app you want to launch.

The app opens.

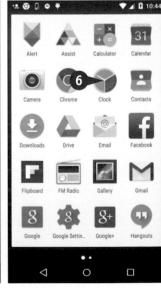

Switch Quickly Among Running Apps

1 From a running app, touch **Overview** (■).

Note: You can also display the Overview screen by touching **Overview** (■) from the Home screen.

The Overview screen appears.

The thumbnails at the bottom of the list are the ones you have used most recently.

2 If necessary, scroll up to reach other apps.

3 Touch the screen you want to display.

The app's screen appears, and you can start using the app.

TIPS

Can I do anything else from the Overview screen?

Yes. You can remove a thumbnail from the Overview screen by either touching **Close** (✖) or simply swiping the thumbnail to the right or to the left, removing it from the list.

Can I close an app from the Overview screen?

No. You can close all the thumbnails for an app by going through the list on the Overview screen, but the app itself remains open. You do not normally need to close apps on Android. However, see Chapter 12 for instructions on how to close an app that has stopped responding.

Explore Google Play and Download Apps

Your Android phone or tablet includes apps such as Chrome, with which you can surf the web, and Calendar, which enables you to keep track of your schedule. You can add other apps for other tasks. Some apps are free; others you must pay for. To get apps, you run the Play Store app and access the Google Play service. Google Play contains hundreds of thousands of apps that Google has approved for use on Android devices. Google Play also offers games, movies, TV shows, music, books, and newspapers and magazines.

Explore Google Play and Download Apps

1 Touch **Home** (⬤).

The Home screen appears.

2 Touch **Play Store** (▷).

Note: If Play Store (▷) does not appear on the Home screen, touch **All Apps** (⬚), and then touch **Play Store** (▷).

The Play Store app opens and displays the Play Store screen.

3 Touch **Apps**.

4 To browse Google Play by categories, touch **Categories** or swipe right.

The Categories screen appears.

5 Touch the category you want to browse. For example, touch **Business**.

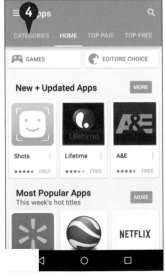

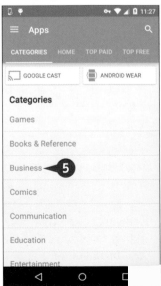

178

The category's screen appears.

6 Swipe left one or more times to display the screen you want to view, such as the Top Free screen.

7 Touch an app you want to learn about.

The app's screen appears.

A You can touch **Read More** to read details and reviews.

8 Touch **Install** if you want to install the app.

The permissions dialog box for the app opens.

9 Read the permissions.

B Touch **Expand List** (⌄) to expand a permission section to see its detail.

C Touch **Collapse List** (⌃) to collapse a section.

10 If you are comfortable giving the app these permissions, touch **Accept**.

Note: For a paid app, choose the means of payment.

Android downloads and installs the app.

11 Touch **Open**.

The app opens.

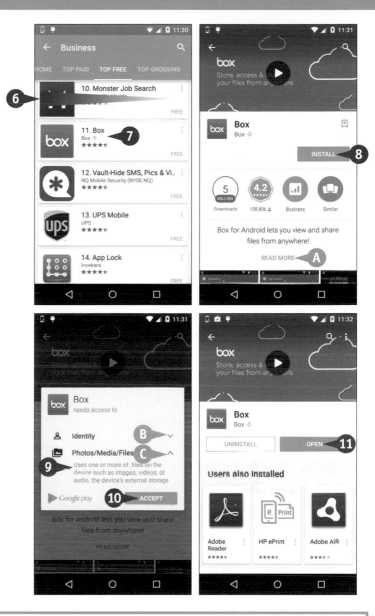

TIPS

How can I see which apps I have previously bought on Google Play?
From the Google Play screen or anywhere in the Apps screens, touch **Menu** (▦), and then touch **My apps**. The My Apps screen appears, showing your Installed list first.

What permissions should I accept for an app?
You must decide depending on what the app does. For example, an app that creates files needs the "Modify or delete the contents of your USB storage" permission; an app that can open e-mail attachments needs the "Read email attachments" permission. Be suspicious of any app that requires access to sensitive data such as your contacts without a compelling reason.

Update Your Apps

Android developers often update their apps to remove bugs and to add new features. To keep your apps running well, you should install app updates when they become available. Most updates for paid apps are free, but you must usually pay to upgrade to a new version of the app. You can update all your apps at once or update a single app at a time. Normally, updating all your apps is most convenient, but you may sometimes need to update a single app without downloading all available updates.

Update Your Apps

1 Touch **Home** (◉).

The Home screen appears.

Note: If Play Store (▶) appears on the Home screen, touch **Play Store** (▶) and skip steps **2** and **3**.

2 Touch **All Apps** (⊞).

The Apps screen appears.

3 Touch **Play Store** (▶).

Note: If Play Store (▶) does not appear on the first Apps screen, swipe left to display the next Apps screen.

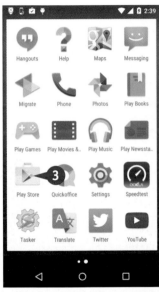

The Play Store app opens and displays the Home screen.

4 Touch **Menu** (☰).

The menu panel opens.

5 Touch **My apps**.

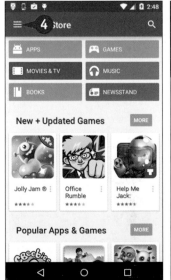

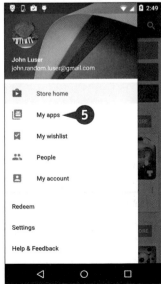

The My Apps screen appears.

Note: If the My Apps screen does not show the Installed list at first, swipe right or touch **Installed** to display the Installed list.

6 Touch **Update All**.

The permissions dialog box for each app opens in turn.

7 Read the permissions, touching **Expand List** (⌄) or **Collapse List** (⌃) as needed.

8 Touch **Accept** to proceed, or touch **Skip** to skip this update.

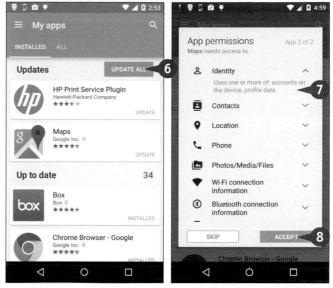

A Android downloads the updates and installs them.

B Each updated app appears in the Recently Updated list.

Note: If the Manual Updates list appears, touch an app's button, and then touch **Update** on the app's screen.

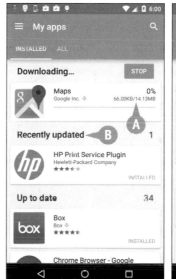

TIPS

How do I update a single app?
Display the Installed list by following steps **1** to **7** in the main text. Touch the app's button to display the screen for the app, and then touch **Update**.

Why must I review the permissions when updating an app?
You need to review the permissions because they may have changed. Developers often add features that need extra permissions — or they may simply change the permissions without adding features. So be on your guard for inappropriate permission requests when updating apps.

Remove Apps You No Longer Need

Each app you install takes up some of your device's storage space and appears on the Apps screen. When you no longer need an app you have installed, you can remove it from your device. The app remains available to you on Google Play, so you can easily reinstall it if necessary. You can remove an app either by using the Apps screen or by using the App info screen for the app, whichever you find easier. You cannot remove the apps that come built in to Android, only the apps you have installed.

Remove Apps You No Longer Need

Remove an App by Using the Apps Screen

1 Touch **Home** (⬤).

The Home screen appears.

2 Touch **All Apps** (⬛).

The Apps screen appears.

3 Touch and hold the icon for the app you want to remove.

The Home screen appears.

Ⓐ The app icon you are holding appears in the main part of the screen.

Ⓑ The Uninstall button and the App info icon appear at the top of the screen.

4 Still holding, drag the app to the Uninstall button.

Ⓒ The app icon and the Uninstall button turn red.

5 Release the app icon.

A confirmation dialog box opens.

6 Touch **OK**.

Android removes the app.

Remove an App by Using Its App Info Screen

1 Touch **Home** (⬤).

The Home screen appears.

2 Touch **Play Store** (▶).

Note: If Play Store (▶) does not appear on the Home screen, touch the **All Apps** button (⚬⚬⚬), and then touch **Play Store** (▶).

The Play Store app opens and displays the Home screen.

3 Touch **Menu** (▤).

The menu panel opens.

4 Touch **My apps**.

The My Apps screen appears.

5 Touch the app you want to remove.

The app's screen appears.

6 Touch **Uninstall**.

A confirmation dialog box opens.

7 Touch **OK**.

Android removes the app.

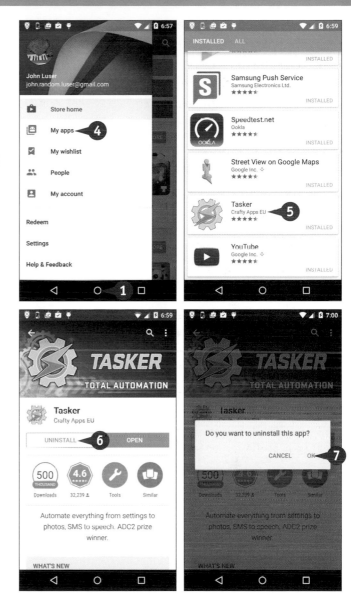

TIP

How do I reinstall an app I have removed?

You can easily reinstall an app by using the My Apps list on the Play Store. Touch **Home** (⬤) to display the Home screen, then touch **All Apps** (⚬⚬⚬) to display the Apps screen. Touch **Play Store**, touch **Menu** (▤), and then touch **My Apps**. Touch **All** or swipe left to display the All list, and then touch the app you want to reinstall. On the app's screen, touch **Install**.

Choose Which Apps to Update Automatically

Keeping your Android apps up to date enables you to take advantage of bug fixes and new features that developers add to the apps. You can set your phone or tablet to update its apps automatically. You can choose to update all apps or just some apps automatically. Automatic updates may involve transferring large amounts of data. To prevent automatic updates from consuming your cellular data plan, you can set your phone or cellular-capable tablet to download updates only when it is connected to a Wi-Fi network.

Choose Which Apps to Update Automatically

Open the My Apps Screen in the Play Store App

1 Touch **Home** (⬤).

The Home screen appears.

2 Touch **Play Store** (▶).

Note: If Play Store (▶) does not appear on the Home screen, touch **All Apps** (⬤), and then touch **Play Store** (▶).

The Play Store app opens and displays the Google Play screen.

3 Touch **Menu** (☰).

The menu opens.

4 Touch **Settings**.

The Settings screen appears.

5 Touch **Notifications** (☐ changes to ☑) if you want to receive notifications about updates.

6 Touch **Auto-update apps**.

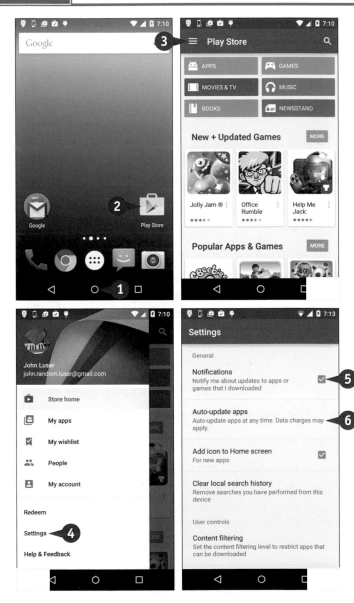

The Auto-Update Apps dialog box opens.

7 Touch **Auto-update apps over Wi-Fi only** (○ changes to ◉) to update apps only over Wi-Fi connections.

8 Touch **Add icon to Home screen** (□ changes to ✓) only if you want an icon on the Home screen for each new app.

Ⓐ You can touch **Clear local search history** to remove details of your searches with this device.

9 Touch **Content filtering**.

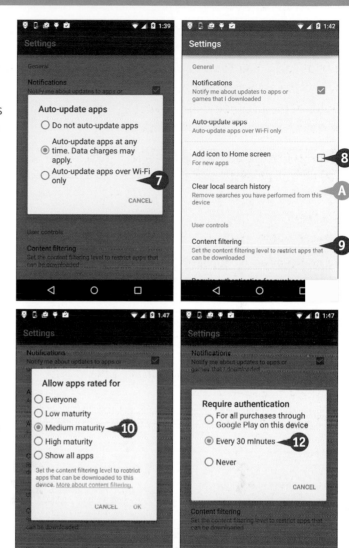

The Allow Apps Rated For dialog box opens.

10 Touch the appropriate option, such as **Medium Maturity** (○ changes to ◉).

11 Touch **Require authentication for purchases**.

The Require Authentication dialog box opens.

12 Touch the appropriate option, such as **For all purchases through Google Play on this device** or **Every 30 minutes** (○ changes to ◉).

13 Touch **Back** (◁).

The Play Store screen appears.

TIP

How do I control updating for a single app?

In the Play Store app, touch **Menu** (☰), and then touch **My apps** to display the My Apps screen. Touch the app you want to affect. On the App Info screen for the app, touch **Menu** (⋮) to open the menu, and then touch **Auto-update** to select it (□ changes to ✓) or deselect it (✓ changes to □).

Move Apps to the SD Card

When you install an app, Android places it in your device's internal storage. Internal storage is normally the best place for apps, and if your device does not have an SD card slot, internal storage is the only option. But if your device does have an SD card slot, you can move existing apps to the SD card. This maneuver is useful when your device's internal storage fills up, but it is available for only some apps. Understandably, apps on the SD card are available only when that SD card is present.

Move Apps to the SD Card

1 Touch **Home** (○).

The Home screen appears.

2 Touch **All Apps** (⠿).

The Apps screen appears.

3 Touch **Settings** (⚙).

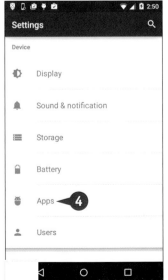

The Settings screen appears.

4 Touch **Apps**.

The Apps screen appears. Normally, the Downloaded tab appears at first.

5 Touch **On SD Card** or swipe left.

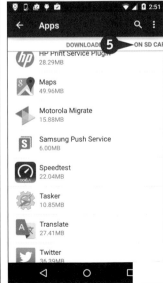

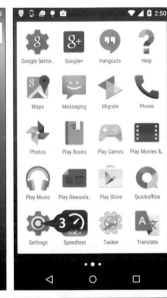

The On SD Card tab appears. This tab shows the apps you can move to the SD card.

Ⓐ A check mark indicates the app is already on the SD card.

⑥ Touch the app you want to move.

The App Info screen for the app appears.

⑦ Touch **Move to SD Card**.

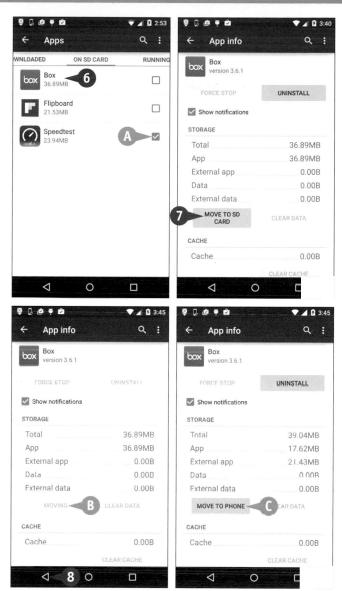

Ⓑ The *Moving* readout appears on the Move To button while Android moves the app. The move may take a minute or more.

Ⓒ The Move to Phone button appears. You can touch this button to move an app from the SD card to internal storage.

Note: On a tablet, the Move to Tablet button appears.

⑧ Touch **Back** (◁).

TIP

Which apps should I move to the SD card?

This depends on how much storage your device has and how frequently – if ever – you switch SD cards. If you use many apps, or apps that store large amounts of data, consider grouping apps that you use together into sets and keeping those sets on different SD cards that you can swap in and out.

If your device has plenty of internal storage, keep all the apps on the internal storage so that they are always available.

Manually Install an App

The normal way to install an app on your Android phone or tablet is by downloading it from the Google Play service using the Play Store app. But you can also load an app onto your device manually by using a technique called *sideloading*. In sideloading, you acquire a package file containing the app you want to install. You then transfer the package file to your phone or tablet, enable installation of apps from unknown sources, and then install the app.

Understanding What Manual Installation Is Useful For

Sideloading is primarily useful for installing apps that are not available on Google Play. For example, you may need to sideload an app that your company or organization provides. Sideloading can also be useful for installing an app that is available for other Android devices but not for your phone or tablet. Be aware that apps you download from sources other than Google Play may contain malevolent code. It is wise to search the web for reviews of an app before installing it.

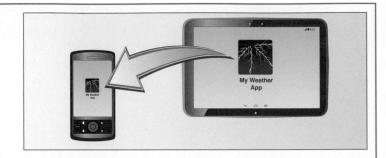

Install an App You Can Use to Sideload

By sideloading an app, you can add functionality to your Android device. The sideloading process requires a file-management app on your Android device. You use this app to install the app you are sideloading. To get your device ready to sideload an app, open the Play Store app and install a file-management app from Google Play. Two good choices are ES File Explorer, shown here, and Astro File Manager. Both these apps are free and easy to use.

Get the App Package File You Need

You can find many apps for sideloading on your Android device to add functionality. Each app comes in a distribution file called a package file from which you install the app. You can acquire a package file in several ways. If you already have the app on another phone or tablet, use a file-management app such as ES File Explorer or Astro File Manager to copy the file to a backup, creating a package file. For an app provided by your company or organization, download the package file from the company or organization's site. For other apps, download the package file from an online repository, but be wary of malevolent software.

Transfer the Package File to Your Phone or Tablet

After acquiring the package file for the app you want to sideload, you need to transfer the file to your phone or tablet. You can transfer the file in several ways. If the package file is on your computer, use a tool such as File Explorer or Windows Explorer on Windows or Android File Transfer on the Mac to copy or move the file. Otherwise, use an online storage service such as Dropbox. If the package file is small, you can also use e-mail.

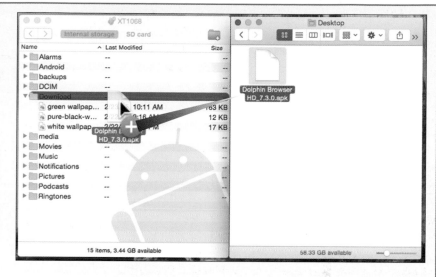

Enable Installation of Apps from Unknown Sources

By default, Android does not permit you to install apps from sources other than Google Play. So before you can sideload an app on your phone or tablet, you must set Android to allow the installation of apps from unknown sources. Touch **Home** (⬤) to display the Home screen, touch **All Apps** (⊞) to display the Apps screen, and then touch **Settings** (⚙). On the Settings screen, touch **Security**, then set the **Unknown sources** switch to On (◯ changes to ⬤). In the warning dialog box that opens, touch **OK**.

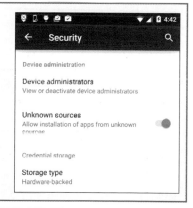

Manually Install the App

After copying the package file to your Android device and setting Android to allow the installation of apps from unknown sources, you can manually install the app. Open the file-management app on your phone or tablet, and then touch the package file. When the screen listing the permissions appears, read the permissions carefully before you decide to complete the installation. After you install the app, you can run it from the Apps screen like any other app.

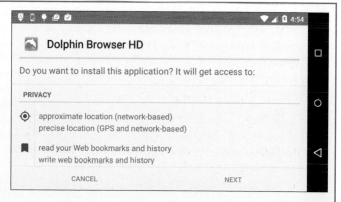

CHAPTER 9

Browsing the Web and E-Mailing

Your Android phone or tablet is fully equipped to browse the web and to send e-mail via either a Wi-Fi connection or a cellular network.

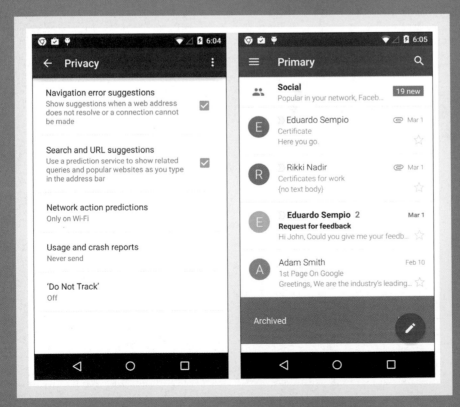

Browse the Web

Your phone or tablet comes equipped with the Chrome app, which you use for browsing the web. You can go quickly to a web page by entering its address in the Chrome omnibox or by following a link from another page. Although you can browse quickly by opening a single web page at a time, you may prefer to open multiple pages in separate tabs and switch back and forth among them.

Browse the Web

Open Chrome and Navigate to Web Pages

1 Touch **Home** (⬤).

The Home screen appears.

2 Touch **Chrome** (◉).

Note: If Chrome (◉) does not appear in the Favorites tray, touch **All Apps** (⸬) and then touch **Chrome** (◉).

Chrome opens.

3 Touch the omnibox. This is a combined address box and search box.

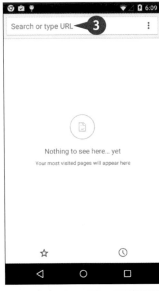

The omnibox expands, and the keyboard appears.

4 Type the address of the page you want to open.

A You can touch **Delete** (✖) to delete the contents of the omnibox.

5 Touch **Go** (➔).

B Alternatively, touch a search result.

Chrome displays the page.

6 Touch a link on the page.

Chrome displays that page.

Note: After going to a new page, you can touch **Back** (◀) to go back to the previous page. You can then touch **Menu** (⋮) and then touch **Forward** (➔) to go forward again to the page.

Open Multiple Web Pages and Switch Among Them

1 Touch **Menu** (⋮).

The menu opens.

2 Touch **New tab**.

Note: Many websites detect that your phone or tablet is a mobile device and so deliver a version of the web page designed or optimized for mobile devices.

Chrome displays the Most Visited screen, which shows pages you have visited most frequently.

3 Touch the omnibox, and then go to the page you want. For example, type the address and touch **Go**.

Note: You can also go to a page by using a bookmark.

The page appears.

4 To switch to another page, touch **Overview** (■).

The list of open screens appears, including the open Chrome tabs.

⊙ You can touch ✕ to close a tab.

Note: You can also close a tab by swiping it left or right.

5 Touch the page you want to display.

Chrome displays the page.

TIPS

What is the Microphone icon in the Chrome omnibox for?

The Microphone icon (🎤) is for searching by voice. Touch the omnibox to select it; if the omnibox contains an address, touch **Delete** (✕) to delete it. Then touch **Microphone** (🎤) and say your search terms when the *Speak now* prompt appears.

How do I get the full version of a web page rather than the mobile version?

To get the regular version of the web page, touch **Menu** (⋮) and then touch **Request desktop site** (☐ changes to ✓). Some sites are programmed to prevent mobile devices from requesting the desktop versions.

Using Bookmarks, Most Visited, and Other Devices

Typing web addresses can be laborious, so Chrome provides features for reducing the number of addresses you need to enter. Chrome for Android can automatically sync your bookmarks, most-visited sites, and recent tabs from Chrome on your computer or other devices via your Google account, giving your phone or tablet quick access to the same web pages and sites. You can also create bookmarks on your phone or tablet and have Chrome sync them back to your computer.

Using Bookmarks, Most Visited, and Other Devices

Open the Bookmarks Screen

1 Touch **Home** (⬤).

The Home screen appears.

2 Touch **Chrome** (◉).

Chrome opens.

3 Touch **Menu** (⋮).

The menu opens.

4 Touch **Bookmarks**.

The Bookmarks screen appears, showing the Mobile Bookmarks folder by default.

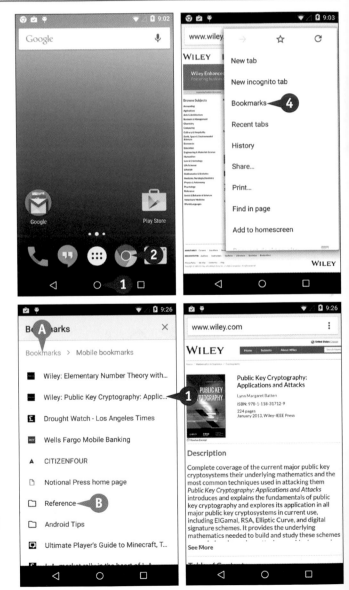

Open a Bookmarked Web Page

A You can navigate to another bookmarks folder by touching **Bookmarks** and then touching the folder.

B You can touch a folder icon to open that folder.

1 Touch the bookmark for the page you want to display.

The web page opens.

Note: You can zoom in and out quickly on a web page by double-tapping it. For a more controlled zoom, place two fingers together on the screen and pinch apart to zoom in, or place two fingers apart and pinch inward to zoom out.

Open a Web Page from the Most Visited List

1 Touch **Menu** (⋮).

The menu opens.

2 Touch **New tab**.

The New Tab screen appears, showing the Most Visited list.

3 Touch the web page you want to open.

The web page opens.

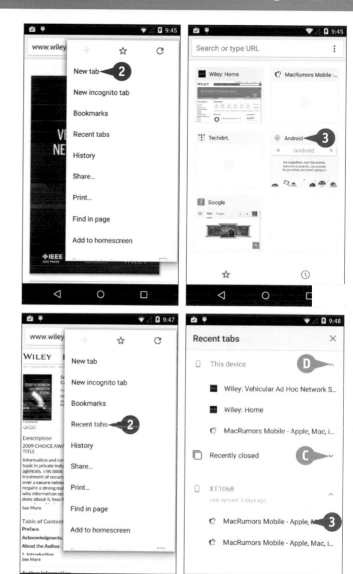

Open a Web Page from the Recent Tabs List

1 Touch **Menu** (⋮).

The menu opens.

2 Touch **Recent tabs**.

The Recent Tabs screen appears.

⊙ You can touch **Expand List** (∨) to expand it (∨ changes to ∧).

⊙ You can touch **Collapse List** (∧) to collapse an expanded list to its heading (∧ changes to ∨).

3 Touch the web page you want to open.

The web page opens.

TIP

How do I make Chrome on my computer sync my data?

Chrome on Windows or OS X automatically syncs your data with your Google account as long as you are signed in to Chrome. To check whether you are signed in, look for a button bearing your first name at the right end of the title bar. If this button does not appear, click **Menu** (≡), click **Settings**, and then click **Sign In**.

Create Bookmarks for Web Pages

W hile browsing the web on your phone or tablet, you will likely find web pages you want to access again later. To easily access such a web page, create a bookmark for it. Chrome automatically makes your bookmarks available to other computers and devices that sign in using the same Google account, so you can easily access your bookmarked pages on your computer and other devices as well.

Create Bookmarks for Web Pages

Create a Bookmark on Your Phone or Tablet

1 Touch **Home** (⬤).

The Home screen appears.

2 Touch **Chrome** (◉).

Chrome opens.

3 Navigate to the web page.

4 Touch **Menu** (⋮).

Note: On a tablet, touch **Bookmark** (☆) at the right end of the Chrome omnibox to open the Add Bookmark screen.

5 Touch **Bookmark** (☆).

The Add Bookmark screen appears.

6 Edit the name as needed.

7 If necessary, edit the address.

A If the Folder box shows the folder in which you want to store the bookmark, touch **Save** and skip the rest of this section.

8 Touch the folder in the Folder box.

The Choose a Folder screen appears.

B To use an existing folder, touch it.

9 To create a new folder, touch **New folder**.

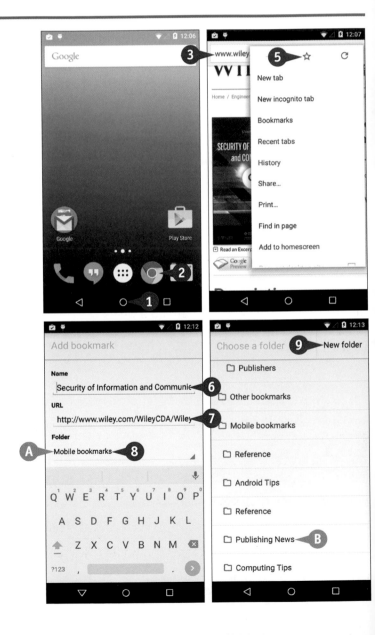

196

The Add Folder screen appears.

10 Touch **Name**.

The on-screen keyboard appears.

11 Type the name for the folder.

12 Touch the **Folder** pop-up menu, which shows the name of the current folder.

The Choose a Folder screen appears.

13 Touch the folder in which you want to create the new folder.

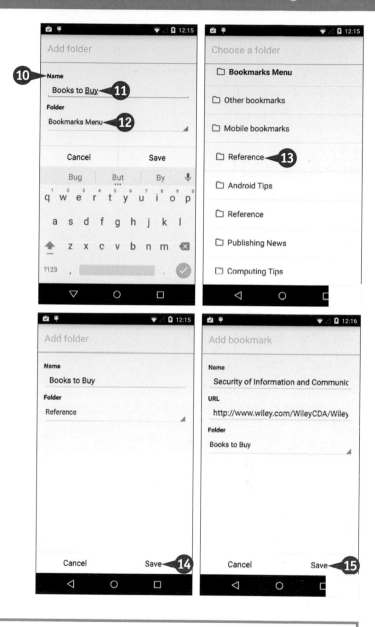

The Add Folder screen appears.

14 Touch **Save**.

The Add Bookmark screen appears.

15 Touch **Save**.

Chrome creates the bookmark.

The web page appears again.

Note: After you create a bookmark for a web page, the Bookmark star on the menu changes from ☆ to ★.

How do I delete a bookmark?

1 Touch **Menu** (⋮) to open the menu.

2 Touch **Bookmarks** to display the Bookmarks screen.

3 Touch and hold the bookmark you want to delete until a pop-up menu opens.

4 Touch **Delete bookmark**.

Configure Your Default Search Engine

To find information with Chrome, you often need to search using a search engine. Chrome's default search engine is Google, but you can change to another search engine. Your choices include major search engines such as Google, Yahoo!, Bing, and Ask. Google, Yahoo!, and Bing compete directly with one another and return similar results to many searches. Experiment with the available search engines to discover which one suits you best.

Configure Your Default Search Engine

1 Touch **Home** (◉).

The Home screen appears.

2 Touch **Chrome** (◉).

Chrome opens.

3 Touch **Menu** (⋮).

The menu opens.

4 Touch **Settings**.

The Settings screen appears.

5 Touch **Search engine**.

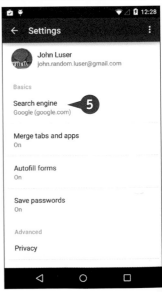

The Search Engine screen appears.

6 Touch the search engine you want to use.

A *Currently selected search engine* appears under the search engine you touch.

7 Touch **Back** (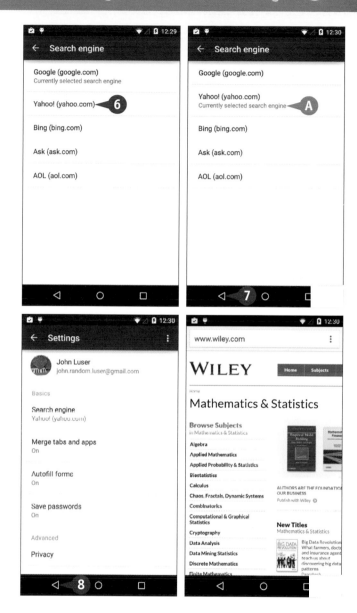).

The Settings screen appears.

8 Touch **Back** (◁).

The web page you were previously viewing appears, and you can continue browsing.

TIP

How can I search using a search engine other than those that appear on the Search Engine screen?
You can search using any search engine you can find on the web. Open a web page to the search engine, and then perform the search using the tools on the page. At this writing, you cannot set any search engine other than those listed on the Search Engine screen as the default search engine on an Android device. But you can easily add the site to your Bookmarks list, and if you use it frequently, it will appear on your Most Visited list.

Fill In Forms Using Autofill

If you fill in forms using your phone or tablet, you can save time by enabling the Autofill feature. Autofill can automatically fill in standard form fields, such as name and address fields, using the information from one or more profiles you enter. Autofill can also automatically store other data you enter in fields, and can store credit-card details to enter them for you automatically. For security, you may prefer not to store your credit-card information in Autofill — but if you do, it can save you time and effort.

Fill In Forms Using Autofill

1 Touch **Home** (◉).

The Home screen appears.

2 Touch **Chrome** (◉).

Chrome opens.

3 Touch **Menu** (⋮).

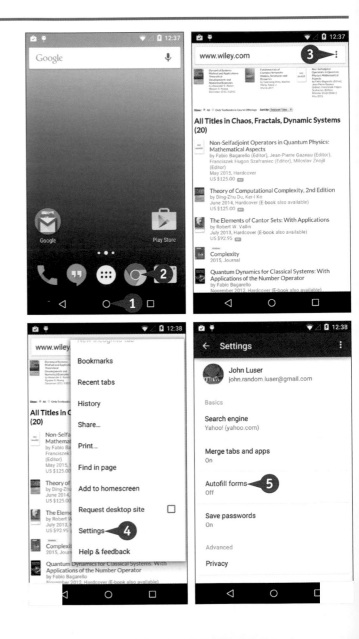

The menu opens.

4 Touch **Settings**.

The Settings screen appears.

5 Touch **Autofill forms**.

The Autofill Forms screen appears.

6 Set the **Autofill** switch to On (⬜ changes to ⬛).

7 Touch **Add profile**.

The Add Profile screen appears.

8 Touch **Country/Region** and then touch your country or region.

9 Type your name and address details.

10 Touch **Next** (➡) to move to the next field.

11 Type your data in the remaining fields.

12 Touch **Save**.

The Autofill Forms screen appears.

Note: You can touch **Add profile** and add another profile. For example, you may need separate Autofill profiles for business use and personal use.

13 Touch **Add credit card**.

The Add Credit Card screen appears.

14 Enter your details.

15 Touch **Save**.

The Autofill Forms screen reappears.

16 Touch **Back** (◀).

The Settings screen appears.

17 Touch **Back** (◀).

The web page you were viewing before appears.

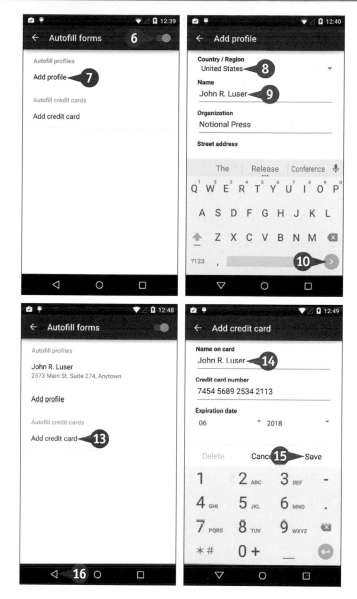

TIP

How else can Chrome save me time filling in my details on the web?

Chrome can also store your passwords and enter them for you. This feature can save you plenty of complex typing, especially if you use strong passwords that include letters, numbers, and symbols, as security experts recommend.

To store passwords, touch **Menu** (⋮), and then touch **Settings**. On the Settings screen, touch **Save passwords** to display the Save Passwords screen, and then set the **Save passwords** switch to On (⬜ changes to ⬛).

Tighten Up Your Browsing Privacy Settings

Along with its many sites that provide useful information or services, the web contains sites that try to infect computers with malevolent software, or *malware*, or lure visitors into providing sensitive personal or financial information. Although Google has built Android to be as secure as possible, it is wise to choose high-security settings. This section shows you how to choose privacy settings, disable JavaScript, and block pop-ups and cookies.

Tighten Up Your Browsing Privacy Settings

1 Touch **Home** (⏺).

The Home screen appears.

2 Touch **Chrome** (◉).

Chrome opens.

3 Touch **Menu** (⋮).

The menu opens.

4 Touch **Settings**.

The Settings screen appears.

5 Touch **Privacy**.

The Privacy screen appears.

6 Touch **Navigation error suggestions** (☐ changes to ✓) if you want to use Navigation Error Suggestions.

7 Touch **Search and URL suggestions** (☐ changes to ✓) if you want to use Search and URL Suggestions.

8 Touch **Network action predictions**.

The Network Action Predictions dialog box opens.

9 Touch **Always**, **Only on Wi-Fi**, or **Never** (○ changes to ◉), as needed.

10 Touch **Usage and crash reports**.

The Usage and Crash Reports dialog box opens.

11 Touch **Always send**, **Only send on Wi-Fi**, or **Never send** (○ changes to ◉), as needed.

The Usage and Crash Reports dialog box closes.

12 Touch **'Do Not Track'**.

The 'Do Not Track' screen appears.

13 Set the **'Do Not Track'** switch to On (☐ changes to ◉).

14 Touch **Back** (◁).

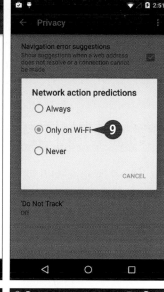

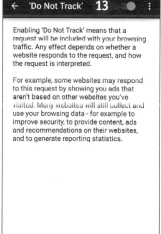

TIP

What are Navigation Error Suggestions and Search and URL Suggestions?

Navigation Error Suggestions are web addresses that Chrome suggests when you request an address that Chrome cannot reach — for example, because you typed the address incorrectly, or because a linked address no longer exists. Search and URL Suggestions are queries and web addresses the search engine considers to be related to those you type in the omnibox.

Both types of suggestions are usually helpful, but they may occasionally display surprising or unsuitable content, so do not follow them blindly.

continued ▶

To enhance your privacy, you can turn on the 'Do Not Track' setting. This setting requests that websites you visit not track your actions — but be warned that websites need not honor this request. When you have browsed sites that you do not want Chrome to retain in your browsing history, you can use the Clear Browsing Data command to purge them. Chrome also enables you to allow sites to use your device's camera and microphone with your permission or simply block sites from using these items.

Tighten Up Your Browsing Privacy Settings (continued)

The Privacy screen appears.

15 Touch **Menu** (⋮).

The menu opens.

16 Touch **Clear Browsing Data**.

The Clear Browsing Data dialog box opens.

17 Touch each item you want to clear
(☐ changes to ☑).

18 Touch **Clear**.

Chrome clears the browsing data for the items you chose.

The Clear Browsing Data dialog box closes.

19 Touch **Back** (◀).

The Settings screen appears.

20 Touch **Site settings**.

The Site Settings screen appears.

21 Touch **Cookies** (☑ changes to ☐) if you want to prevent sites from storing cookies. See the tip for details.

22 Touch **JavaScript** (☑ changes to ☐) if you want to prevent sites from running JavaScript.

23 Touch **Camera or Microphone**.

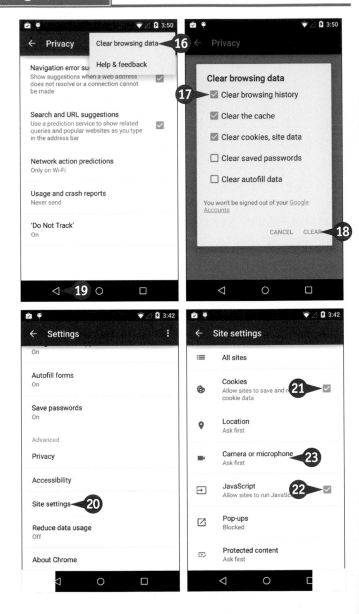

The Camera or Microphone screen appears.

24 Set the **Camera or microphone** switch to On (changes to) if you want Chrome to ask permission before allowing sites to use the camera and microphone. Set the switch to Off (changes to) to block these features.

25 Touch **Back** (◀).

The Site Settings screen appears.

26 Touch **Pop-ups**.

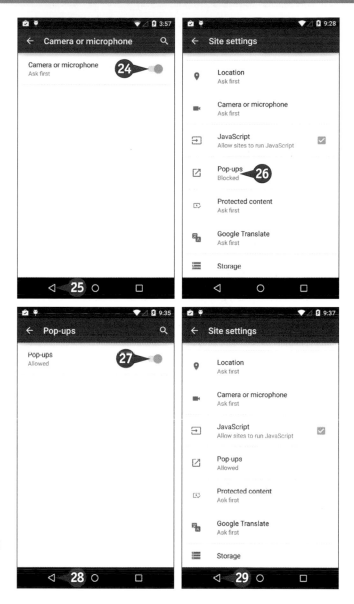

The Pop-ups screen appears.

27 Set the **Pop-ups** switch to On (changes to) if you want to allow pop-up windows. Set the switch to Off (changes to) to block pop-up windows.

28 Touch **Back** (◀).

The Site Settings screen appears.

29 Touch **Back** (◀).

The Settings screen appears.

30 Touch **Back** (◀).

Chrome displays the web page you were viewing before you opened the Settings screens.

TIP

What are cookies and what threat do they pose?

A *cookie* is a small text file that a website places on a computer to identify that computer in the future. This is helpful for many sites, such as shopping sites in which you add items to a shopping cart, but when used by malevolent sites, cookies can pose a threat to your privacy. You can set Chrome to refuse cookies, but this prevents many legitimate websites from working properly. Normally it is best to set Chrome to accept cookies.

Navigate in the Gmail App

The Gmail app enables you to access multiple e-mail accounts using a single streamlined interface. You can switch among accounts as needed. For Gmail accounts, you can switch among the Primary, Social, and Promotions categories of messages.

Normally, you set up your primary Gmail account when you first set up your Android device. You can add other e-mail accounts to the Gmail app as explained in the section "Set Up Your E-Mail Accounts" in Chapter 5.

Navigate in the Gmail App

Open the Gmail App

1 Touch **Home** (⬤).

The Home screen appears.

Note: If the Google folder appears on the Home screen, you can touch **Google** to open the folder and then touch **Gmail** (M).

2 Touch **All Apps** (⚏).

The Apps screen appears.

3 Touch **Gmail** (M).

Note: If Gmail (M) is not on the Apps screen that appears first, scroll left or right until you find Gmail (M).

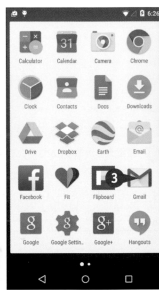

Navigate Among Your Accounts and Categories

Ⓐ The category name appears at the top of the screen.

1 Touch **Menu** (☰).

The menu panel opens.

2 Touch the account name at the top.

Ⓑ The icon indicates the number of messages in the account identified by the picture.

The account-management panel appears.

3 Touch the account to which you want to switch.

The list of messages in the account appears.

4 Touch **Menu** (≡).

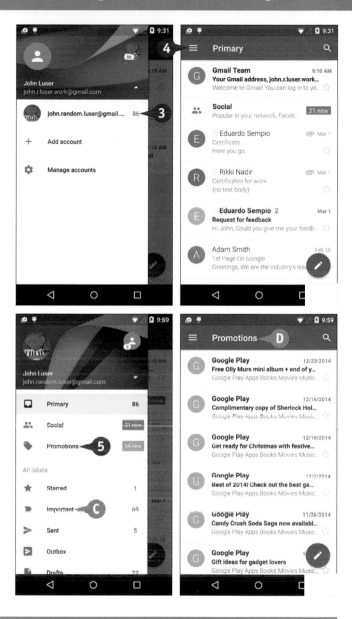

The menu panel opens.

5 Touch the category you want to display, such as **Promotions**.

C Instead of a category, you can touch a label to display the messages marked with that label.

The messages in the category appear.

D The category name appears at the top of the screen.

Read Your E-Mail Messages

Gmail enables you to review and read your e-mail messages quickly and easily. After opening the Gmail app and displaying the appropriate mailbox, you can review the messages by their senders, subjects, and first lines. When you identify a message you want to read, you can open it and then move to earlier or later messages directly from it.

Read Your E-Mail Messages

Open Gmail and the Account You Want to Use

1 Touch **Home** (⬤).

The Home screen appears.

Note: If the Google folder appears on the Home screen, you can touch **Google** to open the folder and then touch **Gmail** (M).

2 Touch **All Apps** (⊞).

The Apps screen appears.

3 Touch **Gmail** (M).

Note: If Gmail (M) is not on the Apps screen that appears first, scroll left or right until you find Gmail (M).

Gmail opens, and your Inbox appears.

A Each message appears as the sender's name followed by a two-line preview showing the subject line and the first part of the message.

B The sender and subject of unread messages appear in boldface.

C The sender and subject of read messages appear in regular, non-bold font.

4 Touch the message you want to open.

The message opens.

D You can touch **Delete** (🗑) if you want to delete the message.

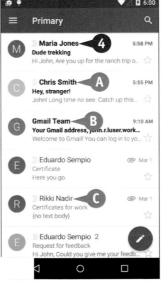

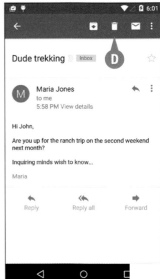

5 When you want to display the next message, swipe left.

The next message appears.

6 If the message is too wide for the screen, or you simply want to view the text at a larger size, rotate your device to landscape orientation.

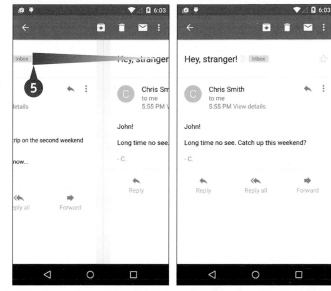

The message appears in landscape orientation.

7 When you finish reading messages, touch **Back** (◀).

Your Inbox appears again.

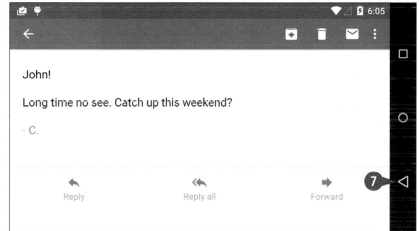

Why do some messages have a gold chevron to the left of the sender in the inbox?
A gold chevron ( ) means that Gmail has marked the message as important. Gmail automatically marks messages as important based on various weighting measures, but you can also manually mark messages as important or not important. To do so, touch and hold the message to select it, touch **Menu** (⋮), and then touch **Mark important** or **Mark not important**, depending on whether the message is currently marked as important. Gmail gradually learns from your marking, so this is well worth the minimal effort involved.

Reply to or Forward an E-Mail Message

You can choose to reply only to the sender of a message you have received, or to reply to the sender and all the other recipients in the To field and the Cc field. Gmail adds Re: to the beginning of the subject line to indicate that the message is a reply. You can also forward a message you have received to one or more other people. In this case, your e-mail app adds Fwd: to the beginning of the subject line to indicate that the message has been forwarded.

Reply to or Forward an E-Mail Message

1 Touch **Home** (⊙).

The Home screen appears.

2 Touch **All Apps** (⊞).

The Apps screen appears.

3 Touch **Gmail** (M).

Note: If Gmail (M) is not on the Apps screen that appears first, scroll left or right until you find Gmail (M).

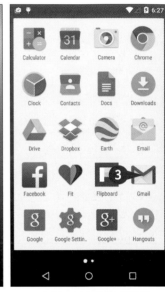

Gmail opens, and your Inbox appears.

4 Touch the message you want to open.

The message opens.

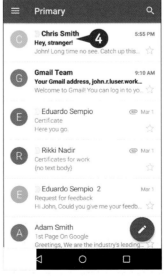

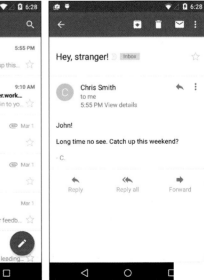

210

Reply to the Message

1 In the open message, touch **Reply** (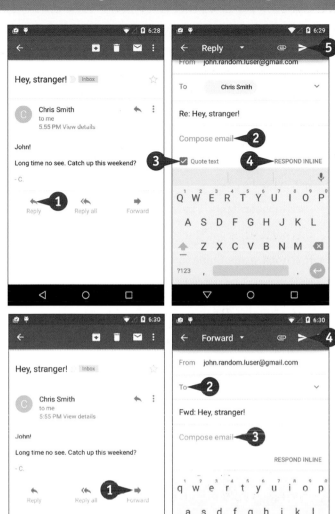).

Gmail creates a reply and displays it.

2 Touch the **Compose email** field and type your message.

3 Touch **Quote text** (☑ changes to ☐) if you do not want to include the original message in the reply.

4 Touch **Respond Inline** if you want to respond to the original message paragraph by paragraph.

5 Touch **Send** (➤).

Gmail sends the message.

Forward the Message

1 In the open message, touch **Forward** (➡).

Gmail creates a forwarded message and displays it.

2 Type the recipient in the To field.

3 Touch the **Compose email** field and type any message needed.

4 Touch **Send** (➤).

Gmail sends the message.

TIPS

What is the point of the Respond Inline feature?

Responding inline is useful when you need to answer an e-mail message one point at a time. When you touch **Respond Inline**, Gmail sets up the reply so that you can edit the original message and add the paragraphs of your reply between the paragraphs of the original for clarity.

How do I reply to all the recipients of a message?

To reply to all recipients of the message, either touch **Reply All** («) or touch **Menu** (⋮), and then touch **Reply All**. You can then compose the reply and touch **Send** (➤) to send it.

Label and Archive Your Messages

To keep your Inbox under control, you should archive each message you no longer need in the Inbox and delete any message you do not need to keep. Before archiving a message, you can apply one or more labels to it. Labels help you categorize messages so that you can find them later. You can label, archive, or delete a single message at a time, or you can select multiple messages in your Inbox and label, archive, or delete them all at once.

Label and Archive Your Messages

Open Gmail

1 Touch **Home** (●).

The Home screen appears.

2 Touch **All Apps** (⊞).

The Apps screen appears.

3 Touch **Gmail** (M).

Note: If Gmail (M) is not on the Apps screen that appears first, scroll left or right until you find Gmail (M).

Gmail opens, and your Inbox appears.

Select Messages, Label Them, and Archive Them

1 Touch the sender image to the left of a message.

A The sender image changes to a gray circle containing a white check mark (✓).

Gmail changes to selection mode.

2 Touch the sender image for each other message you want to select.

B The readout shows how many messages you have selected.

3 Touch **Menu** (⋮).

The menu opens.

4 Touch **Change labels**.

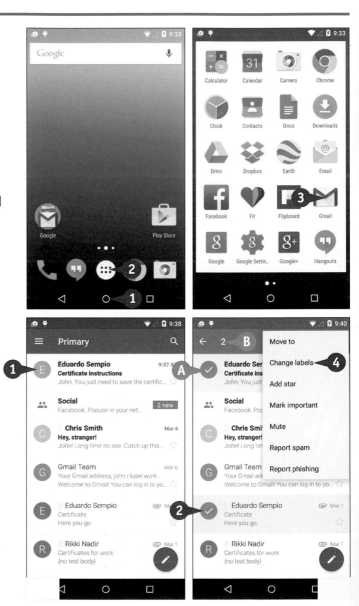

The Label As dialog box opens.

5 Touch each label you want to apply (□ changes to ☑).

6 Touch **OK**.

The Label As dialog box closes.

C The label or labels you selected appear on the messages.

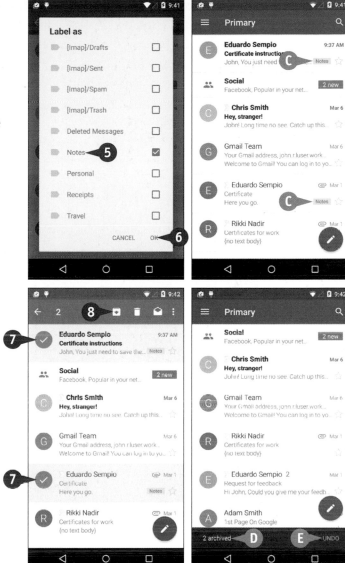

7 Touch the sender image to the left of each message you want to archive.

The sender image changes to a gray circle containing a white check mark (✓).

8 Touch **Archive** (⬇).

Gmail archives the messages and removes them from the Inbox.

D The Archived message appears at the bottom of the screen.

E You can touch **Undo** to undo the archiving.

TIPS

How do I file my messages in folders?

You can select messages as explained in this section, touch **Menu** (⋮), touch **Move to**, and then touch the destination folder in the Move To dialog box. However, you may find it easier simply to assign labels and then browse or search by labels.

How can I create new labels for marking my messages?

At this writing, you cannot create new labels directly in the Gmail app. Instead, open Chrome or another browser, log in to your Gmail account, and create the new labels from there.

Write and Send E-Mail Messages

When you need to write new messages, you can use the data in the Contacts app to address your messages quickly and accurately. If the recipient's address is not one of your contacts, you can type the address manually. You can attach one or more files to an e-mail message to send those files to the recipient. This works well for small files, but many mail servers reject files larger than several megabytes in size.

Write and Send E-Mail Messages

1 Touch **Home** (◉).

The Home screen appears.

2 Touch **All Apps** (⬚).

The Apps screen appears.

3 Touch **Gmail** (M).

Note: If Gmail (M) is not on the Apps screen that appears first, scroll left or right until you find Gmail (M).

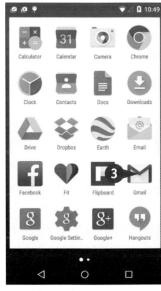

Gmail opens, and your Inbox appears.

4 Touch **Compose** (✏).

The Compose screen appears, with the insertion point in the To field.

5 Start typing the recipient's name or address.

A pop-up menu displays possible matches from your contacts in the Contacts app.

6 Touch the recipient to whom you want to send the message.

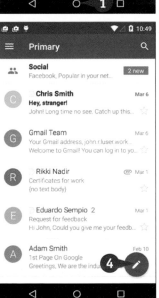

The recipient's name appears as a button in the To box.

Note: You can add another recipient by starting to type his or her name or address.

7 To add Cc or Bcc recipients, follow these substeps:

Ⓐ Touch **Expand** (⌄).

The Cc and Bcc fields appear.

Ⓑ Touch **Cc** or **Bcc**, as needed.

Ⓒ Begin typing the recipient's name.

Ⓓ Touch the correct entry on the pop-up menu.

8 Touch the **Subject** field and type the subject for the message.

9 Touch the **Compose email** field and type the body of the message.

Note: You can also touch **Microphone** (🎤) and dictate the contents of the message.

10 Touch **Send** (➤).

Gmail sends the message.

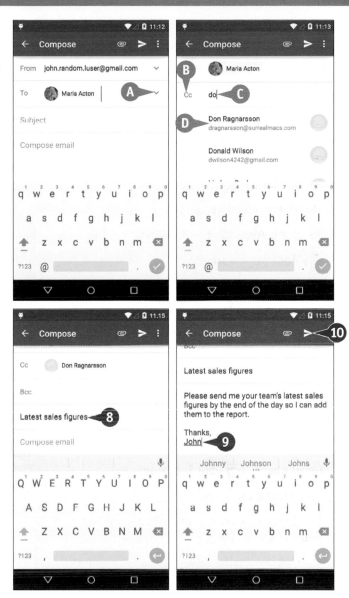

View Files Attached to Incoming Messages

E-mail is not just a great way to communicate, but you can use it to transfer files quickly and easily. When you receive an e-mail message with a file attached to it, you can quickly view the file from the Gmail app. Often, the best approach is to preview the file to get an idea of its contents and check that it is safe to open. Once you know what the file contains, you can choose which app to open the file in.

View Files Attached to Incoming Messages

1 Touch **Home** (◉).

The Home screen appears.

2 Touch **All Apps** (⊞).

The Apps screen appears.

3 Touch **Gmail** (M).

Note: If Gmail (M) is not on the Apps screen that appears first, scroll left or right until you find Gmail (M).

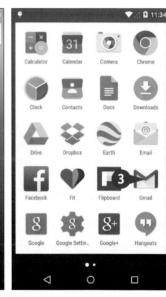

Gmail opens, and your Inbox appears.

Ⓐ A paperclip icon (📎) indicates that a message has one or more files attached.

4 Touch the message you want to open.

The message opens.

5 Touch the button for the attachment.

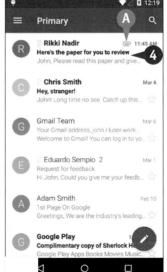

216

The preview of the attachment appears.

6 If you want to save the attachment to Google Drive, touch **Drive** (⚠).

The Save to Drive dialog box opens.

B You can edit the title as needed.

C You can choose a different account if necessary.

D You can touch **Folder** and choose the destination folder.

7 Touch **Save**.

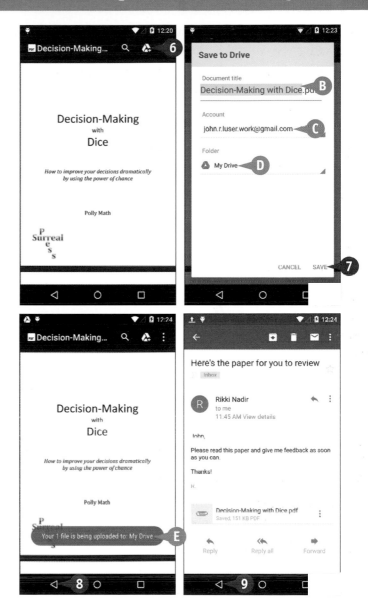

E Gmail uploads the file to Google Drive.

8 Touch **Back** (◀).

The message appears.

9 Touch **Back** (◀).

Your inbox appears, and you can label and archive the message as needed.

TIP

How can I delete an attached file from an e-mail message?

You cannot directly delete an attached file from an e-mail message in the Android Gmail app at this writing. You can delete only the message along with its attached file. If you use an e-mail app such as Apple Mail to manage the same e-mail account, you can remove the attached file using that app. When you update your mailbox on your phone or tablet, Gmail deletes the attached file but leaves the message.

Browse by Labels and Search for Messages

Google's Gmail service uses tags called *labels* to categorize messages instead of filing them into folders, as most other services do. You can apply one or more labels to any message as needed. You can then use these labels to browse through your messages to find the ones you need to work with. Browsing is useful when you need to look at a selection of messages to find the right one. You can also find a particular message by searching for it. Searching is the fastest approach when you can identify one or more keywords contained in the message.

Browse by Labels and Search for Messages

1 Touch **Home** (⬤).

The Home screen appears.

2 Touch **All Apps** (⬛).

The Apps screen appears.

3 Touch **Gmail** (M).

Note: If Gmail (M) is not on the Apps screen that appears first, scroll left or right until you find Gmail (M).

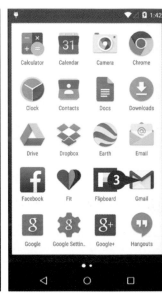

Gmail opens, and your Inbox appears.

4 Touch **Menu** (☰).

The menu panel opens.

5 Touch the label by which you want to browse.

The screen for the label appears, showing the messages that match.

Ⓐ You can touch a message to open it.

❻ To search, touch **Search** (🔍).

Ⓑ The Search Mailbox appears at the top of the screen.

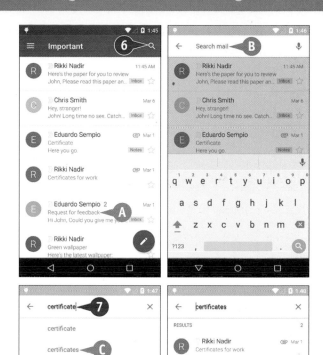

❼ Type your search term.

Ⓒ You can touch a suggestion to search by that term.

❽ Touch **Search** (🔍).

Gmail searches and displays matching messages.

Ⓓ You can touch a message to open it.

TIP

How can I prevent the Search pop-up menu from showing out-of-date suggestions?

❶ Touch **Menu** (▬).

❷ Touch **Settings**.

❸ Touch **General settings**.

❹ Touch **Menu** (⋮).

❺ Touch **Clear search history**.

❻ Touch **Clear** in the Clear Search History dialog box.

CHAPTER 10

Taking and Using Photos and Videos

Most Android phones and tablets include one or more cameras that enable you to take photos and video using the Camera app. You can easily edit your photos and share them with other people.

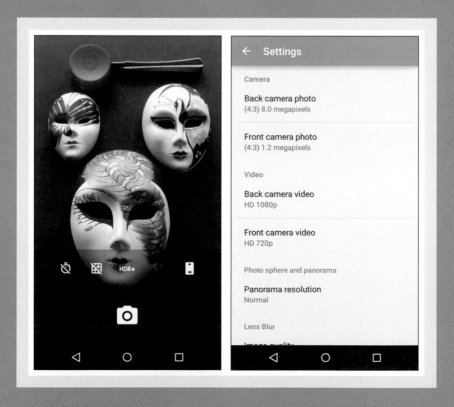

Take Photos with the Camera App

Most Android phones and many Android tablets include a rear camera that you can use to take photos. Most devices have a front, screen-side camera that you can use to take photos and videos of yourself or to enjoy video calls.

To take photos using the camera, you use the Camera app. This app includes zoom and flash capabilities, plus a *High Dynamic Range*, or HDR, feature for improving the exposure in your photos.

Take Photos with the Camera App

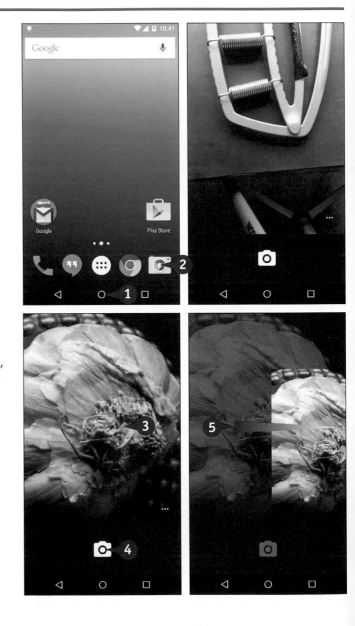

1 Touch **Home** (⬤).

The Home screen appears.

Note: From the lock screen, swipe left to open the Camera app quickly.

2 Touch **Camera** (◯).

Note: If Camera (◯) does not appear on the Home screen, touch **All Apps** (⸬) and then touch **Camera** (◯).

The Camera app opens.

The screen shows what the Camera lens is pointing at.

3 Aim the phone or tablet so that your subject appears in the middle of the photo area.

Note: If you need to take tightly composed photos, get a tripod that fits your phone or tablet. You can find various models on Amazon, eBay, and photography sites.

4 Touch **Shutter** (◯).

The Camera app takes a photo.

5 Swipe left from the Camera screen.

The photo you just took appears as a thumbnail.

6 Scroll left to see other photos on the Camera.

7 Touch the thumbnail for a photo you want to view.

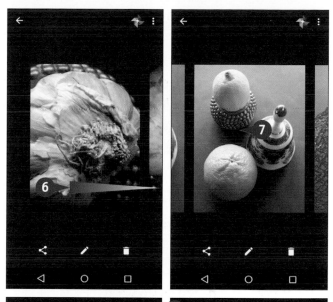

The photo appears, taking up most of the screen but with the controls still appearing at the top and bottom.

Note: You can touch anywhere on the photo to hide the controls.

8 Touch **Menu** (▦) and then touch **Details**.

The Details screen appears, showing the photo's details.

Note: You may need to scroll down to see further details.

9 Touch **Close**.

The photo appears.

10 Touch **Back** (◁).

The Camera screen appears again.

Details

Title: IMG_20150313_104547
Time: Mar 13, 2015 10:45:48 AM
Location: 54.534907, -1.951956
Width: 2448
Height: 3264
Orientation: 0
File size: 1.09MB
Maker: LGE
Model: Nexus 5
Flash: No flash
Focal Length: 3.97 mm
White balance: Auto
Aperture: 2.52

9 CLOSE

TIPS

Why does my phone's Camera app look different from the Camera app shown here?

Some skinned versions of Android include camera apps with different interfaces and other features than those shown here. Consult your device's documentation to learn how to use it and any extra features it offers.

How do I switch to the front-facing camera?

Touch **Options** (⚬⚬⚬) to display the Options bar, and then touch **Front Camera** (⚬) to switch to the screen-side camera. Touch **Options** (⚬⚬⚬) and then touch **Rear Camera** (⚏) to switch back to the rear-facing camera.

Using Zoom and Manual Focus

If your device's camera includes zoom capability, you can zoom in so that your subject appears larger. Zoom is useful when you cannot get the camera close enough to make the subject the size you want. After zooming in, you can zoom back out as needed.

Most devices' cameras focus automatically on the middle of the picture. This works well for many photos, but when your subject is not in the middle of the picture, you can focus manually instead.

Using Zoom and Manual Focus

Use the Zoom Feature

1 Touch **Home** (⬤).

The Home screen appears.

2 Touch **Camera** (◎).

Note: If Camera (◎) does not appear on the Home screen, touch **All Apps** (⸬), and then touch **Camera** (◎).

The Camera app opens.

The screen shows what the Camera lens is pointing at.

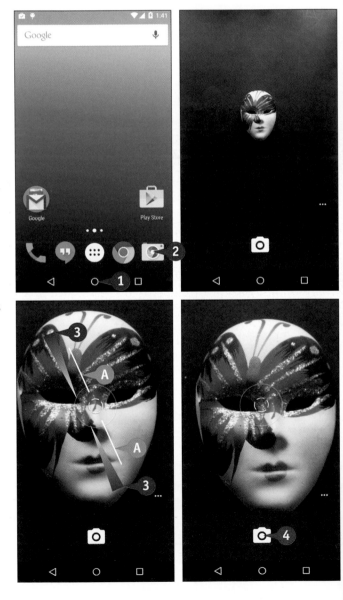

3 If you need to zoom in or out, place two fingers together on the screen and pinch outward.

Ⓐ The zoom lines appear.

4 Touch **Shutter** (◎).

The Camera app takes the photo.

Use Manual Focus

1 Aim the camera lens at your subject.

2 Zoom in as described in the previous subsection if the subject is too far away.

3 Touch the screen where you want to place the focus.

The Camera app focuses on the point you touched.

B The circles indicate that the Camera app is focusing.

4 Touch **Shutter** ($\widehat{\text{o}}$).

The Camera app takes the photo.

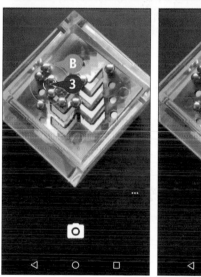

TIPS

Why do my pictures become grainy when I zoom in?
The cameras on most smartphones and tablets use digital zoom rather than optical zoom. Digital zoom zooms in by enlarging the pixels that make up the picture, so when you zoom in a long way, the pictures can become grainy as the pixels become larger. By contrast, optical zoom uses moving lenses to zoom in, thus retaining full quality even at extreme zoom.

Can I add optical zoom to my Android device?
Yes, you can add optical zoom by using an external lens. Some lenses come built in to cases, whereas other stick onto your Android device. To find such lenses, look at specialist photography retailers such as Photojojo (http://photojojo.com).

Using the Flash and the HDR Feature

M ost phones and many tablets include a flash for lighting your photos. You can choose among three flash settings: On forces the Camera app to use the flash for every photo, Auto lets the Camera app decide whether to use the flash, and Off prevents the Camera app from using the flash. You can use the *High Dynamic Range* feature, HDR, to improve a photo's color balance and intensity. HDR takes three photos in immediate succession with slightly different exposure settings, and then combines them into a single photo.

Using the Flash and the HDR Feature

Use the Flash

1 Touch **Home** (⬤).

The Home screen appears.

2 Touch **Camera** (◎).

Note: If Camera (◎) does not appear on the Home screen, touch **All Apps** (⠿), and then touch **Camera** (◎).

The Camera app opens.

The screen shows what the Camera lens is pointing at.

3 Touch **Options** (•••).

The Options bar appears.

Note: You cannot use the HDR feature and the flash at the same time. If the flash icon is grayed out, touch **HDR+** to turn off HDR.

4 Touch **Flash** (⚡A, ⚡, or ⚡) once or twice until the appropriate icon appears: Flash On (⚡), Flash Off (⚡), or Flash Auto (⚡A).

5 Touch **Shutter** (◎).

The Camera app takes the photo.

Take High Dynamic Range Photos

1 Touch **Options** (⦂).

The Options bar appears.

2 Touch **HDR+** (HDR+ changes to HDR+).

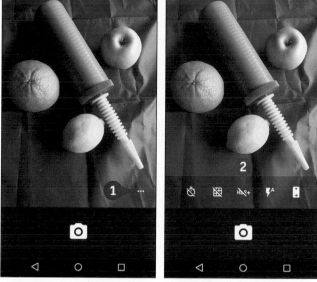

Note: You cannot use the HDR feature and the flash at the same time. Turning on HDR makes the flash unavailable.

Ⓐ HDR+ appears to the left of Options.

3 Compose your photo.

4 Touch **Shutter** (⃝).

The Camera app takes the HDR photo.

Is there any disadvantage to using HDR?

HDR prevents you from using the flash to light your photos. Taking an HDR photo also takes longer than taking a regular photo, so you cannot shoot photos in rapid succession. Whenever possible, use a tripod for your HDR photos to ensure that each photo has exactly the same alignment.

What are the other icons on the Options bar?

Touch **Timer** (◎) to cycle the timer through its three settings: Off (◎), 3 seconds (**3s**), and 10 seconds (**10s**). Touch **Grid** (▦) to toggle on (▦ changes to ▦) or off (▦ changes to ▦) the grid, a composition aid.

Take Panorama, Photo Sphere, and Lens Blur Photos

The Camera app enables you to take panorama photos, Photo Sphere photos, and Lens Blur photos. A panorama photo combines a series of photos taken of your surroundings on the same level, giving a long, low photo looking around a single point. A Photo Sphere photo is similar to a panorama photo, but goes up and down as well as horizontally. A Lens Blur photo records the subject's distance from the background, creating a photo in which you can subsequently change the depth of field.

Take Panorama, Photo Sphere, and Lens Blur Photos

Take a Panorama Photo

1 Touch **Home** (⬤).

The Home screen appears.

2 Touch **Camera** (⭕).

Note: If Camera (⭕) does not appear on the Home screen, touch **All Apps** (⠿), and then touch **Camera** (⭕).

The Camera app opens.

3 Swipe right.

The Camera Mode list appears.

4 Touch **Panorama** (⬙).

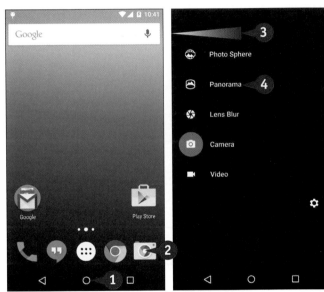

The Camera app switches to Panorama mode.

5 Aim the camera at your subject.

6 Touch **Panorama** (⬙).

The Camera app starts taking the panorama.

7 Turn the camera around you, moving the circle to the next white dot. When the dot turns blue, continue to the next dot.

When you complete the panorama or touch **Done** (✔), the Camera app renders the panorama.

228

Take a Photo Sphere Photo

1 In the Camera app, swipe right.

The Camera Mode list appears.

2 Touch **Photo Sphere** (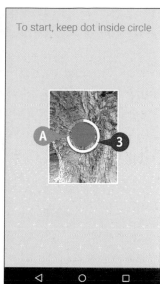).

The Camera app switches to Photo Sphere mode.

The *To start, keep dot inside circle* prompt appears.

3 Move the circle to the blue dot.

The Camera app starts taking the Photo Sphere photo automatically.

A The white ring shows the progress of the current capture.

The blue dot turns white when this part of the capture is complete.

4 Move the circle to the next blue dot in the direction you want to capture next.

5 Touch **Done** () when you finish taking the Photo Sphere photo.

The Camera app renders the Photo Sphere photo.

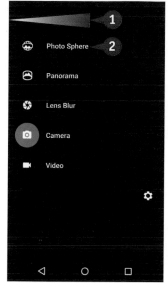

TIP

How do I take and adjust a Lens Blur photo?

In the Camera app, swipe right to open the Camera Mode list, and then touch **Lens Blur** (). Compose your photo with the subject some distance in front of the background, and then touch **Lens Blur** () to capture the photo. Move your device up when the Camera app instructs you to do so. Swipe left to display the image, and touch **Lens Blur** () to display the screen for adjusting the focus. Drag the bottom slider left to decrease the blur or right to increase it. Touch **Done** when you are satisfied with the look.

Choose Settings for Photos and Videos

The Camera app enables you to configure settings to help you shoot suitable photos. You can set the resolution for still photos and for video for both the back camera and the front camera, choose the resolution for panorama and Photo Sphere photos, and set the image quality for Lens Blur photos. You can control whether the Camera app includes location information in each photo. You can also turn on manual exposure when you need to take control of each photo's exposure time.

Choose Settings for Photos and Videos

1 Touch **Home** (⦿).

The Home screen appears.

2 Touch **Camera** (⌾).

Note: If Camera (⌾) does not appear on the Home screen, touch **All Apps** (⊞) and then touch **Camera** (⌾).

The Camera app opens.

3 Swipe right.

The Camera Mode list appears.

4 Touch **Settings** (⚙).

The Settings screen appears.

5 Set the **Save location** switch to On (⬤ changes to ⬤) if you want to save the location in photos, or to Off (⬤ changes to ⬤) if you do not.

6 Touch **Resolution & quality**.

The Resolution & Quality settings appear.

7 Touch **Back camera photo**.

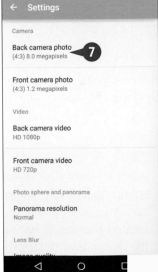

The Back Camera Photo dialog box opens.

8 Touch the resolution you want (○ changes to ◉).

Note: The numbers in parentheses show the aspect ratio, such as 4:3 or 16:9.

9 Touch **Front camera photo**, **Back camera video**, or **Front camera video** and choose the resolutions you want.

10 Touch **Panorama resolution** and then touch **High**, **Normal**, or **Low (fastest)** (○ changes to ◉), as needed.

11 Touch **Image quality** and then touch **Normal** or **Low (fastest)** (○ changes to ◉), as needed.

12 Touch **Back** (◄).

The Settings screen appears.

13 Touch **Advanced**.

The Advanced settings appear.

14 Set the **Manual exposure** switch to On (⬜ changes to 🔵) if you want to control exposure manually.

15 Touch **Back** (◄).

The Settings screen appears.

16 Touch **Back** (◄).

The Camera screen appears.

Note: After turning on manual exposure, touch **Options** (•••), touch **Exposure**, and then touch **−2**, **−1**, **0**, **+1**, or **+2** to control the exposure.

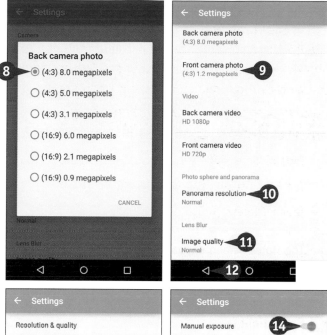

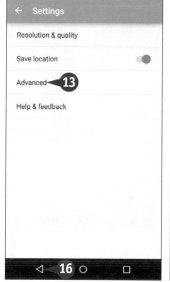

TIPS

What picture size should I choose for my photos?

Shoot most of your photos at the highest resolution the camera on your phone or tablet supports. You can then create lower-resolution versions of your photos if needed. When you need to shoot lower-resolution photos and then use them directly from your phone or tablet, choose the size you need in the Camera app.

What size is CIF?

CIF has a resolution of 352 × 288 pixels. CIF is the acronym for Common Intermediate Format, a longtime standard for making video compatible on different systems. By today's standards, CIF is extremely low resolution, but you may sometimes find it useful.

Android enables you to crop a photo to a square, to the same aspect ratio as the original photo, or to exactly the aspect ratio you choose.

You can apply a preset look, such as monochrome, to change a photo's appearance in an instant. For greater control, you can use the Tune Image feature to separately adjust settings such as Brightness, Saturation, and Warmth.

Edit Your Photos (continued)

Crop a Photo

1. With the photo open for editing, touch **Crop** (⛶).

   The cropping tools appear.

2. Touch **Free** (⟦ ⟧), **Original** (🖼), or **Square** (◻), depending on the aspect ratio you want.

   The crop box changes accordingly.

3. Drag the crop handles to select the appropriate area.

   Note: You can touch inside the crop box and drag to reposition it without moving the handles.

4. Touch **Done** (✓).

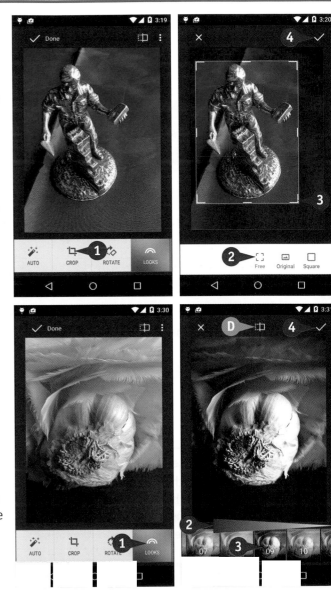

Apply a Look to a Photo

1. With the photo open for editing, touch **Looks** (◎).

   The Looks bar appears.

2. Scroll the Looks bar as needed to find the look you want.

3. Touch the look.

   The Photos app applies the look.

Ⓓ You can touch and hold **Toggle original** (▤) to display the photo without the look to help judge the difference.

4. Touch **Done** (✓).

   The editing controls appear.

Work with the Tune Image Controls

1 With the photo open for editing, touch **Tune image** (⚏).

The Tune Image controls appear.

E The name of the current setting appears.

2 Drag right to increase the setting or left to decrease it.

The Photos app adjusts the setting for the photo.

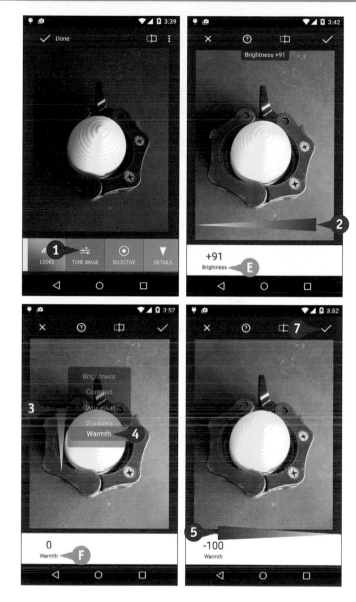

3 Place your finger on the screen and slide it up, keeping it on the screen.

The Settings pop-up menu appears.

4 Slide your finger up or down to highlight the setting you want to change, such as **Warmth**.

F The setting's name appears.

5 Drag right to increase the setting or left to decrease it.

6 Repeat steps **4** and **5** as needed to adjust other settings.

7 Touch **Done** (☑).

The editing controls appear.

TIP

What other editing controls does the Photos app offer?
Touch **Selective** to apply image-tuning effects to the parts of the photo that you select instead of to the photo as a whole. Touch **Details** to adjust the structure or sharpening of the image. Touch a named effect, such as **Vintage** or **Drama**, to apply a preset look and lighting; you can adjust it subsequently if you want. Touch **Frames** to display controls for applying various types of frames to the photo.

Capture Video

Most cameras on Android devices can capture video as well as take photos. Many devices have rear cameras that can capture high-definition video, also known as HD video, and front cameras that can capture lower-resolution video.

To capture video, you use Video mode in the Camera app. After taking the video, you can easily view it on the screen of your phone or tablet. You can also share the video with other people or play it back on your TV.

Capture Video

1 Touch **Home** (⬤).

The Home screen appears.

2 Touch **Camera** (◯).

Note: If Camera (◯) does not appear on the Home screen, touch **All Apps** (⠿) and then touch **Camera** (◯).

The Camera app opens.

3 Swipe right.

The Camera Mode list appears.

4 Touch **Video** (▭).

The Camera app switches to Video mode.

5 Aim the lens at your subject.

A You can touch **Options** (•••) to choose options such as flash. See the tip for more information.

6 Touch **Video** (▭).

The Camera app starts recording video.

B The readout shows the recording time.

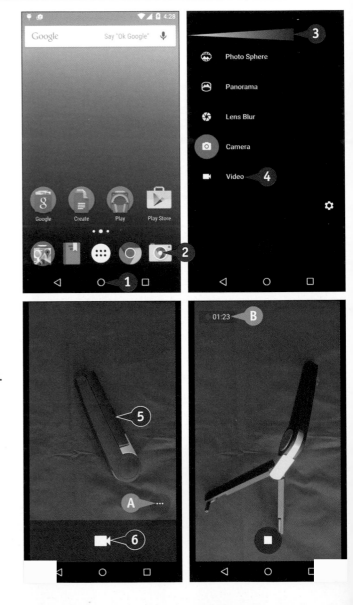

Note: You can shoot a still frame by touching the screen at the appropriate moment. The screen flashes, and a corner of the still frame slides briefly onto the right side of the screen, then disappears.

7 Touch **Stop** (☐).

The Camera app stops recording.

8 Swipe left.

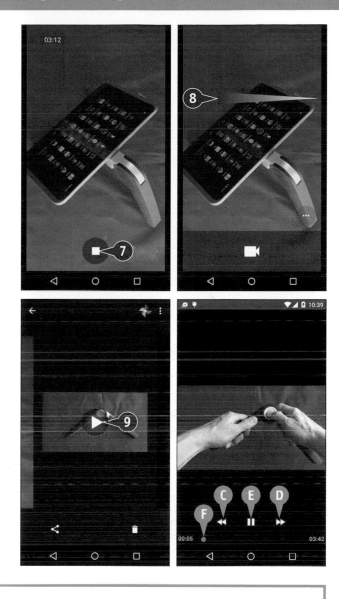

The video you just took appears.

9 Touch **Play** (▶).

The video starts playing.

C You can touch **Rewind** (◀◀) to rewind the video.

D You can touch **Fast-Forward** (▶▶) to fast-forward the video.

E You can touch **Pause** (❚❚) to pause the video.

F You can drag the **Playhead** (●) to move through the video.

TIP

What options can I choose for video?

The options vary depending on your device and the camera app, but typical options include turning the flash on for illumination, turning the grid on to help composition, and switching between the rear camera and the front camera.

Some camera apps enable you to change the white balance among sunny, cloudy, fluorescent, and incandescent; set up time-lapse video recording; and even control the app from another device.

If the camera app supplied with your device does not provide all the features you need, open the Play Store app and browse Google Play for a more suitable app. Many are available, either for free or for modest prices.

Share Your Photos and Videos

Android makes it easy to share photos and videos with other people. You can share photos and videos you take with the Camera app as well as those you load on your device.

You can share photos and videos using built-in apps and features, such as Gmail, Hangouts, and Bluetooth. This sections uses Gmail as the example app. If you have installed other apps that support sharing, such as Facebook, Twitter, or Skype, you can share via those apps, too.

Share Your Photos and Videos

1 Touch **Home** (⬤).

The Home screen appears.

2 Touch **All Apps** (⬚).

The Apps screen appears.

3 Touch **Photos** (🌀).

Note: If Photos (🌀) is not on the Apps screen that appears first, scroll left or right until you find Photos (🌀).

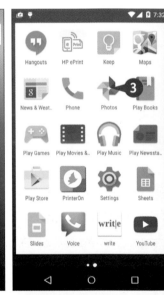

The Photos app opens and displays the All tab.

Ⓐ You can touch **Highlights** to display the Highlights tab.

4 Touch the photo you want to share.

The photo opens.

5 Touch **Share** (◁).

The Share panel appears, showing the most-used sharing apps and features at the top.

6 To see the full range of sharing apps and features, slide your finger up.

The rest of the Share panel appears.

7 Touch the app or feature you want to use, such as **Gmail** (M).

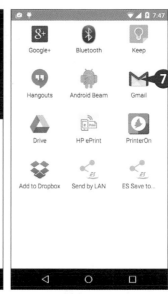

The app opens and displays a screen for sharing the item. For example, Gmail creates a new message.

8 Touch **To** and add the e-mail address.

9 Touch **Subject** and type the subject.

10 Touch **Compose email** and type any text needed.

11 Touch **Send** (➤).

TIP

How large a video can I share?
The maximum video size depends on the means of sharing that you use. It is seldom a good idea to send videos via instant messaging, but sharing videos of up to several megabytes via e-mail is viable. Generally, however, it is better to use a means of sharing that stores the video online, such as Google Drive or Dropbox, or to post the video to social networking sites if you want to share it with many people.

CHAPTER 11

Using Maps, Clock, Play Music, and Videos

Your Android phone or tablet includes Maps for directions, Clock for alarms and timing, Play Music for playing music, and Videos for playing videos.

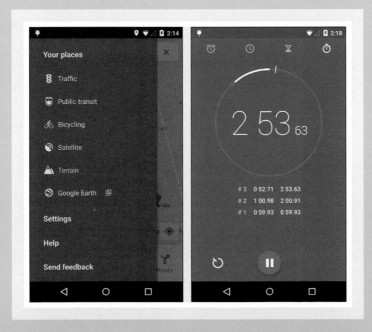

Find Your Location with the Maps App

Your phone or tablet includes a Maps app with which you can pinpoint your location by using the Global Positioning System, known as GPS, or known wireless networks. You can view your location on a road map, a satellite picture, or a terrain map. You can easily switch among map types and add different layers of map information to make the map display exactly what you need. To get your bearings, you can rotate the map to match the direction you are facing.

Find Your Location with the Maps App

1 Touch **Home** (⬤).

The Home screen appears.

2 Touch **All Apps** (⊞).

The Apps screen appears.

3 Touch **Maps** (🗺).

Note: If Maps (🗺) is not on the Apps screen that appears first, scroll left or right until you find Maps (🗺).

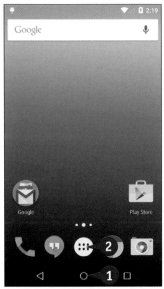

The Maps screen appears.

Ⓐ A blue circle shows your current location.

Ⓑ The blue triangle shows the direction your device is facing.

4 Place two fingers apart on the screen and pinch in.

The map zooms out, showing a larger area.

5 Touch **Menu** (☰).

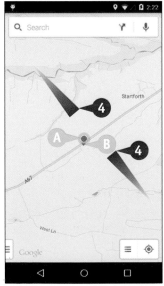

The menu panel opens.

6 Touch **Satellite**.

The menu panel closes.

The satellite map appears with road names and place names overlaid on it.

7 Touch **Menu** (☰) again.

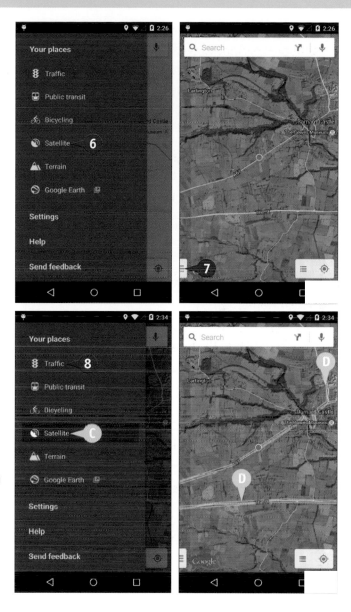

The menu panel opens.

C The darker shading indicates that Satellite is turned on.

8 Touch **Traffic**.

The menu panel closes.

D Colored lines indicating traffic flow appear on the major roads.

Note: Some layers, such as Satellite and Transit, can appear at the same time. Other layers, such as Terrain and Satellite, are mutually exclusive.

TIP

Which is the best view to use in Maps?

That depends on what you are doing. When you need straightforward street navigation, use the regular map without the satellite information or terrain information; you may want to add layers such as Traffic, Public Transit, or Bicycling, depending on your means of transport. When you want to see a picture of the area, add the Satellite layer. And when you want to see the lay of the land, switch to the Terrain layer.

Find Directions with the Maps App

The Maps app enables you to get step-by-step directions to your destination. Maps can also show you current traffic information to help you identify the most viable route for a journey and avoid getting stuck in congestion. Maps displays driving directions by default, but you can also display public transit directions and walking directions. It is wise to double-check that public transit direction and schedules are up to date before using them. You can also use the Navigation feature, which gives you directions as you proceed along your route.

Find Directions with the Maps App

1 Touch **Home** (⬤).

The Home screen appears.

2 Touch **All Apps** (▦).

The Apps screen appears.

3 Touch **Maps** (🗺️).

Note: If Maps (🗺️) is not on the Apps screen that appears first, scroll left or right until you find Maps (🗺️).

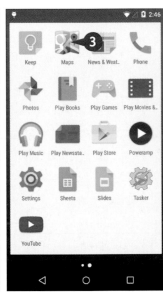

The Maps screen appears.

4 Touch **Directions** (🔀).

The Directions screen appears.

A The upper box shows My Location as the suggested start point.

5 To use another start point, touch the upper box.

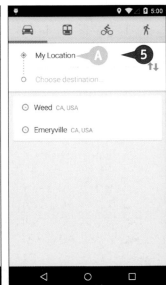

6 Type the starting location.

A list of suggestions appears.

7 If a suggestion is correct, touch it. Otherwise, type the entire address.

8 Touch **Driving** (🚗) for driving directions, **Public transit** (🚆) for public transit directions, **Cycling** (🚲) for cycling directions, or **Walking** (🚶) for walking directions.

9 Touch **Choose destination** and enter the destination.

Maps searches automatically and displays possible routes.

10 Touch the route you want to view.

The route appears on the map.

11 Touch **Preview**.

The first map section and the first direction appear.

12 Swipe left on the gray bar to display the next map section and the next direction. Swipe right on the gray bar to go back to the previous map section and direction.

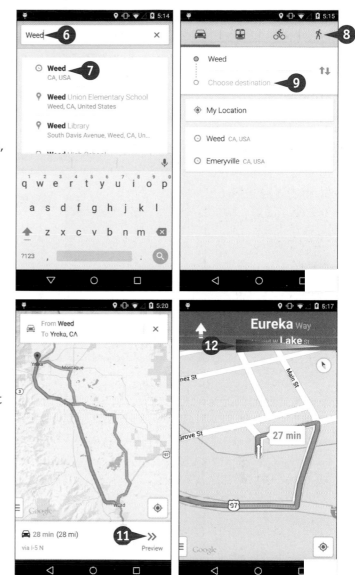

TIPS

Is there an easy way to find my way back to my start point?

After setting your start point and endpoint in the Maps app, touch **Reverse start and end** (⇅).

How accurate are the directions?

The maps are mostly highly accurate, but you should always follow the directions sensibly rather than slavishly. The Navigation feature is in development as of this writing and traffic data is not real time, so be careful when following the navigation instructions. You may also have to adjust your route for detours caused by construction or special events.

Rotate, Zoom, and Tilt the Map

To make the maps easier to use and more helpful, the Maps app lets you rotate, zoom, and tilt the map. Rotating the map enables you to align the map with the direction in which you are looking, which helps you identify your location. Zooming the map lets you move from viewing a large area at a small scale to viewing a small area at a large scale. Tilting the map gives you a better idea of the lay of the land. You can combine the three movements to explore the map in great detail.

Rotate, Zoom, and Tilt the Map

Open the Maps App

1 Touch **Home** (⬤).

The Home screen appears.

2 Touch **All Apps** (⊞).

The Apps screen appears.

3 Touch **Maps** (📍).

Note: If Maps (📍) is not on the Apps screen that appears first, scroll left or right until you find Maps (📍).

The Maps screen appears.

Rotate the Map

1 Place two fingers, or your finger and thumb, apart on the map, and then rotate them in the appropriate direction.

The map rotates.

Ⓐ The compass arrow (◀▬) appears. The red end points north; the white end points south.

2 Touch **Compass arrow** (◀▬) when you want to make the map point north again.

Zoom the Map

1 Place your thumb and index finger together on the screen and then pinch apart (pinch-out zoom).

The map zooms in to a close-up view of the area.

2 Place your thumb and index finger apart on the screen and then pinch together (pinch-in zoom).

The map zooms out to a wide-aerial view.

Note: You can zoom in by increments by double-tapping the area on which you want to zoom. Double-tap with two fingers to zoom out, again in increments.

Tilt the Map

1 Place two fingers near the bottom of the screen and draw them up.

The map tilts away from you, giving a flatter perspective instead of a straight-down perspective.

2 When you finish using the tilted map, place two fingers near the top of the screen and then draw them down.

The straight-down perspective reappears.

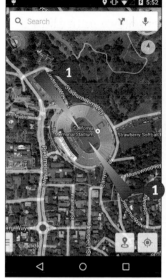

How can I see the scale of the map I am viewing?

Place two fingers on the screen and move them slightly together or apart. A scale appears at the bottom of the screen for a few seconds.

How can I quickly get maps of my home area?

You can enter your home address in Maps. Touch **Menu** (≡) to display the menu panel, and then touch **Settings** to display the Settings screen. Touch **Edit home or work** to display the Edit Home or Work screen, and then touch **Enter home address** or **Enter work address**.

Make a Map Available Offline

Maps enables you to save specific sections of a map to your phone or tablet so you can access them even when the device has no Internet connection. After saving a map to your device, you access it by going to the My Places screen and touching the **Offline** tab. You can keep offline maps for as long as needed and delete those you no longer need.

Make a Map Available Offline

1 Touch **Home** (⬤).

The Home screen appears.

2 Touch **All Apps** (⬚).

The Apps screen appears.

3 Touch **Maps** (🗺).

Note: If Maps (🗺) is not on the Apps screen that appears first, scroll left or right until you find Maps (🗺).

The Maps screen appears.

4 Navigate to the area you want to make available offline.

5 Touch **Menu** (≡).

The menu opens.

6 Touch **Your places**.

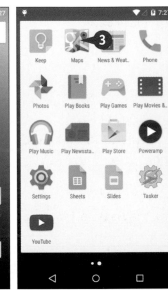
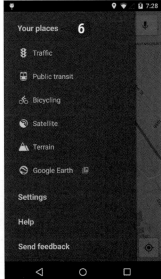

The Your Places screen appears, showing your name at the top.

7 In the Offline Maps section at the bottom of the screen, touch **Save map to use offline**.

The map appears, showing the *Save this map?* prompt at the top.

Note: You can adjust the map by panning or zooming if necessary.

8 Touch **Save**.

The Name Offline Map dialog box opens.

9 Type the name for the map.

10 Touch **Save**.

Ⓐ The Maps app downloads the map.

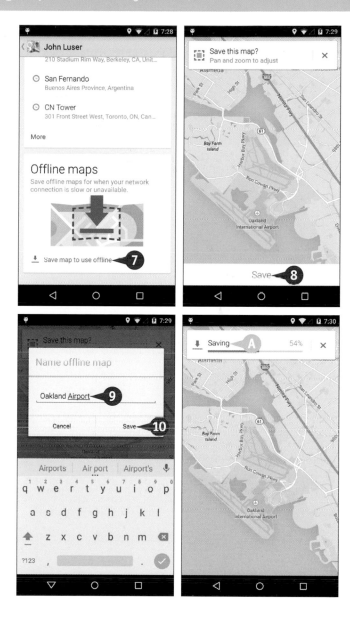

TIP

How do I use and manage my offline maps?

Touch **Menu** (☰) and then touch **Your places** to display the Your Places screen. In the Offline Maps section at the bottom of the screen, you can touch a map to display it, or touch **View all and manage** to display the Offline Maps screen. Here, you can touch **Menu** (⋮) for an offline map and then use the three commands on the menu: Touch **Rename** to rename the map, touch **Update** to update the map with the latest information, or touch **Delete** to delete the map.

Explore with Street View

The Maps app is not only great for finding out where you are and for getting directions to places, but it also enables you to use the Street View feature to explore the view at ground level. Street View displays images from Google's vast database of city streets and rural areas. You can pan around the area at which you enter Street View, move along certain streets almost as if you were walking along them, and look up and down.

Explore with Street View

1 Touch **Home** (⬤).

The Home screen appears.

2 Touch **All Apps** (▦).

The Apps screen appears.

3 Touch **Maps** (▧).

Note: If Maps (▧) is not on the Apps screen that appears first, scroll left or right until you find Maps (▧).

The Maps screen appears.

4 Navigate to the area you want to explore.

5 Touch and hold the place where you want to enter Street View.

A A dropped pin (📍) appears on the map.

B The location bar for the pin appears at the bottom of the screen.

6 Touch the location bar.

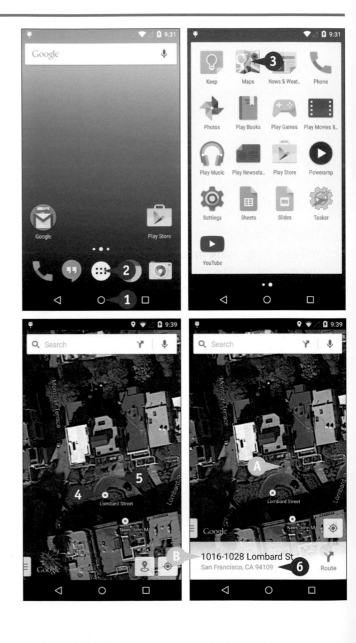

The info page for the place appears.

7 Touch **Street View**.

Street View appears.

Note: The images in Street View may be several years old, so what you see in Street View may be significantly different from reality.

8 You can touch the white arrows to move in the directions they indicate.

9 Drag left to look right, or drag right to look left.

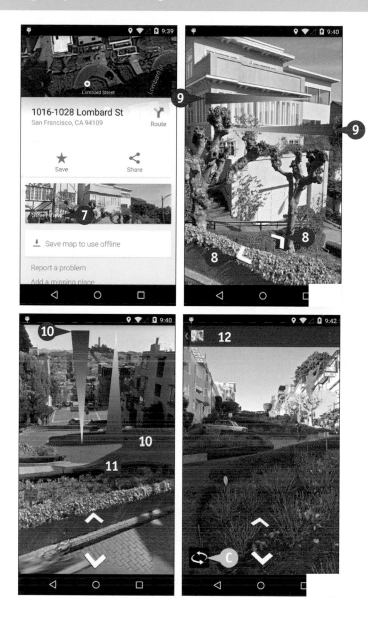

10 Drag down to look up, or drag up to look down.

11 Touch the screen.

The controls appear.

C You can touch **Look around** (🔄) to have the map follow the movements of your device. This feature is useful when you are physically in the place you are viewing.

12 When you are ready to return to the map, touch **Maps** (🗺️).

Maps exits Street View and displays the map instead.

TIP

I have found an error in Street View. How do I tell Google about it?

If you find errors or unsuitable content in Street View, you can report it to Google. With the offensive image on screen, touch **Menu** (≡) and then touch **Send feedback**. On the Send Feedback screen, touch **Report a mapping issue** to report map errors, touch **Add a missing place** to add a new place or business, touch **Send location feedback** to report errors with the blue dot or the location bar, or touch **Send app feedback** to report other issues, such as offensive pictures.

Share a Location with Others

After finding an interesting place in the Maps app, you can easily share it via e-mail, messaging, or other means such as Facebook or Twitter. When you share a place, the Maps app includes a link that the recipient can touch to go straight to that place in a web browser or — if it is available — the Maps app.

Share a Location with Others

1 Touch **Home** (⬤).

The Home screen appears.

2 Touch **All Apps** (⬚).

The Apps screen appears.

3 Touch **Maps** (🗺).

Note: If Maps (🗺) is not on the Apps screen that appears first, scroll left or right until you find Maps (🗺).

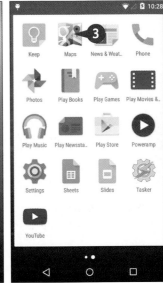

The Maps screen appears.

4 Navigate to the place you want to share.

5 Touch and hold the appropriate place on the map.

Ⓐ A dropped pin (📍) appears on the map.

Ⓑ The location bar for the pin appears at the bottom of the screen.

6 Touch the location bar.

The info page for the place appears.

7 Touch **Share** (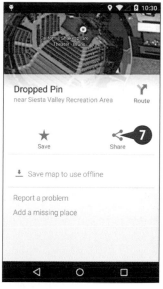).

The Share Via dialog box opens.

Note: The options in the Share Via dialog box vary depending on your device's features and the apps installed on it.

8 Touch the means of sharing you want to use. This example uses **Gmail**.

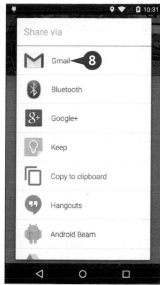

Android opens the appropriate app.

9 Type any necessary text, such as a descriptive subject line, in an e-mail message.

C Maps includes a link that the recipient can use to open the location in a browser or in Maps.

10 Touch **Send** ().

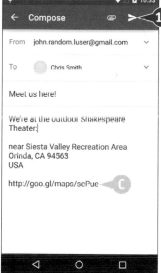

How can I mark a place so that I can go back to it later?

In the Maps app, navigate to the area that contains the place, then touch and hold the place until a dropped pin and the location bar appear. Touch the location bar to display the info screen for the place, then touch the **Save** star (⭐ changes to ⭐).

To return to the place, touch **Menu** (☰) and then touch **Your places** on the menu panel. On the Your Places screen, touch the saved place to which you want to go.

Using the Clock App

A ndroid provides a Clock app that includes alarms, a countdown timer, a stopwatch, and a World Clock. You can set as many alarms as you need and create different schedules for the alarms. For example, you can set an alarm to wake you each weekday but not on the weekend. Using the Timer feature, you can set one or more timers to count down a set amount of time, which is useful for timed activities such as cooking.

Using the Clock App

Open the Clock App

1 Touch **Home** (⬤).

The Home screen appears.

A If the analog clock or digital clock appears on the Home screen, you can touch it to display the Clock app.

2 Touch **All Apps** (⦂⦂⦂).

The Apps screen appears.

3 Touch **Clock** (🕐).

Note: If Clock (🕐) is not on the Apps screen that appears first, scroll left or right until you find Clock (🕐).

The Clock app appears.

Set Alarms

1 Touch **Alarms** (⏰).

The Alarms screen appears.

2 Touch **Add** (▦).

The clock face appears, showing hours.

3 Touch **AM** or **PM**, as needed.

4 Touch the hour.

The minutes appear.

5 Touch the minutes.

6 Touch **OK**.

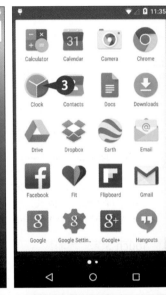

The details screen for the alarm appears.

7 Set the alarm's switch to On (changes to) or Off (changes to), as needed.

8 Touch **Label**, type a name in the Label dialog box, and then touch **OK**.

9 To create a repeating alarm, touch **Repeat** (changes to ✓).

10 Touch the letters for the days on which to repeat the alarm.

11 Touch **Vibrate** (changes to ✓) if you want vibration as well as sound.

Ⓑ You can touch **Delete** (🗑) to delete the alarm.

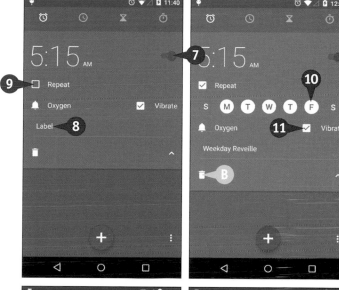

Use the Timer Feature

1 Touch **Timer** (⏳).

2 Touch the buttons to set the countdown time. For example, touch **4** and **3** and **0** to set 4 minutes, 30 seconds.

3 Touch **Start** (▶).

The timer starts counting down.

Ⓒ You can touch **Label** and type a name for the timer.

Ⓓ You can touch **+1'** to add one minute.

Ⓔ You can touch **Delete** (🗑) if you want to clear the timer.

TIPS

How do I change the sound for the alarm?
On the Alarms screen, touch **Expand** (⌄) for the alarm. Touch **Alarm Sound** (🔔) to display the Ringtones dialog box, touch the sound you want to use, and then touch **OK**. You can add your own alarm tones by copying music files to the Alarms folder using Windows Explorer or Android File Transfer.

Can I run multiple timers at the same time?
Yes. Touch **Add timer** (⏳) to start setting up another timer. After you start it, dots (🔵) appear to the right of each timer to indicate how many timers are running. Swipe up or down to switch among the timers.

continued ▶

Watch, Rate, and Flag YouTube Videos

When you find a video that interests you on YouTube, you can watch the video on your phone or tablet. If you have signed in to YouTube using your Google account, you can also give the video a rating. Your ratings can help other people decide whether to view the videos you have watched. If you find a video offensive, you can flag it to help YouTube identify problems with it. For example, if you discover dangerous acts in a video, or if it infringes upon your rights, you can flag it for review.

Watch, Rate, and Flag YouTube Videos

1 Touch **Home** (⬤).

The Home screen appears.

2 Touch **All Apps** (⊞).

The Apps screen appears.

3 Touch **YouTube** (▶).

Note: If YouTube (▶) is not on the Apps screen that appears first, scroll left or right until you find YouTube (▶).

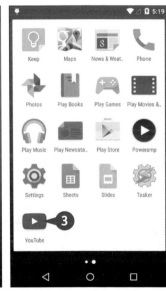

The YouTube app opens, and you can find a video by using the technique explained in the previous section.

4 Touch the video you want to view.

The video's screen appears, and the video starts playing.

Ⓐ You can touch **Like** (👍) or **Dislike** (👎) to give your opinion — preferably after watching the video.

5 Turn your device to landscape orientation.

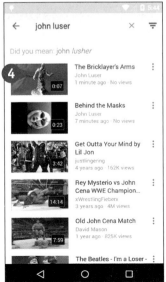

The video appears in landscape orientation, filling the screen.

6 Touch the screen.

The controls appear.

7 Touch **Add video to** (⊞) to add the video to a new playlist or your Watch Later list.

8 Touch **Share** (◁) to share the video's details with others.

9 Touch **Collapse** (∨) to shrink the video to a thumbnail so that you can keep this video available while navigating in the YouTube app.

Note: Turn your device to portrait orientation to return to the video's page with the rating icons and the suggestions for other videos you may want to watch.

TIP

How do I report a problem with a video?

1 On the video's screen, touch **Menu** (⋮).

2 On the menu, touch **Report**.

3 In the Flag This Video dialog box, touch the appropriate option button. For example, touch **Hateful or Abusive Content** or **Harmful Dangerous Acts** (○ changes to ◉).

4 Touch **Flag**.

CHAPTER 12

Troubleshooting Your Device

To keep your phone or tablet running well, you should update its software, keep backups against disaster, and learn essential troubleshooting moves.

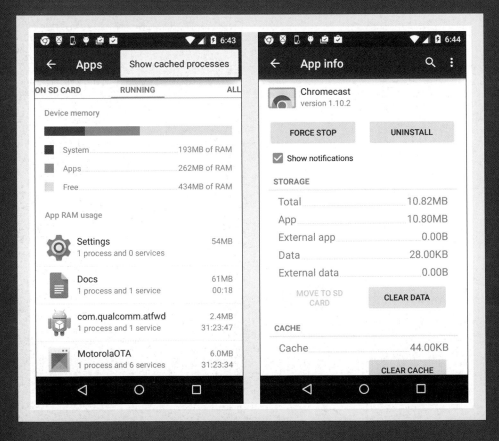

Close an App That Has Stopped Responding

Developers make their apps as reliable as possible, but sometimes an app stops responding to your input. When this happens, you need to close the app and then restart it so that you can continue using it. The easiest way to close an app is by using the Overview screen. If you cannot use this method, you can use the Apps screen in the Settings app to close the app.

Close an App That Has Stopped Responding

Close an App from the Overview List

1 When the app stops responding, touch **Overview** (▣).

The Overview screen appears.

2 Touch and hold the icon at the upper-left corner of the thumbnail for the app that has stopped responding.

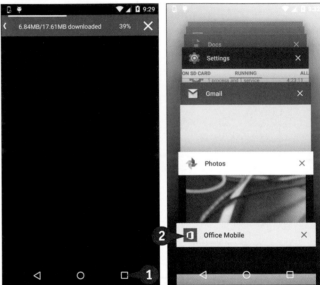

The App Info screen for the app appears.

3 Touch **Force Stop**.

The Force Stop? dialog box opens.

4 Touch **OK**.

Android stops the app. You can then touch **Home** (◉) to display the Home screen, touch **All Apps** (⸭) to display the Apps screen, and then touch the app to restart it.

Close an App from the Apps Screen

1 Touch **Home** (⬤).

The Home screen appears.

2 Touch **All Apps** (⊞).

The Apps screen appears.

3 Touch **Settings** (⚙).

Note: If the Settings icon (⚙) is not on the Apps screen that appears, swipe left or right until you can see it.

The Settings screen appears.

4 Touch **Apps**.

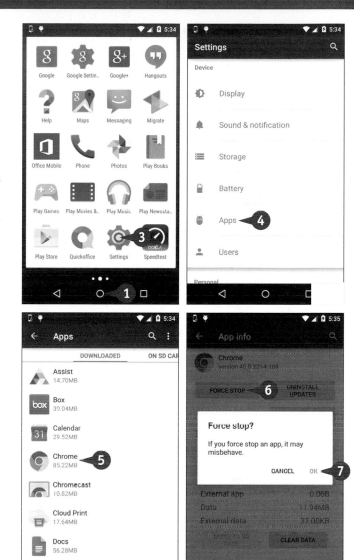

The Apps screen in Settings appears.

5 Touch the app that has stopped responding.

The App info screen for the app opens.

6 Touch **Force Stop**.

The Force Stop? dialog box opens.

7 Touch **OK**.

Android forces the app to stop running.

8 Touch **Back** (◁).

The Apps screen appears.

9 Touch **Back** (◁).

The Settings screen appears.

TIP

What should I do if my Android device stops responding to the touch screen?

If your phone or tablet stops responding to the touch screen, restart it. Press and hold the Power button until the Power Off dialog box opens, then touch **Power off**.

If the Power Off dialog box does not appear, continue to hold the Power button until the device turns off. Wait 10 seconds, then press and hold the Power button until the Google logo appears.

Update Your Device's Software

Google periodically releases new versions of the Android operating system to fix problems, improve performance, and add new features. To keep your phone or tablet running quickly and smoothly, and to add the latest features that Google provides, update the device's software when a new version becomes available. Your phone or tablet checks periodically for new versions of Android and notifies you when they are available. Any companion software you run on a computer may also check for new versions of Android. You can also check manually for new versions of the software.

Update Your Device's Software

A When a system update is available, System Update (🔃) appears in the status bar.

Note: The screens for the update may vary depending on your device's manufacturer and the software version.

1 Drag down the Notification shade.

Note: On a tablet, drag down the left part of the status bar to display the Notification shade.

2 Touch **Download**.

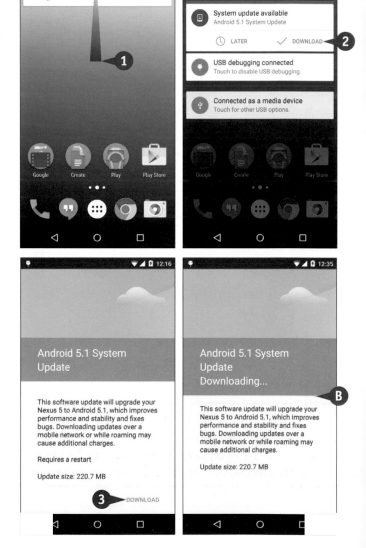

The System Update screen appears.

3 Touch **Download**.

The Downloading screen appears.

B The yellow bar shows the progress of the download.

After Android finishes downloading and verifying the update, the Downloaded and Verified screen appears.

④ Touch **Restart & Install**.

The Power Off dialog box appears briefly.

Your phone or tablet shuts down, and then restarts.

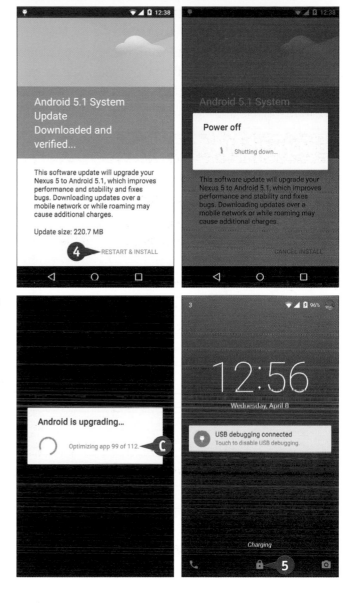

Ⓒ During the upgrade, Android optimizes the apps on your device, reorganizing their placement in the device's storage as efficiently as possible.

After optimizing the apps, Android starts those you were running.

The lock screen appears.

⑤ Drag the **Lock** button (🔒) upward.

Android unlocks the screen.

You can now start using your phone or tablet again.

TIP

How do I check manually for new versions of Android?
Touch **Home** (⊙) to display the Home screen, then touch **All Apps** (⊞) to display the Apps screen. Touch **Settings** (⚙) to display the Settings screen, then touch **About phone** or **About tablet** at the bottom. Touch **System updates** to display the System Updates screen, then touch **Check now**.

Extend the Runtime on the Battery

To keep your phone or tablet running all day, you need to charge the battery fully by plugging the device into an adequately powered USB socket, the charging unit, or another power source. You can extend your device's runtime by reducing the demands on the battery. You can turn off Wi-Fi and Bluetooth when you do not need them. You can dim the screen so that it consumes less power, and you can set the phone or tablet to go to sleep quickly.

Extend the Runtime on the Battery

1 Touch **Home** (⬤).

The Home screen appears.

2 Pull down from the top of the screen with two fingers.

The Quick Settings panel opens.

3 Touch and hold **Brightness** (⚙).

A You can touch **Location** (⚲ changes to ⬙) if you want to turn off location services.

Android hides the Quick Settings panel so that you can see the screen brightness better.

4 Drag the **Brightness** slider left to reduce the brightness.

5 Touch **Bluetooth** (⚹ changes to ⬙) if you want to turn off Bluetooth.

6 Touch the **Wi-Fi** symbol (▽ changes to ⬙) if you want to turn off Wi-Fi.

7 Touch the **Settings** icon (⚙).

The Settings screen appears.

8 Touch **Display**.

The Display screen appears.

9 Set the **Adaptive brightness** switch to On (⬜ changes to 🔵) if you want Android to adjust the brightness automatically to suit the conditions.

10 Touch **Sleep**.

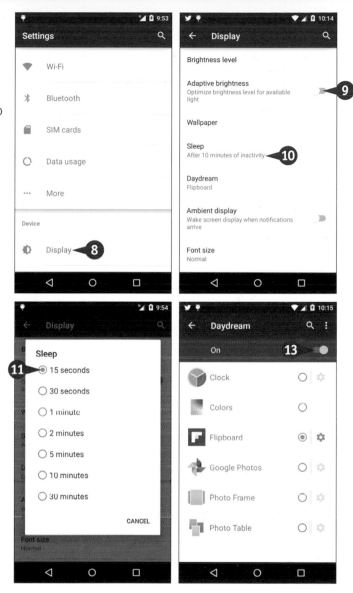

The Sleep dialog box opens.

11 Touch the appropriate radio button to set how long you want your device to remain awake before sleeping (◯ changes to ◉). To save power, choose a short time, such as 15 seconds.

12 On the Display screen, touch **Daydream**.

The Daydream screen appears.

13 Set the **Daydream** switch to Off (🔵 changes to ⬜).

Android turns off the Daydream feature.

TIPS

How can I see which features and apps use the most battery power?

In the Settings app, touch **Battery** to display the Battery screen. The list of features below the battery use diagram shows which apps have used the most power.

What else can I do to get more use of my phone or tablet between charges?

If your phone or tablet's battery is easily removable, carry another fully charged battery with you, and swap batteries when the device runs low on power. If you need more power on the move, buy a case with a built-in battery or a charger for charging the battery in a car.

Reset Your App Preferences

If your phone or tablet starts behaving oddly, you may be able to bring it back under control by resetting your app preferences. This move resets each app's preferences to their default settings. You can then set the preferences for any given app the way you want them. You may also find it useful to reset your app preferences when you have been experimenting with the settings for different apps but cannot find the settings needed to restore normality.

Reset Your App Preferences

1 Touch **Home** (⬤).

The Home screen appears.

2 Touch **All Apps** (⬚).

The Apps screen appears.

3 Touch **Settings** (⚙).

Note: If Settings (⚙) is not on the Apps screen that appears first, swipe left until you find Settings (⚙).

The Settings screen appears.

4 Touch **Apps**.

The Apps screen appears.

5 Touch **Menu** (⋮).

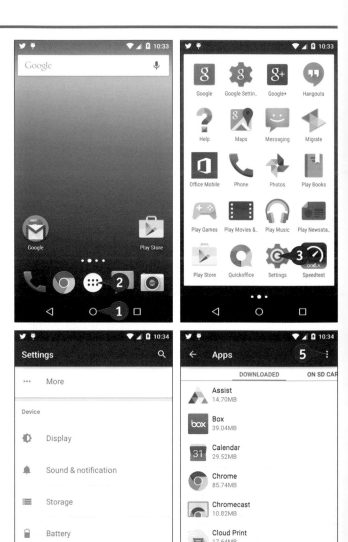

The menu opens.

6 Touch **Reset app preferences**.

The Reset App Preferences? dialog box opens.

7 Touch **Reset Apps**.

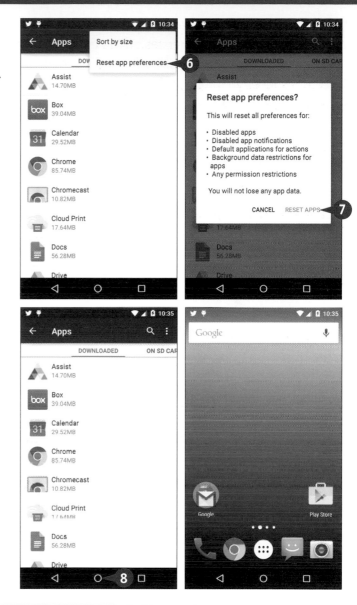

The Apps screen appears again.

The Settings screen appears.

8 Touch **Home** (⬤).

The Home screen appears, and you can start using your phone or tablet to check that you have resolved the problem.

TIP

What other effects does resetting app preferences have?

Resetting app preferences also removes the associations you have made between particular file types and apps. For example, when you first try to open a movie file, Android displays a dialog box showing a list of the available apps. You can then touch the app to use and touch **Always** or **Just Once**. If you touch **Always**, you make an association between the movie file type and the app you chose. The next time you open a movie file of this type, Android uses that app without asking. After you reset app preferences, Android prompts you again to choose which app to use when opening a file.

Check Free Space and Clear Extra Space

I f you take your phone or tablet with you everywhere, you will probably want to put as many data and media files on it as possible. When you do this, your device may run low on free space. This can cause the device to run slowly or be unstable. To avoid problems, you can check how much free space your phone or tablet has. When free space runs low, you can clear extra space to keep your device running well.

Check Free Space and Clear Extra Space

1 Touch **Home** (⬤).

The Home screen appears.

2 Touch **All Apps** (▦).

The Apps screen appears.

3 Touch **Settings** (⚙).

Note: If Settings (⚙) is not on the Apps screen that appears first, scroll left or right until you find Settings (⚙).

The Settings screen appears.

4 Touch **Storage**.

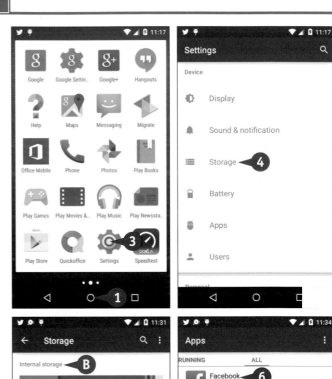

The Storage screen appears.

A Android warns you if storage space is running out.

B The Internal Storage chart shows how much of the storage is in use.

C The *Total Space* readout shows your device's entire memory capacity.

D The *Available* readout shows how much space is free.

E The list breaks down the memory usage by users and categories.

5 To see which apps are installed, touch **Apps**.

The Apps screen appears.

6 To remove an app from your device, touch its name.

The App Info screen for the app appears.

7 Touch **Uninstall**.

A confirmation dialog box opens.

8 Touch **OK**.

9 When you finish managing apps, touch **Back** (◀).

The Storage screen appears.

10 Touch **Downloads**.

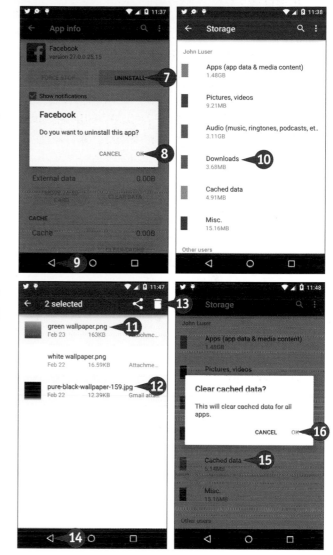

The Downloads screen appears.

11 Touch and hold the first item you want to delete.

Android selects the item, shading its button, and turns on Selection mode.

12 Touch each other item you want to delete.

13 Touch **Delete** (🗑).

Android deletes the files.

14 Touch **Back** (◀).

The Storage screen appears.

15 Touch **Cached data**.

The Clear Cached Data? dialog box opens.

16 Touch **OK**.

TIP

What other items can I get rid of to free up space on my phone or tablet?

You can remove miscellaneous files and media files.

On the Storage screen, touch **Misc.** to display the Misc. files screen. You can then select the check box for each item you want to delete (☐ changes to ☑) and then touch **Delete** (🗑).

Although the Storage screen provides a Pictures, Videos button and an Audio button, it is easier to remove pictures, video, and audio files using File Explorer or Windows Explorer on Windows or Android File Transfer on the Mac than directly using Android. If you have other companion software for your device, you can use it to remove pictures, videos, and audio.

Back Up Your Phone or Tablet Online

To keep your valuable data and carefully chosen settings safe, you can back up your Android phone or tablet online to your Google account. If your device subsequently has problems, you can restore it to factory settings and then restore your data and settings to it. Similarly, if your device gets broken, lost, or stolen, you can restore your data and settings from your Google account to a new device. Restoring your data and settings enables you to implement your preferred setup on your new device without laborious customization.

Back Up Your Phone or Tablet Online

① Touch **Home** (⬤).

The Home screen appears.

② Touch **All Apps** (⦿).

The Apps screen appears.

③ Touch **Settings** (⚙).

Note: If Settings (⚙) is not on the Apps screen that appears first, scroll left or right until you find Settings (⚙).

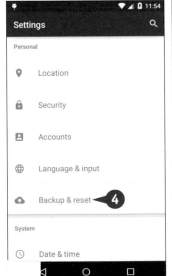

The Settings screen appears.

④ Touch **Backup & reset**.

Note: On a phone, you may have to scroll down to display the Backup & Reset button.

The Backup & Reset screen appears.

⑤ Set the **Back up my data** switch to On (⬭ changes to ⬤).

Note: When setting up your phone or tablet, you may already have set it to back up to your Google account. If the **Back up my data** switch is already set to On (⬤) and **Backup account** shows the right e-mail account, you are all set.

6 Touch **Backup account**.

The Set Backup Account dialog box opens.

7 Touch the appropriate account.

Note: If the account does not appear, touch **Add account** and follow the instructions on the Add Your Account screen. You can touch **Or Create a New Account** to start creating a new account from here.

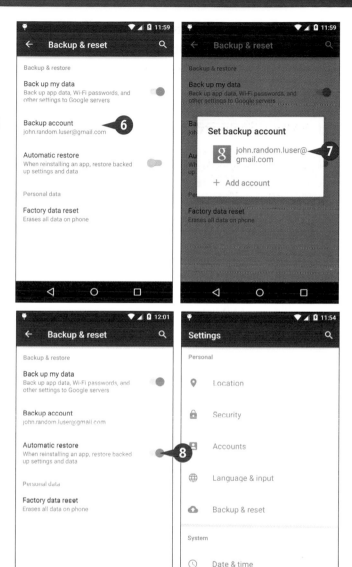

The Set Backup Account dialog box closes.

8 Set the **Automatic restore** switch to On (⬜ changes to ⬤) if you want to restore your settings and data when you reinstall an app.

9 Touch **Back** (◁).

The Settings screen appears.

10 Touch **Home** (⬤).

The Home screen appears.

Your Android device now backs itself up periodically to the account you designated.

TIPS

What settings does my Android device back up to Google?
Android backs up your personal data, such as your contacts, web bookmarks, Wi-Fi passwords, and custom dictionaries. Android also stores the list of apps you have bought or downloaded from the Play Store and your customized settings — for example, your Display settings and Sound settings.

Why does the Backup & Reset button not appear on the Settings screen?
Most likely because you have a nonowner account on the device. On a device set up for multiple users, only the owner — the first account set up — has access to the Backup & Reset commands.

Restore Your Device to Factory Settings

Google makes Android as reliable as possible, but sometimes problems occur that need your intervention. If your computer has companion software for your phone or tablet, connect your device to your computer and try using the software to reset or restore the device. If those moves fail, or if you do not have companion software, you may need to restore the device to factory settings. Restoring to factory settings is an operation you perform on the phone or tablet itself to resolve severe problems. After restoring to factory settings, you can restore data to your device from your Google account.

Restore Your Device to Factory Settings

1 Touch **Home** (⬤).

The Home screen appears.

2 Touch **All Apps** (⠿).

The Apps screen appears.

3 Touch **Settings** (⚙).

Note: If Settings (⚙) is not on the Apps screen that appears first, scroll left or right until you find Settings (⚙).

The Settings screen appears.

4 Touch **Backup & reset**.

Note: On a phone, you may have to scroll down to locate the Backup & Reset button.

The Backup & Reset screen appears.

5 Touch **Factory data reset**.

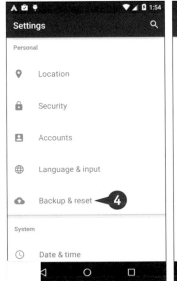

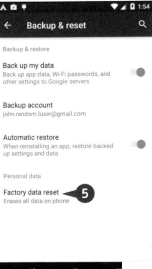

The Factory Data Reset screen appears.

6 Touch **Reset Phone** or **Reset Tablet**.

Note: If the phone or tablet has a PIN or password, the Confirm Your PIN screen or Confirm Your Password screen appears. Type your PIN or password and then touch **Next**.

The Reset? screen appears.

7 Touch **Erase Everything**.

Your phone or tablet restarts and restores its factory settings.

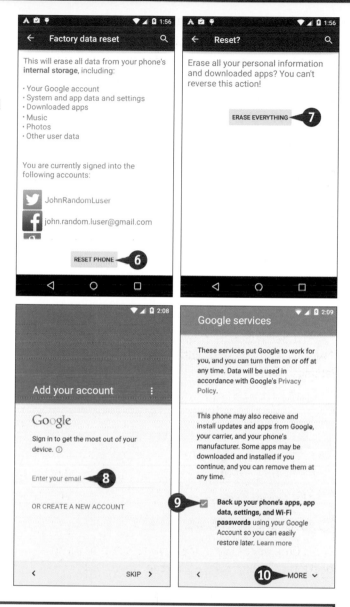

The Add Your Account screen appears.

8 Touch **Enter your email**, type your e-mail address, and then enter your password.

The Google Services screen appears.

9 Touch **Back up your phone's apps, app data, settings, and Wi-Fi passwords** (☐ changes to ✓) if you want to restore your data.

10 Touch **More** to display the remaining options.

11 Touch the **Next** button and allow setup to finish.

TIPS

What if I do not want to restore data from my Google account to my device?

Deselect the **Back up your phone's apps, app data, settings, and Wi-Fi passwords** check box (✓ changes to ☐) on the Google Services screen. You can then set up your device manually.

Are there other reasons for restoring a device to factory settings?

Other than software problems, there are two other common reasons for restoring a device to factory settings. First, if you have encrypted the device, you can restore it to factory settings to remove the encryption. Second, if you plan to give or sell the device to someone else, you restore it to factory settings to remove all your data and settings.

Troubleshoot Charging Problems

If your computer is a few years old and you are having problems charging your phone or tablet, the USB ports on your computer may not supply enough power to meet the device's needs. In this case, you can use a USB charger to charge your phone or tablet from an AC outlet to see if that solves the problem. Another option is a powered USB hub.

If you are having problems charging your device, you can try several moves to troubleshoot the issue. These moves can help you determine whether the problem is trivial or you need to get the device's battery replaced.

Check Your Cable Connections

If your phone or tablet does not charge, first check that the cables are actually connected and secure. Make sure that the micro USB connector is attached firmly to your device's SlimPort and that the USB end is firmly connected to your computer or charger. Verify that the connectors are free of any dirt or dust that could break the connection. If possible, try another charger or another wall socket in case the one you are using is faulty.

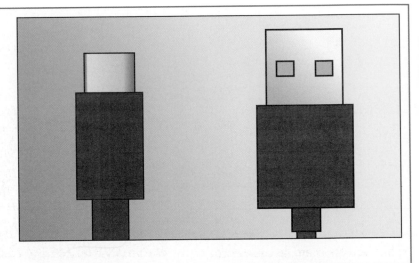

Switch USB Ports

If you are using your USB cable to connect your phone or tablet to your computer, you can also try connecting to a different USB port. Be aware that the USB ports on some keyboards do not provide enough power to charge a phone or tablet. If you are connecting to a keyboard USB port, try connecting to a USB port located on the computer instead. If you have a powered USB hub, you can try that, too.

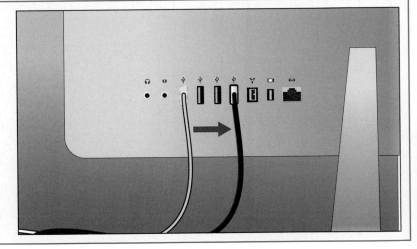

Update to a New Computer

If your Mac or PC is long out of date
and you have tried using a powered
USB hub but found it unsatisfactory,
another solution is to update to a new
computer. This is an expensive option,
so normally you will want to exhaust
all other charging options first. The
built-in USB ports on a computer more
than a few years old may not supply

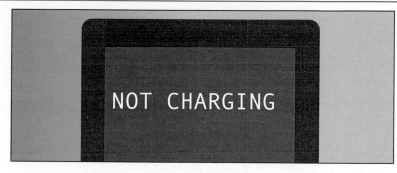

enough power to your phone or tablet. In this case, the USB ports may be good only for syncing your device
with your computer, and you will need to use another power source to charge the device.

Wake Up Your Computer

Some computers do not charge
connected USB devices such as phones
and tablets when the computers are
asleep; others do. If your computer
does not charge your device when
asleep, you can simply wake it up and
configure your computer not to sleep
while you are charging the device.

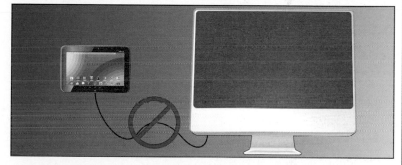

Some laptop computers will charge connected USB devices only when plugged into a power source, not when
running on the battery. In this case, you can plug in the laptop computer to make it charge your device.

Replace the Battery

If you still cannot charge your phone
or tablet, you may need to replace the
battery. How easy this is depends on
the device. Some phones and tablets
have easily removable backs that
enable you to replace the battery in
seconds. Others require surgery by a
trained technician. If your device has

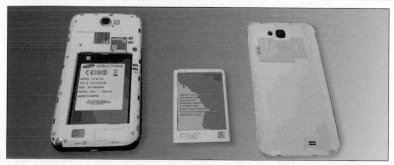

no obvious way of accessing the battery, consult its documentation before attempting to open it, because
opening a device that is not designed to be user-serviceable may void the warranty.

Troubleshoot Wi-Fi Connections

To get the most out of your phone or tablet, use Wi-Fi networks whenever they are available. This is especially important for cellular-capable Android devices with meager data plans. Normally, your phone or tablet establishes and maintains Wi-Fi connections without problems. But you may sometimes need to tell your device to forget a network, and then rejoin the network manually, providing the password again. You may also need to find your device's IP address or its MAC address, the unique hardware address of its wireless network adapter.

Troubleshoot Wi-Fi Connections

Reestablish a Faulty Wi-Fi Connection

1 Touch **Home** (⬤).

The Home screen appears.

2 Touch **All Apps** (⬡).

The Apps screen appears.

3 Touch **Settings** (⚙).

Note: If Settings (⚙) is not on the Apps screen that appears first, scroll left or right until you find Settings (⚙).

The Settings screen appears.

4 Touch **Wi-Fi**.

The Wi-Fi screen appears.

5 Set the **Wi-Fi** switch to Off (⬤ changes to ⬤).

Android turns Wi-Fi off.

6 Set the **Wi-Fi** switch to On (⬤ changes to ⬤).

Android turns Wi-Fi on and tries to reestablish the previous wireless network connection.

Note: If the Wi-Fi connection is now working satisfactorily, skip the rest of these steps.

7 Touch the network marked **Connected**.

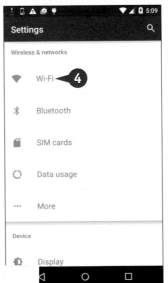

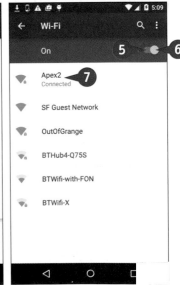

A dialog box opens showing the connection details, including the IP address.

8 Touch **Forget**.

The dialog box closes, and Android forgets the network.

9 Touch the network's button again.

A dialog box opens, prompting you for the password.

10 Type the password.

11 Touch **Connect**.

The dialog box closes, and your device connects to the network.

Find Out Your Device's MAC Address

1 From the Wi-Fi screen, touch **Menu** (▤).

The menu appears.

2 Touch **Advanced**.

The Advanced Wi-Fi screen appears.

3 Look at the MAC address readout.

Note: MAC is an acronym for Media Access Control. It has nothing to do with Apple's Mac computers.

4 Touch **Back** (◁).

The Wi-Fi screen appears again.

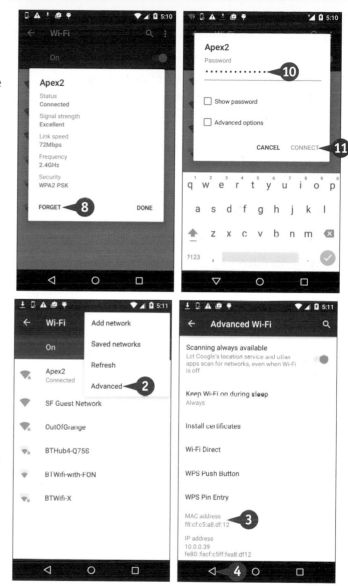

TIP

Why may I need to know my device's MAC address?

Many Wi-Fi networks use a whitelist of MAC addresses to control which computers and devices can connect to the network. Any device with a MAC address on the list can connect, while devices with other MAC addresses cannot.

A MAC address whitelist is a useful security measure, but it is not foolproof. This is because, although each network adapter has a unique MAC address burned into its hardware, software can *spoof*, or imitate, approved MAC addresses.

Index

Teach Yourself VISUALLY™

Read Less-Learn More®

Are you a visual learner? Do you prefer instructions that *show* you how to do something — and skip the long-winded explanations? If so, then this book is for you. Open it up and you'll find clear, step-by-step screen shots that show you how to tackle more than 120 Android phone and tablet tasks. Each task-based spread covers a single technique, sure to help you get up and running on Android phones and tablets in no time.

You'll learn to:

- Customize your phone or tablet
- Work with text, voice, and apps
- Use maps and play music and videos
- Browse the web and e-mail
- Take photos and shoot videos

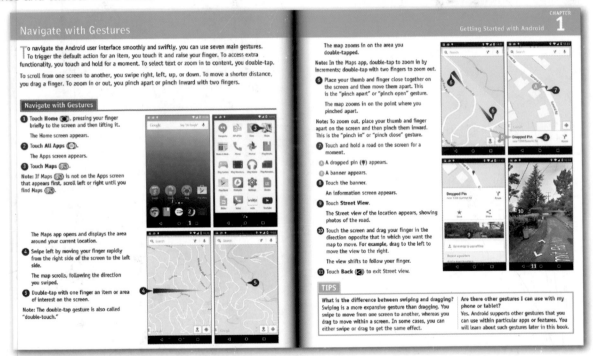

Designed for visual learners

- Two-page lessons break big topics into bite-sized modules
- Succinct explanations walk you through step by step
- Full-color screen shots demonstrate each task
- Helpful sidebars offer practical tips and tricks

Also available as an e-book

ISBN 978-1-119-11676-9

52999

9 781119 116769

Visual A Wiley Brand

www.wiley.com/go/visual

Computers/Hardware/Mobile Device

$29.99 USA • $35.99 CAN • £19.99 U